THE
GOOD
NEIGHBOR

HOW THE UNITED STATES
WROTE THE HISTORY OF
CENTRAL AMERICA AND
THE CARIBBEAN

GEORGE BLACK

PANTHEON BOOKS
NEW YORK

Black, George, 1949—
The good neighbor.
(A new look at history)
1. Central America—Politics and government—
1979– . 2. Central America—Foreign public
opinion, American.   3. Public opinion—United
States.   4. Central America—History—1951–
—Pictorial works.
I. Title.   II. Series.
F1439.5.B55   1988   972.8'05   88-9919
ISBN 0-394-75965-6

Manufactured in the United States of America
98765
Book design by Chris Welch

FRONTISPIECE:

AMERICAN TOURIST IN CUBA, 1948.

CONTENTS

Contents

FIVE

SIX

ACKNOWLEDGMENTS

The first person I ever met in Nicaragua, back in the latter days of the Somoza regime, was an American. His name was Joe Damico. Joe was a former cop in the Los Angeles Police Department. He had grown tired of police work and come to Nicaragua in the late 1950s, just after the violent death of old man Anastasio Somoza García. Twenty years later Joe owned 350 acres of rich, red land in the department of Carazo. He drove me the length and breadth of his property one day, stopping occasionally to wave an arm across the landscape. "Mine, all mine," he told me. He had left the United States because, he said, you couldn't realize dreams like this any longer there. The distant germ of this book lies in that meeting, ten years ago, and there are echoes of Joe Damico throughout its pages.

In a more immediate sense, a number of acknowledgments are in order. Bill Buzenberg, Dan Hallin, Jim Lobe, John Spicer Nichols, and Jon Snow were valuable sounding boards for an earlier version of this project and helped me understand the best direction for it to take. The Fund for Investigative Journalism provided financial support for some of my initial research. Eddie Becker and Karen Glynn gave me generous access to their personal archives and were wonderfully helpful in assembling material from the 1920s and 1930s. I am grateful to Lynne Barbee for her patience and darkroom skills, especially with some of the rare early photographs. Susan Meiselas lent an expert and sympathetic eye to the final selection of images and made a number of valuable suggestions.

I'm grateful to Victor Navasky for allowing me a well-timed leave of absence to work on the manuscript, and to Elsa Dixler, Phillip Frazer, Mark Schapiro, Micah Sifry, and Katrina vanden Heuvel for graciously assuming additional work as a result. I would like to thank Robin Epstein and Mark Gevisser for research assistance, and above all for their help with the arduous business of copyright permissions. I also appreciated Laurie Parsons's advice on navigating the copyright labyrinth.

The staffs of the Library of Congress, the New York Public Library, the Columbia University School of Journalism Library, and the Peace Corps were invariably courteous, efficient, and indulgent of my more arcane requests. Sarah Beckjord, Elvis Brathwaite, George Cohen, Martha Doggett, Marian P. Francois, Elizabeth Gallin, Scot Jahn, Peter Kornbluh, Sandra Levinson, M. G. Lord, Peter Raymont, Barbara Shattuck, Denise Smith, and Martin Smith were all helpful in tracking down particular images and pieces of information.

To Andre Schiffrin at Pantheon, my appreciation for his faith in this project in its various incarnations. Wendy Wolf has provided the perfect blend of critical intelligence and boundless good humor; a marvelous editor and friend throughout the process. Tony Borden, a gifted and exacting copy editor, improved the manuscript in many small ways. Chris Welch took raw words and images and put them together with elegance and imagination.

Appropriately enough, it was a photograph from Central America that first introduced me to my wife, Anne Nelson, and her visual, editorial, and political sensibilities have enriched every part of this project. The result is for her.

THE
GOOD
NEIGHBOR

"ANY AGGRESSIVE NORTH AMERICAN . . . LOOKS UPON
THE SPLENDID AREAS OF LAND, THE FINE RIVERS,
THE DENSE FORESTS, AND THE OTHER UNTOUCHED
RESOURCES OF THIS RICH COUNTRY WITH
AMAZEMENT, AND BEGINS TO PLAN DEVELOPMENT
PROJECTS AND DREAM OF ORGANIZING SYNDICATES,
BUT THE NATIVE LOSES NO SLEEP OVER SUCH VAIN
IMAGININGS. IF HE DREAMS AT ALL, IT IS OF HIS FOOD
IF HE BE POOR, AND OF POLITICS IF HE BE RICH."
—GEORGE A. MILLER, 1919.

INTRODUCTION

AFTER ALL, HISTORY IS IN OUR MINDS. IT IS WHAT
WE THINK HAPPENED.
—JOHN KING FAIRBANK,
THE GREAT CHINESE REVOLUTION, 1800—1985

Ever since the approach of the U.S. Civil War, the countries of Central America and the Caribbean have occupied a special place in the American psyche. Cuba, Nicaragua, Panama, and their neighbors have been a magnet for adventurers and pioneers, a proving ground for grand abstractions of democracy and freedom, and frequently a refuge for scoundrels. For most of the twentieth century they were known derisively as "banana republics"; by the 1980s, that name had been adopted by a chain of clothing stores for affluent travelers.

This was frontier territory, a land where the whim of the adventurer was often the only law, where Americans were deemed to have limitless prerogatives, and outside intruders only malicious intentions. As early as the mid-nineteenth century, Senator E. A. Hannegan of Indiana fancied he saw Britain hastening "with race-horse speed" to seize the entire isthmus of Central America, along with Mexico's Yucatán Peninsula and Cuba. Spain was the target of similar suspicion at the turn of the century, to be succeeded in turn by Germany, Mexico, and, since the end of World War II, the Soviet Union. Each of these foreign powers was charged with importing ideologies alien to the natural order of the region.

Of these, none has been more menacing than socialism. An everyday fact of political life in Western Europe, socialism has always been regarded as something close to a national heresy in the United States, and therefore in the rest of the Western Hemisphere, whose political interests the United States has declared, unilaterally, to be the same as its own. In the early part of the century, Edward Bellamy wrote that the average American "conceived of a socialist . . . as a mysterious type of desperado, reputed to infest the dark places of continental Europe and engaged with his fellows in a conspiracy as monstrous as it was futile, against civilization and all that it implied." The United States's experiences since World War II in Guatemala, Cuba, the Dominican Republic, and Nicaragua suggest that little has changed.

Bellamy's socialist is only one of a number of stereotypes that inhabit the historical landscape of Central America and the Caribbean. They tend to share two principal characteristics, irrational violence and feckless indolence —"Latin" challenges to North American ingenuity and order. The purpose of this book is not, however, to compile a catalogue of Latin stereotypes, which in themselves do not necessarily provide a guide to events. One only has to think of French cancan dancers and Spanish bullfight posters to conclude that countries larger and better able to take care of themselves can also

UNCLE SAM'S HELPING HAND.

—BOSTON HERALD AMERICAN, 1960.

"THEY HAVE NOT THE FIRST

ELEMENTS OF GOOD OR FREE

GOVERNMENT. ARBITRARY POWER,

MILITARY AND ECCLESIASTICAL,

WAS STAMPED UPON THEIR

EDUCATION, UPON THEIR HABITS,

AND UPON ALL THEIR INSTITUTIONS.

CIVIL DISSENSION WAS INFUSED

INTO ALL THEIR SEMINAL

PRINCIPLES. WAR AND MUTUAL

DESTRUCTION WAS IN EVERY

MEMBER OF THEIR ORGANIZATION,

MORAL, POLITICAL, AND PHYSICAL."

—JOHN QUINCY ADAMS

ON LATIN AMERICA, 1821.

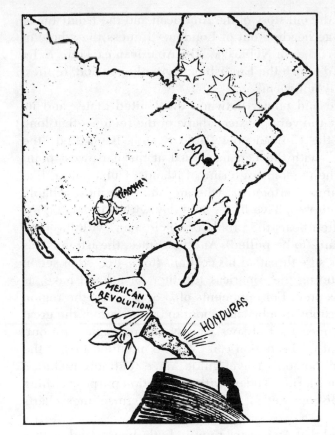

"ANOTHER TOUCH OF SORE
THROAT."
—LOUISVILLE TIMES, 1924.

be the victims of cliché. But what makes Central America and the Caribbean different is the degree to which their entire modern history has been held hostage to the demands of the American imagination.

The region spent most of the twentieth century as an obscure backwater, trapped in a kind of political time warp, which size, location, and poverty left it powerless to resist. Yet in the late 1980s, the United States's inability to work its will on one of its puniest neighbors, Nicaragua, came close to destroying the most popular presidency of the postwar years. The failure to prevail in such an unequal contest, especially when the great universal ideals of freedom and democracy were said to have been at stake, led to a devastating loss of the superpower's most precious asset—its credibility.

The imbalance of scale and power between the United States and the straggle of countries along its southern border has always fascinated and unsettled Americans. It is a kind of ritual among journalists to remind their readers that Nicaragua is the size of Wisconsin, El Salvador of Massachusetts, Grenada of Manhattan. This undeniably serves some educational purpose, but the compulsion to measure and compare seems to stem, too, from the United States's awe at its own vast expanses, and the dilemma superpowers (including the Soviet Union and China) perceive in coexisting with smaller, politically unstable neighbors. It is a difficult attitude for a European to grasp, and always reminds me of the old story of the American and the Englishman who share a railway carriage heading out of London. "I guess the whole of England could fit into one corner of Nebraska," the American exclaims as he looks out of the window. To which the Englishman, greatly puzzled, replies, "Perhaps, but to what *end*, young man?"

The disparities of scale and power between the United States and its neighbors are suggested by the very physical shape of the region—that long connecting sliver of land the Chilean poet Pablo Neruda has called "the delicate waist of America," with the Panama Canal at the narrowest point between the two oceans; the random scattering of islands; Cuba poised like a scimitar above the sea-lanes. Cartoonists, who are often the most reliable barometer of a society's neuroses, have had a field day with this geography. The United States itself often bears the profile of Uncle Sam, with the peninsula of Florida as his beard (to be pulled). At other times, the isthmus has been drawn as Uncle Sam's sore throat, or his coattails (to be tugged or set on fire), or a fragile chain binding the Americas together, or a handshake, as likely to be spurned as accepted. For opponents of U.S. policies, the region has been depicted as a footstool, or a banana about to be devoured; the great landmass to the north becomes a set of jaws, or a swooping eagle with outstretched talons. The layout of the region can even be modified to suit the ideological demands of the moment. Travel guides once routinely included Cuba as a part of the map of Florida. Today, with its vacation purpose a thing of the past, the island has disappeared altogether from the cruise lines' charts of the Caribbean.

Emerson once suggested that Americans require both dreams and mathe-

••••••

"THROAT TROUBLE."

—*OREGON JOURNAL*, 1927.

matics, with the added complication that they need both at once. It is worth looking at U.S. images of Central America and the Caribbean in that light. It was not sufficient for Americans to know that the Gatun Locks or the Culebra Cut in Panama were the pinnacle of engineering skill, or that they embodied the selfless destiny of American enterprise. It was also necessary to calculate that the earth dug out of Panama would fill enough freight cars to circle the globe four times, or that it would build sixty-three replicas of the Pyramid of Cheops along Broadway from the Battery to Harlem.

This compulsion to quantify grand abstractions is, of course, intimately tied up with the desire to exercise control, and it was much in evidence at the beginning of the century, when the United States's sense of its own world role was still in embryo. It has resurfaced whenever American self-confidence has ebbed, or when the country has felt itself at odds with a hostile outside world. Thus, it was not enough to hail the 1954 coup in Guatemala or the invasion of the tiny island of Grenada in 1983 as symbolic triumphs of democratic light over communist darkness. It was also necessary for high U.S. officials to make on-site inspections, to review and quantify the caches of communist weapons and literature that had been discovered. Not enough for the Peace Corps to counter the threat of Fidel Castro with the noblest ideals of John Kennedy's Camelot; it also had to provide an exact count of all the latrines and artesian wells it had dug in the Dominican Republic, a habit which eventually made the agency something of a laughingstock in Washington.

An important clue to U.S. attitudes toward the country's southern neighbors lies in the word "backyard," used since time immemorial to describe the countries of the Caribbean Basin. The backyard is, after all, a vital part of the American family's geography. It is a place that evokes complex feelings about control and ownership—taken for granted, yet crucial to the family's security; if it is not safe, then nothing is safe. The backyard is a space that is walled off against intruders. The rich, who have a lot to protect, patrol it with guard dogs and cordon it off with electronic fences and hidden cameras. The backyard, to pursue the metaphor further, is an area where one can act without inhibitions—sunbathe nude, relax with a barbecue, let the pets run wild, allow the kids to take the training wheels off their bicycles for the first time. It is also where the garbage is dumped, and in the old days it doubled as an outhouse. It is an area for play, experimentation, and control, a place where the owner makes his own laws, a laboratory for ideas that will be tried out later on the broader world beyond its walls.

Within the fractious Republican coalition that came to power in 1981, Central America was a bone thrown to the extreme right wing—with the blessing, to be sure, of a president who shared its (self-destructive) passion for the cause. The terms of the debate were set from the beginning by those who had an ax to grind: the Cuban-American exiles, who saw Castro's betrayal as the key to modern history; the *Soldier of Fortune* crowd, who wanted a second crack at winning Vietnam; and the assortment of Washington pundits and intellectuals, many of them one-time liberals, who

"WEAKENING LINK," MAY 1954. IN THE SAME WEEK AS THIS CARTOON APPEARED, CRITICS REVIEWED 'THE NEW SCIENCE-FICTION MOVIE *THEM!* IN WHICH GIANT MUTANT ANTS, THE PRODUCT OF ATOMIC-WEAPONS TESTS, TAKE OVER THE SEWERS OF LOS ANGELES.

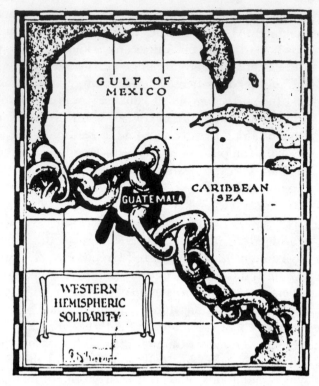

saw the conduct of the Sandinistas in Nicaragua as a lightning rod for their own political conversion.

But their rancor did not spring out of thin air. It has speckled the ideological landscape of the United States for more than a century. One has only to consider how many of the cardinal events of modern American history have taken place in the Caribbean region to grasp what a role the apparent backwater has played in the construction of the United States's self-image, and to realize why, by the 1980s, U.S. policy-makers' feelings about Central America should have come to be such a cluster of raw nerves, an undiagnosed obsession.

In the years immediately before the Civil War, the Caribbean Basin was looked on by the southern states as a promising site for a new slave empire. Forty years later, it was where the expansionists turned when the western frontier was exhausted. With the Spanish-American War of 1898 and the siezure of Puerto Rico and Cuba, the United States gained its first taste of blood as a world power, both naval and commercial. Since the early part of the twentieth century, Central America and the Caribbean have been the arena for a series of grand foreign-policy doctrines—the Big Stick, Dollar Diplomacy, the Good Neighbor Policy, the Alliance for Progress—as well as for the greatest of all feats of American enterprise, the Panama Canal, which subsequently became the cornerstone of U.S. national defense. It was in Nicaragua, between 1927 and 1933, that the United States had its first experience of a stalemated guerrilla war. A generation later, in 1954, the overthrow of the Guatemalan government became the textbook case of a successful covert operation, and a paradigm of U.S. power at its most absolute. Then came Cuba: the indelible image of humiliation at the Bay of Pigs in 1961, the nightmarish spasm of the Missile Crisis the following year, and the constant affront since then of a communist state ninety miles from the Florida shore. After that, the fear of a "second Cuba": first, in 1965, in the Dominican Republic, and now in Nicaragua.

In the long interludes between these political crises, the region often appeared to slump into a condition of benign neglect, to be treated as a kind of comic opera. Search the catalogue for travel books on Central America and the Caribbean, and the titles say it all: G. L. Morrill's *Rotten Republics: A Tropical Tramp in Central America* (1916), Harry L. Foster's *A Gringo in Mañana Land* (1924), Alfred Batson's *Vagabond's Paradise* (1931), and more recently, A. B. Cox's *Siestas and Fiestas* (1961). "Readers of our newspapers might have imagined revolutions and volcanic disturbances were the chief product of Latin America," Calvin Coolidge remarked back in 1926, and for decades at a time, his comment remained true.

Benign neglect and extreme forms of crisis management have always co-existed in the U.S.–Central American relationship, the impulse to "go in" perpetually at war with the desire to stay out. Going in, to do for the hapless natives what they seem incapable of doing for themselves, has been an ever-present temptation since 1898, the natural outgrowth, as Louis Hartz wrote, of Americans' unshakable belief in their own moral rectitude and the universal appeal of the U.S. political system. All of the United States's major policy initiatives in the region have been presented in part as grand rhetorical gestures and in part as technical exercises in problem-solving. After all, as Hartz

••••••

"CENTRAL AMERICA . . . IS SO CLOSE
—SAN SALVADOR IS CLOSER TO
HOUSTON THAN HOUSTON IS TO
WASHINGTON, D.C. CENTRAL
AMERICA IS AMERICA."
—RONALD REAGAN, 1984.

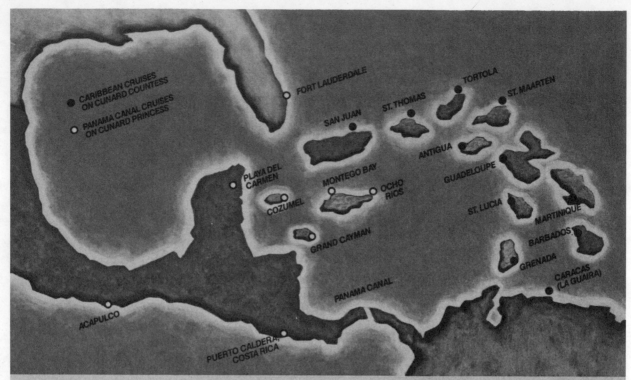

- - - - - -

"IT WILL NOT DO TO SAY WE HAVE
NO BUSINESS IN CUBA. WE HAVE
MUCH BUSINESS THERE. THE CUBAN
MARK IS IN OUR HISTORY AS
PLAINLY AS THE ISLAND APPEARS
ON THE MAP OF THE AMERICAS."
—MURAT HALSTEAD,
THE STORY OF CUBA:
HER STRUGGLES FOR LIBERTY, 1896.

pointed out, "It is only when you take your ethics for granted, that all problems emerge as problems of technique."

In small countries like Cuba, Panama, or Nicaragua, the appeal of a good dose of Yankee tinkering has proved almost irresistible. In earlier times, a team of customs collectors or road-builders could be counted on to bring an unruly local situation under control; it was all in a day's work. More recently, a group of fact-finding senators, a delegation of election monitors, or a team of military advisers are called on to provide some lessons in human rights. The serious problems arise when these quick-fix solutions fail to work, when the structural flaws they have disguised can be camouflaged no longer.

George Kennan once wrote of Americans' "inveterate tendency to judge others by the extent to which they contrive to be like ourselves." The word "contrive" is important, for local leaders who stood to enhance their own power by enlisting U.S. sympathies quickly mastered the game of appearances. Although their commitment to democratic ideals often was only skin-deep, they became excellent mimics. Even the crudest of dictators, like Rafael Leonidas Trujillo, learned the right code words. He would refer to his Dominican tyranny as "freedom and democracy in the Caribbean," and for three decades Washington found it convenient to let the lie stand.

U.S. policies have also been based on a less cynical belief that democratic freedoms would inevitably take root, if only the basic right of free enterprise were guaranteed. But the evidence of history suggests that just the opposite is true. "The myth that we could develop in the image and likeness of the centers is being exploded," wrote the great Argentine economist Raúl Prebisch in 1981, shortly before he died. Prebisch understood very well that those most eager to behave like Americans were often the least likely to bring about democratic capitalism. In Latin America, he wrote, the fruits of free enterprise were not productively invested but "earmarked by the upper strata for the imitation of the consumption patterns of the centers." The result was "inadmissible social inequality."

The continuing U.S. attachment to this cherished illusion has had two consequences. The first is a distinctive kind of historical amnesia, which has sought to preserve the myth of American innocence at all costs. Where the evidence of past U.S. wrongdoing is too great to be ignored, it is explained as an aberration. The past, which sadly offers little but a parade of U.S. support for dictators, can therefore be written off as a repeated cycle of aberrations; anyone who attempts to demonstrate that history is a living chain of causes and effects is characteristically dismissed as a Monday-morning quarterback.

The second result, which also reflects the technical, ahistorical approach to managing political crises, has been an extraordinarily fluid set of loyalties to those who proclaim themselves America's allies. Machado and Batista in Cuba, like Somoza in Nicaragua and Duvalier in Haiti, were all unceremoniously dumped once they had ceased to serve Washington's purposes. In the case of Trujillo, the CIA even gave the nod to his assassination. Nowhere in the world has the United States turned its back on embarrassing clients as regularly as in Central America and the Caribbean, and to conservatives, these betrayals in the name of *Realpolitik* are object lessons in the cowardice of liberalism and the failures of American will. They help explain why the region became a favorite cause of the angry right wing long before Vietnam.

-- -- --

My intention here is to isolate the threads of neurosis that run through this history, and to ask, as in a psychiatrist's word-association test, what responses the words "Cuba," "Nicaragua," and "Panama" have triggered in the minds of Americans. I found myself turning quite quickly from the written word to the visual image, beginning with cartoons but then casting the net much more widely to take in official government records and propaganda, military archives, school textbooks, travelers' tales, scholarly articles, popular journalism, maps, and song lyrics, as well as all manner of printed emphemera, from corporate publicity and tourist guides to postcards and movie stills. These soon revealed an almost uncanny consistency, a shared set of attitudes that

WASHINGTON POST, 1988.

alternated between breezy complacency and intense anxiety in a way that strongly suggested that these were the two sides of a single coin.

In recent years—say, since the mid-1960s—there is little new imagery in a strictly documentary sense: the region is still depicted as a theater for apparently senseless violence, better at self-destruction than at self-reliance. What is more distinctive about the modern images is how they show the propagandist's ability to play on deep-rooted fears. Many of the images in this book were originally used for deliberate political effect—whether or not it was the effect intended by the photographer or artist. Some of them set myths in stone. Others changed the course of history, or fixed its official meaning in a single moment—Cuban or Nicaraguan equivalents of the flag-raising on Iwo Jima or the Vietnamese child burned by napalm. There are pictures here that helped start wars, made some great reputations, destroyed others. Some were willfully misused, others were outright fabrications.

The result is not intended as a parade of U.S. villainies or a gallery of grotesques, though some readers, as a reflex, may see it that way. There are quiet Americans here as well as ugly ones, and in the almost childlike image of Teddy Roosevelt in his steam shovel, the serviceman buying remembrance poppies in wartime Trinidad, the honeymooning gamblers in Havana, even in the desolate face of the captured Eugene Hasenfus, there is that quality of innocence that proves to have such devastating consequences when it confronts the intractable realities of the outside world.

New York
January 1988

"REMEMBER THE *MAINE!*"

ONE

INNOCENTS
ABROAD

1898–1918

LET OUR STRENGTH BE THE MEASURE OF OUR VIRTUE,

SINCE WEAKNESS ARGUES ITS OWN FUTILITY.

—BOOK OF WISDOM, II:ii

At a little after nine o'clock on the evening of February 15, 1898, the twenty-four-gun battleship *Maine* exploded in Havana Bay, killing 260 American sailors. The ship had been stationed there for three weeks on a "courtesy visit," to show concern for U.S. lives and property during the Cuban war of independence from Spain, which was approaching the end of its third year.

William Randolph Hearst's *New York Journal* splashed news of the disaster across its front page. The headline read, "The War Ship *Maine* Was Split in Two by an Enemy's Secret Infernal Machine." To illustrate its point, the paper accompanied the story with a half-page sketch, concocted entirely from the artist's imagination, that purported to show the location of the mine that had ripped through the ship, and of the wires that linked it to the *Maine*'s engine room. Only seventy-eight years later, in 1976, did a report by Admiral Hyman Rickover conclude that the explosion was probably caused by spontaneous combustion inside the ship's coalbins, a common problem of the day. Hearst was soon publishing photographs of the broken hulk lying in the shallow waters of Havana Bay, and offering a reward of $50,000 "for the detection of the perpetrator of the *Maine* outrage."

The perpetrator was never found, and six weeks later, a report to Congress concluded that there was no evidence of Spanish involvement. But by this time, hard facts were of little relevance. The cry "Remember the *Maine!*" had entered the American vocabulary, and President William McKinley, criticized by his opponents as hesitant and weak, eventually bowed to the pressure for revenge. On April 25, Congress declared that a state of war existed with Spain.

The *Maine* explosion, and the war it triggered, held up a mirror to the important changes that had taken place in the United States during the preceding decade. The five years 1893–97 had been a period of terrible economic depression, and U.S. business, crying out for new markets, turned its eyes southward. The *New York Commercial Advertiser* boasted in March 1898 of "a new Monroe Doctrine, not of political principles, but of commercial policy principles. . . . Instead of laying down dogmas, it figures up profits." Admiral Alfred Thayer Mahan, whose 1890 book *The Influence of Sea Power Upon History* had caused a storm, held that new markets had to go hand in hand with an expanded navy, which would protect trade and keep European "outsiders" from making unwelcome inroads. And according to Mahan, the string of naval bases necessary to defend foreign trade would be secure only if the United States also controlled the political affairs of the countries where they were located. The Caribbean—which Mahan called America's Mediterranean—was the cornerstone of this scheme. Building a canal to link the Atlantic and Pacific oceans (an idea that caught the fancy of the young Theodore Roosevelt) would, Mahan believed, be just the thing to rouse Americans' dormant "aggressive impulses."

The country was also urbanizing swiftly. The limits of the western frontier had been reached, and cities in the Northeast and Midwest were filling with European immigrants looking for a brighter future. With the growth of the cities came a new generation of newspapers, the mouthpieces of powerful publishers like Joseph Pulitzer, who owned the *New York World,* and Hearst, who started his *New York Journal* as competition in 1896. The *World's* attachment to the cause of Cuban independence dated back to 1884, when Spanish authorities on the island banned Cuban papers that reprinted Pulitzer stories about negotiations for the island to be sold to the United States. An editorial in the *World* commented, "It strikes us that when journals are not permitted to carry the *World's* news with due credit, it is time for a revolution. We are for Free Cuba henceforth."

The xenophobic Pulitzer and the still more lurid Hearst continued to report—and where necessary invent—Spanish atrocities. Hearst fanned his readers' passions with the case of "the Flower of Cuba," Evangelina Cosio y Cisneros, a young woman jailed by the Spanish, and dispatched one of his reporters, Karl Decker, as an undercover agent to help her escape. Another

Hearst reporter was imprisoned in the fortress of El Morro in Havana; yet another was sent to deliver a jeweled sword to the rebel leader Máximo Gómez.

McKinley had a healthy distaste for this kind of journalism but found it hard to resist the groundswell of congressional and public feeling that it captured. Intolerance and jingoism were loose on the land, and there was a public clamor for war—against the right enemy. There was a sweeping, if somewhat nervous, sense that America was coming of age as a nation, and an urge to flex the country's muscles abroad and dramatize its superiority over the old, European ways from which it had cut free. History, for Americans of the 1890s, was a tide to be seized, a physical force that would sweep them on to higher things. "We are face to face with a strange destiny," mused an editorial in the *Washington Post*. "The taste of Empire is in the mouth of the people even as the taste of blood in the jungle."

While the explosion of the *Maine* anchored in the national psyche the idea of treacherous foreign enemies, the war in Cuba soon brought forth an equally resonant symbol of heroism and assertiveness—the charge up San Juan Hill on July 1, 1898, by the Rough Riders, under the command of Lieutenant Colonel Theodore Roosevelt. Whole generations of American schoolchildren have been brought up on that image, so central to the country's mythology.

Assistant Secretary of the Navy Roosevelt had taken his commission very seriously, and had himself photographed striking a fierce pose in a brand-

"I DO BELIEVE THAT WE MAY DOMINATE THE WORLD, AS NO NATION HAS DOMINATED IT IN RECENT TIME."
—TEDDY ROOSEVELT, ROUGH RIDER.

new uniform supplied by Brooks Brothers. (He had sent the company a telegram of inquiry: "Can you make me, so I shall have it by next Saturday, a blue cravenette lieutenant colonel's uniform, without yellow on the collar, and with leggings? If so, make it. Charge Theodore Roosevelt.") A 1986 ABC documentary, *The Indomitable Teddy Roosevelt,* showed how potent the myth of San Juan Hill has remained, almost a century later. "Miraculously unhurt," exclaimed the narrator, George C. Scott, "Roosevelt on horseback leads his men in the long charge that will be celebrated in art and legend."

Certainly the Rough Riders demonstrated bravery in battle, in keeping with their motto, "Rough, tough, we're the stuff. We want to fight, and we can't get enough. Whoo-pee!" They were the first all-volunteer regiment. Most of them were Indian fighters from the frontier lands of Arizona, Oklahoma, and New Mexico, mixing uneasily with patrician volunteers from the northeastern states. The Rough Riders were the first to raise the Stars and Stripes in Cuba, the first to fire a shot in the Spanish-American War, and the first to sustain casualties. But they did not charge up San Juan Hill behind Roosevelt on horseback. The heroic image, and the tremendous mythological baggage that went with it, were in fact largely manufactured.

The original story of the charge was distilled from the reports of several contemporary journalists and the vivid pictorial record of Frederic Remington, who had earlier chronicled the conquest of the western frontier. Five hundred reporters covered the fighting, and virtually to a man, they were bent on celebrating the symbolic dimensions of the conflict: its valor, the vanquishing of Old World colonial power in the Western Hemisphere, the emergent figure of Roosevelt as an incarnation of the new national will. (A rare exception was the report in Pulitzer's *World* by Stephen Crane suggesting that the Rough Riders had briefly panicked under fire, a story that infuriated Roosevelt.) The famous Richard Harding Davis was also on hand to describe the events on San Juan Hill, "appearing on the battlefield wearing a straw boater with a wide ribbon around it and taking notes from those still alive." Edward Marshall, a reporter for Hearst's *Journal,* provided one of the fullest accounts of the battle—even though he did not witness it, but described it from the hospital ship *Olivette,* where he was lying with his spine shattered by a bullet.

Roosevelt in fact led a charge not up San Juan Hill but up the nearby Kettle Hill, which Marshall described as "a little preliminary hill," separated from San Juan Hill by a depression in the ground and a small pond. To this point, the Rough Riders were on their own, out ahead of the other U.S. troops (but not, incidentally, on horseback—the horses had been left behind). By the time they reached the blockhouse on top of San Juan Hill, however, they had been joined by a number of other regiments, who overwhelmed the Spanish defenders with vastly superior firepower. Though it was on Kettle Hill that the Rough Riders made their solo charge, David McCullough, biographer of the young Roosevelt, explained that "San Juan Hill sounded like a better name, a more Spanish name, a more romantic and exotic name to the people who were covering that event—the newspaper people—and that war was covered as few wars have been. So San Juan Hill it became."

A few commentators were suspicious of TR's propensity for mythmaking. The philosopher William James thought Roosevelt was "still mentally in the *Sturm und Drang* period of early adolescence." He "gushes over war as the ideal condition of human society, for the manly strenuousness which it involves, and treats peace as a condition of blubberlike and swollen ignobility, fit only for huckstering weaklings, dwelling in gray twilight and heedless of the higher life." But Roosevelt was in tune with the mood of the country; James was not. Only a small minority of Americans dissented from the virtues that Roosevelt espoused: the militarism and romantic nationalism, the sense of destiny, the cult of virile strength and personal leadership, all tinged with a distinctive edge of racial purity. "Americanizing of the world is our destiny," said Roosevelt. Cuba and Puerto Rico were the places to start; Panama would soon follow.

Although the Spanish-American War had given the United States its first taste of world power, the impulse to expand into the Caribbean and Central America was nothing new. As early as 1823, the Monroe Doctrine had warned the European colonial powers to keep their hands off the Western Hemisphere, and when John Quincy Adams became president two years later, his first foreign-policy crisis arose over the extent of British influence in Nicaragua. Twenty years later, the phrase "Manifest Destiny" entered the language, signifying a God-given right to extend democratic, republican government, by violent means if necessary. Manifest Destiny was a driving force behind the Polk administration's Mexican War in 1846, the first conflict ever covered by the U.S. press. Stories about the exploits of the volunteer troops, together with artists' impressions, reached readers in as little as two weeks via fast steamer from Veracruz and a network of pony riders called Kendall's Express, for the publisher of the *New Orleans Picayune*.

Toward the middle of the century, Nicaragua began to tug at the minds of the expansionists with a special urgency, both as a commercial hub and as a plantation paradise. It was the likeliest crossing point between the two oceans and, for the southern slave states, a new source of political power. John Lloyd Stephens, a red-bearded adventurer, was among the first to travel there, in 1840, describing his experiences in the best-selling *Incidents of Travel in Central America and Yucatan*. Stephens was particularly taken with the smoking volcano of Masaya, and climbed down into the crater. "At home," he wrote, "this volcano would be a fortune, with a good hotel on top, a railing to keep the children from falling in, a zigzagging staircase down the sides, and a glass of iced lemonade at the bottom." He thought the entire site could probably be bought for $10.

Ephraim George Squier, an amateur archaeologist and agent for Zachary Taylor's Whig administration, published a two-volume book on Nicaragua in 1852. He called the country "the key to the continent, destined to unlock the riches of two hemispheres, and which eager nations even now are aiming to snatch, with felon hand, from its rightful possessors." In Squier's code, "eager nations" meant the British, who had just set up a protectorate over Nicaragua's eastern half, the Mosquito Coast. Its "rightful possessors," of course, were the United States, and Nicaragua would "unlock the riches of two hemispheres" by means of an interoceanic canal, for which it was the obvious location. Already, Cornelius Vanderbilt, the richest man in America, was running a thriving business ferrying adventurers across Nicaragua by steamboat and carriage on their way to the newly discovered California gold fields.

•• •• ••

With the approach of the U.S. Civil War, the stakes in Nicaragua escalated, and the country became a battleground for the forces that were tearing American society apart. The South urgently needed an outlet into which the plantation system could expand, but the Kansas Civil War that began in 1854 showed the degree of resistance to any northward expansion at home. So the slave states looked farther south, dreaming of new plantations in Cuba and Central America. With the Ostend Manifesto, President Franklin Pierce tried to placate the South, recommending that, if Spain refused to sell Cuba, the island should be taken by force. When Europeans and abolitionists protested, the South turned its attention instead to Nicaragua and the exploits of the Tennessee soldier of fortune, or "filibuster," William Walker.

Nicaragua was in a perpetual state of war between rival factions of Conservatives and Liberals, having had fifteen governments in the previous six years. In 1855, the Liberal (also known as Democratic) leader Francisco Castellón concluded that he could unseat the Conservative (or Legitimist) ruler of the day only with outside aid. Walker, with a fifty-eight-soldier army called the Phalanx of Immortals, was his man. Walker spoke almost mystically of his mission to bring peace and democracy to Central America, but his mercenary followers, unemployed louts recruited off the wharves of San Francisco, were less interested in politics than in the legendary sexual allure of Nicaraguan women. Squier had written about them frankly three years earlier, recalling his encounters with women "of all shades from white to ebon black, straight as arrows, lithe yet full-figured, with quick, mischievous eyes."

It took Walker just four months to rout the Nicaraguan Conservatives, whereupon he turned on the Liberals and had himself declared commander-in-chief of the Nicaraguan Army, then, a year later, president. He issued a set of decrees—all, he said, "intended to place a large portion of the land in the hands of the white race." These made English an official language with the same standing as Spanish, instituted forced labor, and legalized slavery.

The impact in the United States was tremendous. The South understood that support for Walker was crucial to its success in the coming conflict at home. The *New Orleans Delta* wrote, "The fate of Cuba depends upon the fate of Nicaragua, and the fate of the South depends upon that of Cuba. This is the hour of destiny. We must live now or have no life. We must do or die." The *Richmond Enquirer* hailed Nicaragua as "a new State soon to be added to the South, in or out of the Union"—meaning that it would either restore

the South's dominance at home, or give the slave states a powerful overseas empire if they chose to secede. Walker was a hero to many Northerners too, and millions, steeped in the culture of individualism, thought of him as "America's Grey-Eyed Man of Destiny." *Harper's Weekly* wrote, "We have again and again called Walker a hero. . . . We are obliged to recognize a persistence, an endurance, a resolute heroism which merit a higher place in human esteem than can be ceded to all the knights errant of history and Faerydom." *Frank Leslie's Illustrated Newspaper* published a set of dramatic drawings of Walker's exploits, and the *New York Daily News* lauded his *mission civilisatrice*, exclaiming, "*Los yankis* . . . have burst their way like a fertilizing torrent through the barriers of barbarism. . . . Nicaragua is at peace."

But not for long. The new administration of James Buchanan, while sympathetic enough to Walker's goals, was opposed to leaving wars of conquest to private enterprise. The president believed that "it would be far better and more in accordance with the bold and manly character of our countrymen for the Government itself to get up such expeditions." Walker also made the mistake of crossing Vanderbilt, who turned against him. And he aroused the first real stirrings of anti-*yanqui* nationalism, as the armies of the other Central American countries overcame their differences to get rid of him—though not before Walker's forces had razed Nicaragua's ancient colonial city of Granada. Returning defeated in May 1857 to New Orleans, the metropolis of the South and hub of the cotton trade, Walker was received as a hero and given front-page treatment in the newspapers.

After a futile attempt at a comeback, the filibuster was finally executed by a Honduran firing squad, in 1860. But his escapades, and the needs of the South in the Civil War, left a number of lasting effects. Nicaraguan politics would remain distorted for the rest of the century. Walker's Liberal paymasters, discredited by the association, were kept out of office until 1893. And Nicaraguan nationalists had their first symbolic rallying point against U.S. interference.

•• •• ••

The same Conservative-Liberal feud that racked Nicaragua had to be resolved in each of the Central American countries. In Guatemala, the largest, the Liberals came to power in 1871. They were believers in modern capitalism, infatuated with Positivism and the grand nineteenth-century idea of Progress, keen to imitate North American and European consumer styles. And their wealth was based on a new crop, coffee.

Eadweard Muybridge, the great English photographer, set sail for Guatemala in 1875 from his home in San Francisco, where he had just been acquitted of murdering his wife's lover. He photographed Guatemala City, the second city, Quezaltenango, and the dirt-poor villages of the Indian highlands. But his main achievement was a portfolio depicting every stage of the coffee-growing cycle, from the preparation of the ground and planting of the seeds to picking, drying, and packing for export.

The most striking sequence was made at the *finca* of Las Nubes, the property of William Nelson, commercial agent in Guatemala for the Pacific Mail Steamship Company. Pacific Mail had in fact sponsored the photographer's trip. The company was watching its profits evaporate in the face of competition from the newly opened railroad across the United States. It used Muybridge's photographs to attract tourists and, more important, investors in Guatemala's booming coffee crop. The country's coffee exports tripled between 1870 and 1880, with almost two-thirds destined for the United States —a figure that made Guatemala more dependent on the U.S. market than any other Latin American nation. Pacific Mail held the monopoly on the transportation of Guatemalan exports.

••••••

FIRST DAY OF THE COFFEE SEASON, LAS NUBES, GUATEMALA. "THE OWNERS ARE GENERALLY WEALTHY MEN, EITHER SPANIARDS OR GERMANS, AND ALWAYS RECEIVE VISITORS WITH THE GREATEST PLEASURE AND CORDIALITY, SHOWING THEM ALL ABOUT THE ESTATES AND SENDING THEM AWAY LOADED WITH FLOWERS."
—HELEN J. SANBORN, *A WINTER IN CENTRAL AMERICA AND MEXICO*, 1886.

By the end of the century, the Atlantic and Caribbean shipping lines, out of New Orleans, Baltimore, and New York, and the Pacific lines out of San Francisco were buzzing with passengers. One of these was the popular writer Richard Harding Davis, who wrote a highly colored account of his travels in an 1896 book, *Three Gringos in Venezuela and Central America*. He was particularly struck by Panama, where he observed the melancholy remains of French heavy machinery, abandoned after the failed attempt to dig a canal across Panama, and declared the isthmus "unholy ground."

In both *Three Gringos* and the novel *Captain Macklin* (a great favorite of John Hay, secretary of state under Teddy Roosevelt) Davis described Central America as a paradise of untapped potential. "There is not a fruit nor a grain nor a plant that you cannot dig out of it with your bare fingers," he wrote in his novel. "It has great forests, great pasture-lands, and buried treasures of silver and iron and gold. But it is cursed with the laziest of God's creatures, and the men who rule them are the most corrupt and the most vicious. . . . They are a menace and an insult to civilization, and it is time that they stepped down and out, and made way for their betters, or that they were kicked out."

Davis was soon followed by O. Henry, whose first book of short stories, *Cabbages and Kings,* was published in 1904. The tales were set in the Caribbean port of Trujillo, Honduras, where Will Porter (the author's real name) had fled from New Orleans to escape an embezzlement charge. By this time, a number of Americans had taken up residence in Central America. They found it a region perpetually caught up in what they called revolutions—in reality no more than a game of musical chairs played by a narrow circle of soldiers and landowners. The expatriates relished their own role in these events, and sent home an image of Central America as an exotic refuge— especially from the law. It was a place where local authorities were too weak or compliant to interfere, an unregulated new frontier for intrigue, adventure, and the making of quick fortunes.

"Coralio," explains Goodwin, the hero of one O. Henry story: "Not much of a town. A banana town, as they run. Grass huts, 'dobes, five or six two-story houses, accommodations limited, population half-breed Spanish and Indian, Caribs and blackamoors. No sidewalks to speak of, no amusements. Rather unmoral. . . . There is an American colony. Some of the members are all right. Some are fugitives from justice from the States. I recall two exiled bank presidents, one army paymaster under a cloud, a couple of manslayers, and a widow—arsenic, I believe, was the suspicion in her case."

The American Republic was dependent, it would seem, on the existence of territory for expansion. The West was no longer available after 1890, when the Census Office declared the frontier closed. "With its going," declared Frederick Jackson Turner, the great chronicler of the frontier, "has closed the first period of American history." Safeguarding the special character of American values and institutions now meant looking beyond the country's borders,

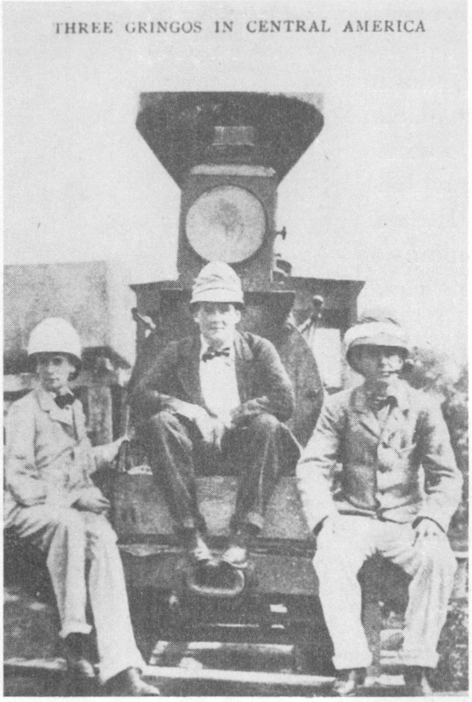
THREE GRINGOS IN CENTRAL AMERICA

"AWAY FROM THE COASTS, WHERE THERE IS FEVER, CENTRAL AMERICA IS A WONDERFUL COUNTRY, RICH AND BEAUTIFUL, AND BURDENED WITH PLENTY, BUT ITS PEOPLE MAKE IT A NUISANCE AND AN AFFRONT TO OTHER NATIONS."

—RICHARD HARDING DAVIS,
THREE GRINGOS IN VENEZUELA AND CENTRAL AMERICA, 1896.

"MOST OF HONDURAS IS A NATION OF EMPTY FORESTS, SWAMPY COASTS, AND SIEVE-LIKE BORDERS. IT IS A LAND MADE FOR SMUGGLERS AND CONSPIRATORS."

—CHRISTOPHER DICKEY,
WITH THE CONTRAS, 1985.

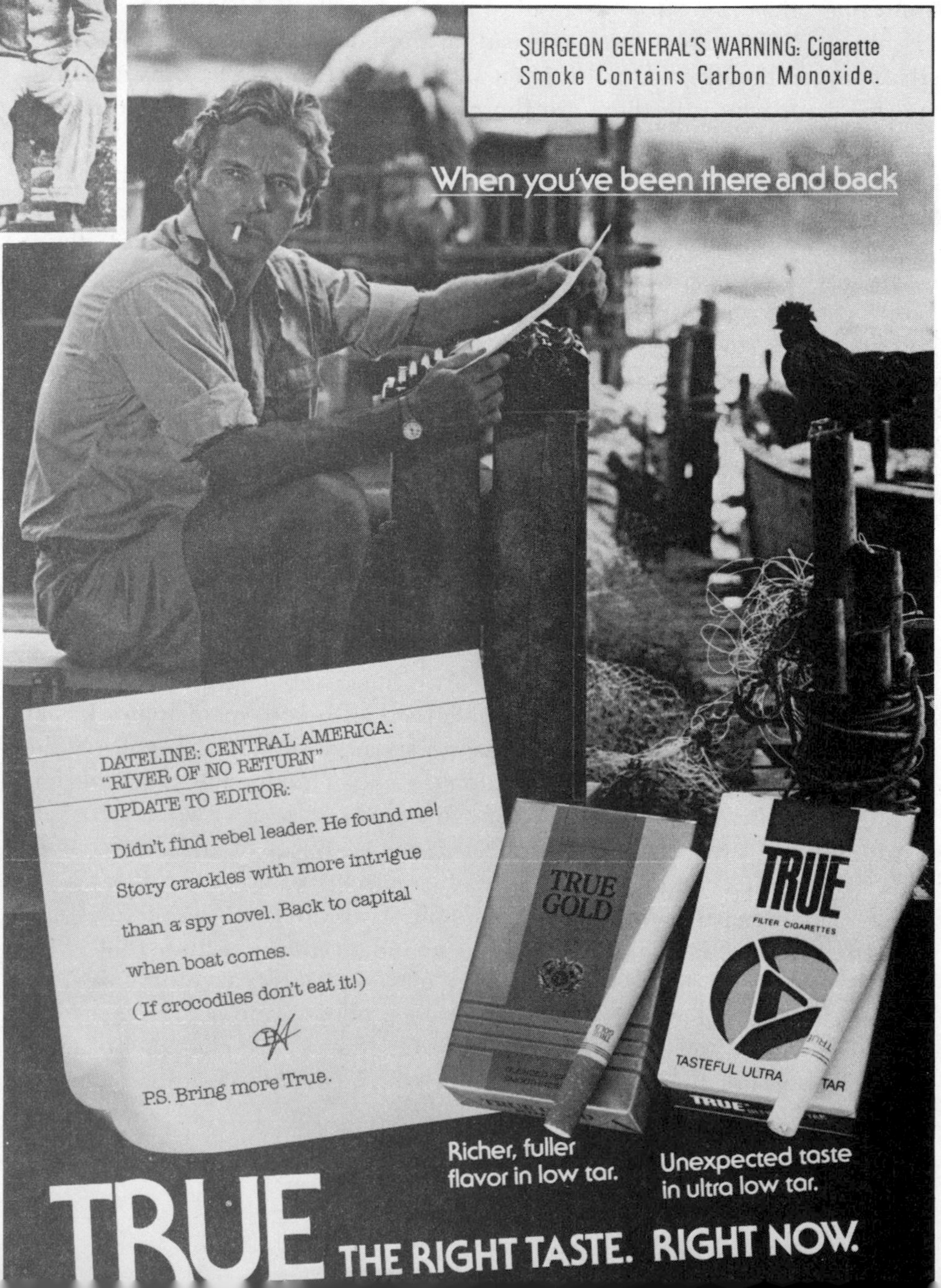
SURGEON GENERAL'S WARNING: Cigarette Smoke Contains Carbon Monoxide.
When you've been there and back
DATELINE: CENTRAL AMERICA:
"RIVER OF NO RETURN"
UPDATE TO EDITOR:
Didn't find rebel leader. He found me!
Story crackles with more intrigue
than a spy novel. Back to capital
when boat comes.
(If crocodiles don't eat it!)
P.S. Bring more True.
TRUE GOLD
TRUE
FILTER CIGARETTES
TASTEFUL ULTRA
Richer, fuller flavor in low tar.
Unexpected taste in ultra low tar.
TRUE
THE RIGHT TASTE. RIGHT NOW.

southward to the Caribbean, and at the same time spreading those values and institutions, missionary fashion, to the benighted nations lying in the path of expansion. But from the very outset, there was a schizophrenic quality to this sense of mission. In the tradition of Walker's Immortals, many of the settlers in Central America were criminals, mercenaries, and freebooters, who found it convenient to claim that they were acting in the service of the noblest ideals. Like the Rough Riders, many came fresh from the conquest of the West, and any half-breeds, Caribs, and blackamoors who stood in the way could expect much the same treatment as that meted out to the American Indian.

Contemplating events on their southern doorstep in the closing years of the nineteenth century, Americans saw alien disorder: savage Spanish colonial rule in Cuba and Puerto Rico, lawless frontier lands in Central America. There were two ways to respond: go in and clean these countries up, or stay out for fear of being contaminated. Confident in its own morality, the United States increasingly viewed the world, in the words of historian Richard Hofstadter, in terms of "simple virtues and unmitigated villainies." To explain the iniquities of the world beyond its borders, he wrote, "A villain was needed, marked with the unmistakable stigmata of the villains of melodrama."

Certainly, there was no shortage of external enemies in Central America and the Caribbean, where the United States saw one example after another of unwelcome European intrusion. The British, with their island colonies and their settlements in British Honduras (now Belize) and eastern Nicaragua, were accused in the Senate of "a series of exploits to gain the control of the Isthmus." The German kaiser was a newer adversary. In 1897, a minor diplomatic skirmish involving a German citizen in Haiti was blown up by the *New York World* into "a first step toward aggression and the acquisition of territory on this side of the ocean." The ill-fated French attempt to dig a canal in Panama finally collapsed in financial ruin and scandal in 1893—proof that France, if not an active menace, was at least guilty of incompetence, corruption, and meddling where it had no business.

-- -- --

As the enemy in a morality play, however, nothing fit the bill so perfectly as the decadent colonial rule of the aging Spanish monarchy. Hatred for the "corpse" of the Old World was widespread, but Spain had always been held in special contempt. Catholicism was seen as bigoted, lazy, and venal—the antithesis of the Protestant spirit of enterprise that had made the New World. "Naturally weak and effeminate," wrote the Reverend Jedediah Morse in one typical nineteenth-century textbook, the Spanish "dedicate the greatest part of their lives to loitering and inactive pleasures. Luxurious without variety or elegance, and expensive with great parade and little convenience, their character is nothing more than a grave and specious insignificance."

Nowhere was Spanish rule more abusive, and nowhere did it seem more of an affront to Americans, than on the island ninety miles from the shores of

Florida. Cuba had always had a special meaning to its northern neighbor. Back in 1823, John Quincy Adams had referred to it as a ripening apple, which "cannot choose but fall to the ground." Cuba, he believed, had "an importance in the sum of our national interests, with which that of no other foreign territory can be compared." The slave states saw the sugar island as an enticing addition to their ranks, and in 1859, Congress considered a bill to annex Cuba, and Santo Domingo (now the Dominican Republic). The idea of taking possession of these countries, and also Haiti, resurfaced in 1895, when a midwestern populist writer named Mary E. Lease produced a proposal— reeking of paranoia about European designs on the New World—for partitioning the globe along racial lines.

The United States convinced itself that its intervention in 1898 was on strictly humanitarian grounds. The purpose of the war would be to export freedom and to liberate Cubans, as well as Puerto Ricans, from their servitude. For many legislators, a fact-finding visit to Cuba was enough to change their votes to the war party. Senator Redfield Proctor, an antiwar conservative from Vermont, declared after such a trip that the United States had an obligation to deliver Cubans from "the worst misgovernment of which I ever had knowledge." The main object of disgust was General Valeriano Weyler, the brute of a Spanish military governor who turned entire Cuban cities into concentration camps. The newspaper headlines, carefully leavening circulation-boosting sensationalism with pious morality, shrieked out Spanish atrocities: the slaughter of innocent noncombatants, firing squads working overtime, bodies thrown into mass graves. Pulitzer's *World* worked itself into a frenzy: "Blood on the roadsides, blood in the fields, blood on the doorsteps, blood, blood, blood. Is there no nation wise enough, brave enough, and strong enough to restore peace in this bloodsmitten land?" Americans decided that there was.

But if the Spanish were unfit to rule, it did not mean that the local population itself was any more suited to the task. Even lower than Europeans in the hierarchy of capable self-government were the blacks and mulattoes who inhabited the region. Illustrators of the day showed Spain as a stage villain, all black cloak and twirling mustachio. Cuba was a slender young woman—the kind who gets tied to railroad tracks. And the native population was portrayed as squalling, watermelon-eating imbeciles and infants—transplanted southern blacks, in other words, or "pickaninnies," a word derived

•—••••••

DISPLAYS OF GRATITUDE FOR LIBERATION: CUBA 1898, GRENADA 1983.

"O CUBA! RAREST, BRIGHTEST GEM THAT DECKS ATLANTIC'S DIADEM! O STAR OF CONSTELLATION BRIGHT THAT BEAMS UPON OUR RAVISHED SIGHT!"
—JEANIE MORT WALKER, 1873.
"IT CERTAINLY IS A LOVELY PIECE OF REAL ESTATE."
—SECRETARY OF STATE GEORGE SHULTZ IN GRENADA, 1983.

from the Spanish *pequeño*, for little child. This image persisted for decades, in the minds of statesmen as well as cartoonists. In 1921, Ferdinand Mayer of the State Department's Division of Latin American Affairs explained that Haitians were "negro for the most part" and therefore "almost in a state of savagery and complete ignorance"; they required "control." "Dear me," said William Jennings Bryan, secretary of state under Woodrow Wilson, when he was briefed on this state of affairs, "think of it—niggers speaking French!"

The Spanish-American War confronted the United States with a dilemma: Left to themselves, the natives were likely to lapse into the cardinal sins in the Yankee canon, instability and inefficiency. The alternative was direct colonial rule on the European model, which asked the Cubans and Puerto Ricans to stand aside while Americans demonstrated the principles of proper government. In the end, the belief in American goodness, tainted though it was with racism, outweighed the risks of mimicking European behavior. The popular syndicated "Mr. Dooley" satirized the attitude perfectly: "Naygurs . . . ye mis'rable, childish-minded apes, we propose f'r to larn ye th' uses iv liberty. In ivry city in this unfair land we will erect schoolhouses an' packin' houses an' houses iv correction; an' we'll larn ye our language, because 'tis aisier to larn ye ours than to larn oursilves yours."

Along with schoolhouses, the Americans built drains, paved roads, and sewers, and public-health services. General Leonard Wood, governor of Cuba, punished offenses against the sanitation laws with a public whipping. The centerpiece of the sanitation crusade was Dr. Walter Reed's program to eradicate yellow fever in Havana (which, together with malaria and typhoid, had killed a dozen times more Americans than enemy gunfire). Official photographers were on hand to record every step for the public at home, emphasizing the natives' wonderment at American ingenuity. The fact that neither the Puerto Ricans nor the Cubans actively resisted the U.S. occupation was taken as further proof of its benevolence (even if many of them privately felt cheated of the fruits of their victory over Spain, and nationalists like José Martí in Cuba saw the Americans as the problem rather than the solution). The faith in the exportability of the American way never faltered: rather than wait for local conditions to allow democracy to develop, the United States simply decided to transplant the seedling without first checking the condition of the soil.

••   ••   ••

The emergence of the United States as a global power did provoke an impassioned, if limited, debate about the nature of its society and institutions, and its future world role. Could the United States remain unique if it acquired an empire? The argument was less about the logic of expansion, or even the subjugation of "inferior peoples," than about the risks of direct colonial rule.

A *Detroit News* cartoon of 1898 summed up these fears about the growing responsibilities of Uncle Sam, the figure who came of age with the Spanish-American War. In other cartoons of the day, he appeared in a variety of stern and kindly guises as the dispenser of punishment and reward: parent, policeman, and baby-sitter; guardian, schoolteacher, and sentry. Whether Uncle Sam's new charges exasperated him or moved him to compassion, there was little disagreement that they were helpless. According to the partisans of empire, the United States had a moral duty to uplift them. Like Asiatics, Mary Lease wrote in 1895, Latins were fit to be "tillers of the soil" in the Caucasian-owned tropics. This would not be an ignoble arrangement, but one they should "hail with joy." The few anti-imperialists of 1898, on the other hand, were convinced that incompetent savages had no place in the American system. For both sides, the ultimate concern was less the welfare of the colo-

•-••••

"HOW SOME APPREHENSIVE PEOPLE
PICTURE UNCLE SAM
AFTER THE WAR."
—*DETROIT NEWS, 1898.*

nized than the constitutional health of the United States. The country already
had a "black elephant" in the South, said a *New York World* editorial. Why
should it get mixed up with "a brown elephant in Porto Rico and perhaps a
yellow elephant in Cuba?"

These arguments had been heard before. Thirty years earlier, E. L. Godkin, editor of the *Nation*, had deplored the plan to annex Santo Domingo as a
"policy of absorbing semicivilized Catholic states." When the administration
of Chester Arthur tried to acquire rights to a Nicaraguan canal, Godkin was
alarmed at the prospect of fifteen million "slightly catholicized savages" becoming U.S. citizens. Central America, he believed, contained "more 'rum,
Romanism, and rebellion' to the square mile than probably any other part of
the world."

•• •• ••

These racial fears were particularly strong when it came to the Philippines.
Even the official chroniclers of the new empire could summon little enthusiasm for "barbarous Asiatics." Another photograph from the lavish two-volume
book *Our Islands and Their People*, which sold in 1899 for the enormous sum
of $15, depicts a group of Filipino prisoners of war. The caption reads: "When
at rest, these people rarely stand or sit down, but, on the contrary, squat like
animals, this peculiarity being one of the indications of their low state of
civilization. The whole nation is not worth the life of one American soldier."

Some opponents of annexation saw a clear moral difference between seiz-
ing the Philippines and taking Puerto Rico and Cuba. For one thing, the
Caribbean islands were so *small*—an argument that would later be applied
to each of the countries that lay across the United States's ragged southern
rim, with the exception of Mexico. They also possessed no "national aspira-

••••••

"NATIVES NEAR MANILA: THESE
PEOPLE REPRESENT THE LOWER
ORDERS AND MIXED RACES. THEIR
SQUATTING POSITIONS, SIMILAR TO
THE MONKEY'S FAVORITE
ATTITUDE, INDICATE A NO-DISTANT-
REMOVAL FROM THE 'CONNECTING
LINK.' "
—*OUR ISLANDS AND THEIR
PEOPLE,* 1899.

tions"—if they had, their people would not have turned out to welcome U.S. troops as liberators. Others believed that climate, biology, and politics were linked: no "tropical" people could ever become self-governing. Look at the experience of the British colonies, said the editor and senator Carl Schurz. Schurz posed the following dilemma: If Caribbean countries were annexed, the logic of American democracy would mean granting them statehood. But that would contaminate the American system. "Have you thought of it, what this means? . . . Fancy ten or twelve tropical States added to the Southern States we already possess; fancy the Senators and Representatives of ten or twelve millions of tropical people, people of the Latin race mixed with Indian and African blood; . . . fancy them sitting in the Halls of Congress, throwing the weight of their intelligence, their morality, their political notions and habits, their prejudices and passions, into the scale of the destinies of this Republic. . . . Tell me, does not your imagination recoil from the picture?"

In the end, Washington agreed that acquiring foreign territory was an "un-American" habit, reminiscent of the old European empires, and that the United States would instead exercise its control over the Caribbean and Central America indirectly. Otherwise the dissent counted for little. In the immortal phrase of Secretary of State Hay, 1898 had been a "splendid little war," a resounding military triumph with few casualties, popular at home. Faced with that kind of conflict, which was so vividly recalled by the invasion of Grenada eighty-five years later, dissenting voices were easily overwhelmed. Certainly the "anti-imperialists" did nothing to block the United States's next great stride to world power: Teddy Roosevelt's Panama Canal.

-- -- --

It is only accurate to call it Roosevelt's canal, even though he never saw the work completed and his successor, William Howard Taft, gave the project more time and attention. The entire enterprise bore the stamp of Roosevelt's personality, as much as San Juan Hill, and the images that surrounded it were engineered for public consumption in much the same fashion. It was Roosevelt who "took the isthmus," regardless of the niceties of international law and congressional debate. It was Roosevelt who grasped the military importance of the canal after the cruiser *Oregon* took nearly ten weeks in 1898 to complete its journey from San Francisco and around the Horn in order to reach Cuba and play a part in the battle at Santiago Bay. And it was Roosevelt who colluded with the Frenchman (and Panamanian agent) Philippe Bunau-Varilla to back the secession of Panama from Colombia in 1903, recognizing the rebel regime less than ninety minutes after it seized power and guaranteeing its survival by sending ten U.S. gunboats to stand offshore at Colón and Panama City. (The new republic's declaration of independence and its draft constitution were concocted by Bunau-Varilla in a Washington hotel room, and its first flag was sewn in Highland Falls, New York, by his wife.)

Everything in Panama was on an epic scale. The canal was wrapped in myth. It was the greatest feat of engineering in history: a victory for American technology and know-how, a taming of the jungle wilderness, and a triumph

"UNCLE SAM'S NEXT DUTY."
—*MINNEAPOLIS TRIBUNE*.
"AN INTEROCEANIC CANAL . . .
WILL BE THE GREAT OCEAN
THOROUGHFARE BETWEEN OUR
ATLANTIC AND OUR PACIFIC SHORES
AND VIRTUALLY A PART OF THE
COASTLINE OF THE UNITED
STATES."
—PRESIDENT RUTHERFORD B.
HAYES, 1880.

SPRAYING TO CONTROL
MOSQUITOES, PANAMA. "GENERAL
GORGAS SAID THAT THERE WERE
THREE CAUSES FOR WHICH THE
AMERICANS LEFT PANAMA IN THE
OLD DAYS: YELLOW FEVER,
MALARIA, AND COLD FEET, AND
THAT OF THE THREE THE LAST
CAUSED MORE DESERTIONS THAN
THE OTHER TWO COMBINED."
—GEORGE A. MILLER, *PROWLING
ABOUT PANAMA*, 1919.

••••••

"A GRAPHIC COMPARISON: THE
'SPOIL' TAKEN FROM THE CANAL
WOULD BUILD SIXTY-THREE
PYRAMIDS THE SIZE OF CHEOPS'
ON BROADWAY FROM THE BATTERY
TO HARLEM."
—*SCIENTIFIC AMERICAN*, 1912.

over disease. Travelers to the California goldfields reported that the construction of the Panama railroad alone had cost a dead man for every tie—some said a dead Irishman, others a dead Chinaman. Other mythmakers outdid themselves with tales of what could be done with all the excavated earth: it was enough to build a Great Wall of China stretching from San Francisco to New York; a train of railroad cars filled with the dirt would circle the earth four times; piled in a solid heap the size of a city block, it would form a tower reaching nineteen miles high.

Like Cuba, Panama was a symbolic victory for the New World. All the contemporary literature stressed how the industrious and upright Americans had succeeded where the dissolute French had failed. The French years, wrote Roosevelt biographer Joseph Bucklin Bishop, had been "a genuine bacchanalian orgy" of vice and incompetence—though U.S. engineers eventually appreciated the magnitude of what the French had accomplished two decades earlier.

The most surprising thing about the Panama Canal was its location. Until 1902, it was taken for granted that a Central American canal would follow the route of Cornelius Vanderbilt's old Nicaragua crossing: up the Río San Juan and across Lake Nicaragua, leaving only a sixteen-mile channel to be cut across dry land. Even as the final Senate vote on a canal site approached, the betting was still strongly on Nicaragua. But on May 8, nature took a hand. A catastrophic volcanic eruption wiped out the city of St. Pierre on the French Caribbean island of Martinique. Six days later, the volcano of Momotombo on Lake Managua followed suit. Even though Momotombo lay a full ninety miles north of the canal route, the Nicaraguan government tried hard to hush it up. Bunau-Varilla, who was in Washington to lobby the United States to buy the unfinished French workings at Panama, seized his opportunity. Three days before the decisive June 16 vote, he got hold of ninety copies of a recent Nicaraguan postage stamp showing Momotombo in vivid eruption— one for each senator. Pasting each on a separate sheet of paper, he typed underneath, "An official witness of the volcanic activity on the isthmus of Nicaragua."

MISS NICARAGUA: "O SAM, YOU
FICKLE THING! THEY TELL AWFUL
STORIES ABOUT HER!"
—*COLUMBUS DISPATCH*, ca. 1902.

"LOOK AT THE NICARAGUAN
POSTAGE STAMPS. YOUNG NATIONS
LIKE TO PUT ON THEIR COATS OF
ARMS WHAT BEST SYMBOLIZES
THEIR MORAL DOMAIN OR
CHARACTERIZES THEIR
NATIVE SOIL."
—PHILIPPE BUNAU-VARILLA.

The tactic depended heavily on senatorial ignorance, for volcanoes were a source of national pride throughout Central America, as postage stamps from almost any country in the region could have shown. Salvadoran stamps of the period show the smoking cone of Izalco; Costa Rican stamps, the eleven-thousand-foot peak of Irazú. Panama itself had no volcanoes—just earthquakes. A severe one had hit Panama City in 1902, and another, more powerful than the San Francisco quake of 1906, struck the canal itself just four days after the first ship passed through the great Gatún locks in 1913. But Bunau-Varilla's ploy worked. In the legislators' lurid but imprecise mental landscape of Nicaragua, geological upheaval meshed with political turbulence, and the Senate voted 42–34 in favor of the site in Panama.

In 1906, as work on the canal pressed ahead, Teddy Roosevelt himself paid a visit—the first foreign trip ever by a sitting U.S. president. The event was superbly stage-managed, as TR demonstrated that he was the first president to grasp the power of technology and the mushrooming influence of the press. Roosevelt understood that most readers cared more about news stories and headlines than about editorial comment, and he saw that a modern president could generate news events at will in order to dominate the front pages. He "played upon the correspondents as if they constituted a human typewriter," wrote press historians John William Tebbel and Sarah Miles Watts.

To dramatize his own adventurous spirit and the challenge involved in building the canal, Roosevelt deliberately chose to travel at the height of Panama's legendary rainy season, when conditions would be at their worst. The deluge on his second day was the heaviest in fifteen years, hurling down three inches of rain in two hours. In the midst of the downpour, the president hoisted himself into the cab of a ninety-five-ton Bucyrus steam shovel. Wearing a white suit and a broad Panama hat (actually manufactured in Ecuador), he remained perched there for twenty minutes while the cameras snapped away—in modern parlance, a photo opportunity. The picture made the front page of the *New York Times* and quickly became part of American folklore.

"I TOOK THE CANAL ZONE AND LET THE CONGRESS DEBATE; AND WHILE THE DEBATE GOES ON, THE CANAL DOES ALSO."
—TEDDY ROOSEVELT, PICTURED HERE AT CULEBRA CUT, PANAMA, 1906.

In the first decade of the new century, Uncle Sam continued to face the problem of how far to trust his squalling infant charges to walk by themselves. The most radical solution was applied to Puerto Rico (or, as Americans insisted on calling it, Porto Rico), which was simply handed over by Spain "as compensation for the losses and expenses occasioned . . . by the war." But Washington expressly disclaimed any idea of direct rule in Cuba, and said it intended "to leave the government and control of the island to its people." Only up to a point, however. An amendment inserted into the new Cuban constitution in 1903 by Senator Orville Hitchcock Platt gave the United States "the right to intervene for the preservation of Cuban independence, [and] the maintenance of a government adequate for the protection of life, property and individual liberty." The United States also granted itself the right to build a naval base at Guantánamo Bay on Cuba's southeastern coast, a crucial defense for the new canal. (It is still there today, almost thirty years after Fidel Castro's revolution.) As General Leonard Wood, U.S. military commander in Cuba, acknowledged, "The Platt amendment has left Cuba with little or no independence."

The right of intervention was invoked whenever Washington felt the Cubans needed to be rescued from their propensity to chaos. The marines went in in 1906, when civil war seemed in the air, and stayed for more than two years. In 1912 they were back, landing on Daiquiri Beach to put down a rebellion of ex-slaves and protect the sugarcane fields of the Cuban-American Sugar Company, whose president, Mario García Menocal, also became president of the country the following year. They landed for a third time in 1917,

THE PHILIPPINES: "WHAT YER GOT?"

CUBA: "PIE."

THE PHILIPPINES: "WHERE'D YER
GIT IT?"

CUBA: "MAH UNCLE SAM GIN IT TO
ME; AN' MAYBE EF YOU WAS HALF
WAY DECENT HE GIN YOU SOME."
—*MINNEAPOLIS TRIBUNE*, 1901.

this visit to guarantee sugar supplies after the United States had entered World War I. On each occasion, the occupation forces announced that their presence was temporary, and their intentions benign—to restore stability—but the net effect was to stunt the growth of strong local authority and ensure that stability was delayed a little longer.

When Theodore Roosevelt read the dispatches from his ministers in the region, he saw Cubans and Dominicans, Haitians and Nicaraguans, collectively refusing to behave like Americans; instead they seemed to be acting like characters from a Richard Harding Davis novel. The vision provoked one of his most common emotions—exasperation—and he responded, in his annual message to Congress in 1904, with his famous corollary to the Monroe Doctrine: "Chronic wrongdoing, or an impotence which results in a general loosening of the ties of civilized society, may in America, as elsewhere, ultimately require intervention by some civilized nation, and in the Western Hemisphere the adherence of the United States to the Monroe Doctrine may force the United States, however reluctantly, in flagrant cases of such wrongdoing or impotence, to the exercise of an international police power."

The proximate cause of this announcement was the situation in Santo Domingo, which had degenerated into factional mayhem since the assassination of the dictator Ulises Heureaux in 1899. Runaway foreign loans had pushed the country to the edge of bankruptcy; worse, Roosevelt invoked the

••••••

UNCLE SAM: "MAYBE I'LL HAVE TO BRING THE BOY INTO THE HOUSE TO KEEP HIM QUIET."
—*ST. PAUL PIONEER PRESS*, 1904.
"I CAN'T TALK YOUR LINGO BUT I'LL DO MY BEST—BY JINGO, STOP THAT FIGHTIN', SAN DOMINGO!"
—WALLACE IRWIN, 1904.

old specter of foreign intervention in the chaos, with European gunboats steaming in to collect their unpaid debts. Riding roughshod over congressional protests, Roosevelt sent in American customs agents to take over the government's finances, holding back 55 percent of its customs revenues to pay off its creditors.

This model of control also appealed to Roosevelt's successor, Taft, though he refined it further. Where TR had stressed the raw pioneer example of the American way—its racial virility, its technological prowess—Taft's particular contribution was his belief in the power of the dollar. In 1912, he told Congress, "The diplomacy of the present administration has sought to respond to modern ideas of commercial intercourse. This policy has been characterized as substituting dollars for bullets." He and Philander Chase Knox, his secretary of state, believed with apparent sincerity that U.S. capital, if allowed to spread freely, would eradicate the evils of poverty and unstable government. They chose the same part of the world Roosevelt had as their guinea pig, though concentrating more on the Central American mainland than the Caribbean islands.

-- -- --

As work got under way on the Panama Canal, U.S. warships were sent to patrol the coasts of Central America, with standing orders to land troops at the discretion of the ship's captain or the local U.S. consul at any sign of unrest—a not infrequent occurrence. In 1907, the marines went ashore when the Honduran government fell after a pitched battle with its more powerful neighbor Nicaragua, which had been ruled since 1893 by José Santos Zelaya, a Liberal in the same mold as the Guatemalan coffee-growers. Washington convened a Central American peace conference and diplomatically banged heads together. The 1907 intervention was of the routine sort that was regularly applied in Cuba: it lasted only a short time, involved little or no bloodshed, and was designed to remind the locals of the realities of power.

In March 1909, however, after Taft entered the White House, Zelaya fell victim to a second, more far-reaching kind of intervention, which radically altered the course of Nicaraguan history. Among other things, his reforms had involved an effort to tax the banana companies and other U.S. businesses that had sprung up along Nicaragua's remote Atlantic coast (a move that may have seemed a personal affront to Knox, whose law firm represented the owners of one of the corporations there, the La Luz and Los Angeles Mining Company). The companies, in turn, had more than once helped to underwrite Conservative uprisings against the Managua government, to the tune of perhaps $1 million. When the U.S. chargé d'affaires urged intervention by the marines ("for there is nothing these people respect and follow like power"), Taft and Knox were not unsympathetic.

Zelaya's crime was nationalism. It was not the patriotic fervor of the Cuban *independentistas* but a more matter-of-fact attempt to diversify the trading relationships of a small country trying to make its way in the modern world—a distinction that was lost on Washington. As part of his long-term plan to develop a modern capitalist economy, Zelaya contracted loans with a British-French syndicate, and engaged a German company to build a railroad linking the Pacific and Atlantic coasts. To the U.S. press, this was enough to convict him of frenzied "anti-Americanism." The *New York Times* accused Zelaya, entirely without foundation, of "advocating an offensive and defensive alliance with Japan, aimed against this country." Rumors also flew that Zelaya was urging the Japanese to build a canal in Nicaragua, though it was

"A HINT."
—*WASHINGTON STAR*, 1907.

never explained why they, or anyone else, should contemplate the folly of competing with the U.S. enterprise in Panama.

The crunch came when a Nicaraguan court-martial found two of the businessmen involved in helping the rebels, Virginian Lee Roy Cannon and Texan Leonard Groce, guilty of attempting to mine a riverboat full of government soldiers. Cannon and Groce were executed by firing squad in November 1909. With a note that condemned the Zelaya regime as "a blot upon the history of Nicaragua," the United States broke off diplomatic relations, which was enough to force Zelaya to resign. Fresh contingents of U.S. troops landed in 1910 to guarantee the survival of the new Conservative government, which agreed in return to tie itself to the United States by a financial pact similar to that applied to the Dominican Republic five years earlier.

The surrender of the national economy to Washington, as well as the venality and incompetence of the new president, Adolfo Díaz (former treasurer of the La Luz and Los Angeles Mining Company), quickly gave rise to a wave of protest against the Conservatives. Almost three thousand marines and navy bluejackets arrived in 1912 to shore up the inept government they had brought to power. They placed the country under martial law and declared that new elections would resolve the crisis. Less than four thousand people were allowed to vote, and there was one candidate—Díaz.

After the voting, a small guard of a hundred marines stayed behind, until 1925. For most of that time, martial law remained in force; there were at least ten attempts at revolution. The American manager of the National Bank of Nicaragua (which paid Díaz's salary) later told Senate hearings, "I think the present government would last until the last coach of marines left Managua station, and I think President Díaz would be on that last coach." During the thirteen-year occupation, the United States sent in whole teams of tinkerers and technicians—election experts to arrange fresh votes, monetary wizards to regulate the currency, military advisers to create a "native constabulary" called the National Guard—all in an effort to restore some natural rhythm to the national development that had been disrupted by the overthrow of Zelaya.

Woodrow Wilson, who restored the Democrats to the White House from 1913 to 1920, presided over most of that period of turmoil in Nicaragua. He was, wrote Hofstadter, "a would-be dispenser of sanity and justice to a world maddened by wartime hatreds . . . preached of a mission of world service to the most insular and provincial people among all the great powers." He believed fervently that American democracy was unique: "There was nothing revolutionary about its movements," Wilson wrote, "it had not to overthrow other polities; it had only to organize itself. It had not to create, but

U.S. MARINES HEAD FOR CORINTO,
NICARAGUA, 1910.
"EVEN THOUGH YOU COUNT ON
EVERYTHING,
YOU STILL LACK ONE THING: GOD."
—RUBÉN DARÍO,
"ODE TO ROOSEVELT."

only to expand, self-government. It did not need to spread propaganda: it needed nothing but to methodize its way of living."

As early as 1902, writing on the Spanish-American War, Wilson had moralized that it was "our peculiar duty" to teach the peoples who inhabited the new U.S. colonial frontiers "order and self-control," and to "impart to them, if it be possible, . . . the drill and habit of law and obedience." With this kind of moral antipathy to disorder, he looked to the Caribbean, where he executed a foreign policy with the zeal of a temperance crusader. And though he decried the vulgar power of the dollar that his predecessor had preached, he was responsible in the end for more (and more prolonged) armed interventions in the region than Taft and Roosevelt combined.

Between 1912 and 1915, Haiti saw six presidents come and go; not one served out his term peacefully. In July 1915, the government collapsed altogether, when President Guillaume Sam was dragged into the street by a mob and torn to pieces. Within a year, President Juan Isidro Jiménez of the Dominican Republic was impeached, and renewed rebellion broke out. The marines went into both countries. Haiti became a protectorate. Its president was barred from entering the U.S. Officers' Club in Port-au-Prince because he was black. An American military government was installed in Santo Domingo, staying there until 1924, and next door in Haiti until 1934.

At first the dispatch of the Marines was relatively popular at home, al-

HAITIAN GENDARMES AT SCHOOL, RECEIVING INSTRUCTION FROM MARINE CORPS OFFICERS. "IT SHALL NOT LIE WITH THE AMERICAN PEOPLE TO DICTATE TO ANOTHER PEOPLE WHAT THEIR GOVERNMENT SHALL BE OR WHAT USE THEY SHALL HAVE OR WHAT PERSONS THEY SHALL ENCOURAGE OR FAVOR." —WOODROW WILSON, DRAFT MESSAGE TO CONGRESS, 1916. "HAITI, S. DOMINGO, NICARAGUA, PANAMA." —SECRETARY OF STATE ROBERT LANSING'S MARGINAL NOTE.

though some publications, like the *Nation,* carried investigative reports on the brutality—and thinly concealed racism—of the occupation. Troops hunting the Haitian rebels sang "Damn, damn, damn the Haitian cacos," to the tune of the old Spanish-American War verse, "Damn the Filipino!" To break the back of the resistance, Marines in blackface surprised and killed the rebel leader Charlemagne Péralte and strapped his body to a door, leading to the persistent belief among Haitians that he had been crucified.

Whenever this kind of gap opened up between the language of pure intentions and actions of pure expediency, Wilson tried to bridge it by invoking external enemies who might threaten the "independence" of these small neighbors. The enemy of the day was Germany, and in the year before the United States entered the Great War, anxiety about the kaiser's intentions in the Western Hemisphere was intense, and not without foundation. Mexico, which was openly pro-German, was the most worrisome. When the rebel Pancho Villa attacked U.S. citizens in 1916, James Gerard, the ambassador to Berlin, cabled the State Department, "Am sure Villa's attacks are made in Germany." The *Buffalo Express* conjured up the image of "hordes of Mexicans under German officers, sweeping into Texas, New Mexico, and Arizona." In Haiti, anxiety slipped over into delusion. Wilson saw the chaos there as an invitation for Germany to move in and build submarine bases. Marine Corps Commander George Thorpe was convinced that "whoever is running this revolution is a wise man; he certainly is getting a lot out of the niggers. . . . It shows the handiwork of the German." He told new marine recruits that the Great War would last long enough "to give every man a chance against the Hun in Europe and the Hun in Santo Domingo."

For domestic consumption, the occupations were portrayed as acts of unimpeachable altruism. In 1916, *National Geographic* dispatched a journalist to write an article about Haiti, Nicaragua, and the Dominican Republic titled "Wards of the United States." His report was a classic of Wilsonian prose: "The Black Republic of Haiti and the Mulatto Republic of Santo Domingo" were "the scene today of one of the most interesting experiments in government that may be found anywhere in the world." Military rule was giving "results of which a nation which covets no territory, which seeks only its own security and the welfare of its unfortunate neighbors, may well be proud. . . . Wherever America has gone, whether to Cuba, whether to Panama, whether to Santo Domingo, Porto Rico, Nicaragua, the Philippines, or Haiti, the welfare of the people has been her first concern, and while all colonial history shows that the tares of evil are never absent from the wheat of good, our nation's record of help given where most needed is one that may well challenge our admiration and quicken our patriotism."

"COME ALL YE GOOD CITIZENS,
RAISE YOUR LOUDEST HOSANNAS,
WITH PAEANS OF POPULAR PRAISE
FOR TAXLESS BANANAS."
—E. T. NELSON, 1913.

TWO

·–·–·–·

BANANA
REPUBLICS

`1918–33`

AN ABSOLUTE NATIONAL MORALITY IS INSPIRED
EITHER TO WITHDRAW FROM "ALIEN" THINGS
OR TO TRANSFORM THEM: IT CANNOT LIVE IN COMFORT
CONSTANTLY BY THEIR SIDE.
—LOUIS HARTZ,
THE LIBERAL TRADITION IN AMERICA

In the early decades of the twentieth century, it seemed as if all America, caught up in a new dietary fad, agreed with Benjamin Disraeli's conviction that "the most delicious thing in the world is a banana."

When domestic sales taxes on bananas were removed in 1913, there was an outpouring of festive verse in the newspapers, and banana recipes abounded. The fruit was cheap, exotic, and nutritious, and the region it came from would henceforth be wrapped in cliché as the land of the "banana republics."

The first samples of the fruit—just thirty bunches—had reached New York from Havana aboard the schooner *Reynard* in 1804, but it remained a rare luxury until the turn of the century. The most famous of the banana giants, the United Fruit Company of Boston, was incorporated in March 1899; with operations soon in place in Cuba, Jamaica, Guatemala, Honduras, Costa Rica, Panama, and Colombia, it was the largest agricultural enterprise in the world. Its rival, Standard Fruit, controlled the banana trade in Nicaragua.

•• •• ••

With the Spanish-American War behind it, and advantageous financial arrangements worked out with the countries of Central America and the Caribbean during the Taft years, the federal government stepped into the back-ground, to be called upon as an enforcer only when necessary. Americans in the region devoted themselves enthusiastically to Calvin Coolidge's belief that the business of America was business. The image they presented to Central Americans was the man in the white tropical business suit, with the marine uniform held in reserve.

Minority opinion in the United States, echoing a widespread sentiment in Latin America, saw the fruit companies as the ugly face of Yankee imperialism. But the businessmen could always rely on a steady stream of favorable publicity—much of which they generated themselves. A typically lyrical account of the banana trade was Frederick Upham Adams's 1914 *Conquest of the Tropics,* which Doubleday Books of New York published as the first volume in a series titled "The Romance of Big Business." For at least four decades, United Fruit and its competitors appeared as the emblems of progress in the tropics. Although in one sense they were the direct descendants of the southern plantation expansionists of the mid-1800s, the fruit companies represented a new kind of corporate enterprise. Their shareholders reaped enormous profits from the companies' use of advanced agrarian technologies and their embrace of the new ideas of labor efficiency that made Frederick Winslow Taylor a household name. Like the builders of the Panama Canal, the fruit giants imposed order on a vast scale. Where there had been wilderness, they built schoolhouses and hospitals and workers' settlements of neat wooden houses, turning inhospitable jungles into company towns.

The arrival of the fruit companies often brought the host countries their first real infrastructure. In Guatemala, for example, United Fruit built (and owned) the main highways, the railroads, and the only port on the Caribbean coast. It handled cable communications throughout the region, and traveling news reporters relied on the company's Tropical Radio to send their dispatches. "It is in Guatemala," wrote W. J. Showalter in *National Geographic,* "that one begins properly to appreciate the great civilizing influence of a much-maligned American corporation—the United Fruit Company. . . . It is the advent of such organizations as these—powerful enough to protect their own interests when disputes with local government arise—that spells the economic salvation of these countries and promises an honest wage to the laboring classes." Sovereignty, in other words, was a lower priority than progress and order.

The other side of the coin for Showalter was that the natives showed no sign of this entrepreneurial drive. In Nicaragua, which most commentators of the day agreed was a special basket case, "they have had revolutions since the memory of the inhabitants runneth not to the contrary. There seems to be

WHERE THE BANANAS COME FROM

Here is the key to the above map:
No. 21, "Almirante," a bay and also a town in Panama.
No. 22, "Santa Marta," a city on the north coast of Colombia.
No. 23, "Metapan," a town in San Salvador.
No. 24, "Zacapa," an important railroad centre in Guatemala.
No. 25, "Pastores," a town in the western part of Gautemala.
No. 26, "Tenadores," the junction of two rivers in Central Guatemala.
No. 27, "Calamares," a town in Colombia.
No. 28, "Miami," a bay and town in Florida.
No. 29, "Manistee," from several sources in the United States.
No. 30, "Aracataca," a town in Colombia.
No. 31, "Chagres," the Panama River that the engineers of its canal had to harness.
No. 32, "Patuca," a river in Spanish Honduras.
No. 33, "Manzanares," a river in Colombia.

•••••

"THE FRUIT COMPANY, INC.
RESERVED FOR ITSELF THE MOST
   SUCCULENT,
THE CENTRAL COAST OF MY OWN
   LAND,
THE DELICATE WAIST OF AMERICA.
IT RECHRISTENED ITS TERRITORIES
AS THE 'BANANA REPUBLICS'
AND OVER THE SLEEPING DEAD,
OVER THE RESTLESS HEROES
WHO BROUGHT ABOUT THE
   GREATNESS,
THE LIBERTY AND THE FLAGS,
IT ESTABLISHED THE COMIC OPERA."
—PABLO NERUDA.

••••••

"BRINGING BANANAS TO THE
AWAITING FRUIT SHIP. HERE ARE
FIVE BANANA TRAINS WHERE A FEW
YEARS AGO WAS AN UNBROKEN
AND DEADLY WILDERNESS."
—*CONQUEST OF THE TROPICS*, 1914.

"THE DIFFERENCE BETWEEN THE
JUNGLE AND THE DIVIDEND-PAYING
PLANTATION IS ONE OF
ORGANIZATION, CAPITAL,
ADMINISTRATION, AND TOIL. ADD
THESE TO THE JUNGLE AND YOU
HAVE THE PLANTATION."
—GEORGE A. MILLER, 1919.

little hope that they will ever be able to give themselves a good government."
Such a waste, Showalter lamented, for "here one sees a thousand opportunities for the development of great wealth. . . . Given good governments, then no countries on the map would afford greater opportunities for profitable investments than those of Central America." Good governments or not, U.S. corporate investments blossomed twentyfold between 1897 and 1929. The largest share, more than $80 million, was in Honduras, the quintessential banana republic.

•• •• ••

Though the companies and their propagandists spoke loudly of order and progress, their operations in the field were often run by cowboys and rogues.

If any one man gave birth to the banana-republic stereotype, it was Sam (the Banana Man) Zemurray, a Bessarabian immigrant to the United States who started his career by buying overripe bananas from United Fruit and peddling them in New Orleans. In 1910, he bought up fifteen thousand acres of Honduras's Caribbean coast. The following year he joined forces with former president Manuel Bonilla and an American mercenary named Lee Christmas to overthrow a Liberal regime that had offended the State Department by getting up to its neck in debt to Britain and becoming too friendly with the Nicaraguan leader Zelaya. Zemurray, Bonilla, and Christmas landed their troops at Trujillo, O. Henry's old stamping ground, and the U.S. consul named a new president of Honduras.

In their north-coast enclave, the banana companies received five hundred hectares of free land for every kilometer of railroad they built. The result was a serpentine maze of tracks that crisscrossed the flatlands of the coast, but no railway was ever laid to serve the capital city, Tegucigalpa. In this splendid isolation, the companies ran Honduras much more effectively than the central government. U.S. dollars became legal tender. Lee Christmas was named commander-in-chief of the Honduran Army, and later was rewarded with the post of U.S. consul.

Until 1929, when United Fruit bought out Zemurray, Honduran politics were little more than disputes between elite factions loyal to one or another fruit company. United Fruit's dominance after 1929 was mirrored by the emergence of the National Party of Tiburcio Carías Andino, the first of the great dictators who ruled the region through the 1940s. Though visitors like Showalter lamented the lack of "good government," the companies seemed

GENERAL LEE CHRISTMAS, 1907.

"WHAT A MAN—WHAT A FIGHTER! A REVOLUTION WAS INCOMPLETE WITHOUT HIM."
—F. A. MITCHELL-HEDGES.

to do their utmost to prevent it from taking root, locking local politicians into the parasitic behavior the Americans claimed to deplore. H. V. Rolston, of United Fruit's Cortes Development Company in Honduras, told his lawyer in 1920 that it was "indispensable to capture the imagination of these subjugated peoples, and attract them to the idea of our aggrandisement. . . . It is in our interest to make it our concern that the privileged class, whom we will need for our exclusive benefit, bend itself to our will; in general, none of them has any conviction or character, far less patriotism; they seek only position and rank, and on being granted them, we will make them hungry for even more."

The companies proposed to "capture the imagination of the subjugated peoples" in the same way they won the admiration of readers back home— through material improvements, social benefits, and high wage rates in a country where most of the population faced a life of squalor and disease. But the paternalism must be kept in perspective: the high wages were designed to attract the best workers to the torrid lowlands and then keep them out of the clutches of labor unions. A large slice of their wages went straight to the company store. Even as it provided benefits that no local employer could match, United Fruit shipped out profits that were almost equal to the entire Honduran national budget.

Bananas were not United Fruit's only crop. In Cuba, the company ran two great sugar mills, the Central Boston and the Central Preston. The company town was Birán, just outside Mayarí. "Few places in Cuba were quite so dominated by the North American presence," wrote Hugh Thomas. "The United Fruit Company's employees had a polo club, swimming pools, shops for U.S. goods. Even the post office and rural-guard headquarters were on company land. The company had its own force of twenty field soldiers, licensed to bear arms. At both Boston and Preston there were schools and hospitals, and every possible amenity." One worker on the United Fruit railroad was an immigrant from Galicia in Spain named Ángel Castro, who looked after company property after the marine intervention of 1917. In 1926, on the family farm at Birán, Ángel Castro's second wife and former cook, Lina Ruz González, gave birth to a son, Fidel.

•• •• ••

Besides being the sugar bowl of the Caribbean, Cuba had another destiny in the minds of Americans. Its potential as a tourist paradise had been foreseen in 1898. As José de Olivares, one of the official chroniclers of the Spanish-American War, had predicted, "With the ultimate success of the sanitary and moral reforms which are now being introduced, it must eventually become one of the most attractive and popular winter resorts." Just a steamship ride away from the ports of the eastern seaboard, there were beaches and golf courses and a country club, the finest tobacco in the world, and "the most charming trolley line in the tropics." The accommodations, transportation, and services were U.S.-owned; the waiters and drivers spoke English. As an educational bonus for the children, there were wartime battlefields to visit,

•—•—•—•

"SEND THREE CENTS IN STAMPS FOR

OUR BEAUTIFULLY ILLUSTRATED

BOOKLET DESCRIBING ABOVE

AND OTHER INTERESTING TRIPS

TO CUBA, TO UNITED RAILWAYS

OF HAVANA."

From Florida to Cuba.

OFF FOR CUBA

like San Juan Hill and, until it was dredged up in 1911, the wreck of the *Maine*. Above all, there were the glories of the capital city, which de Olivares called "beautiful, iniquitous Havana—the Nineveh of the closing century, the Gilead of the next."

The Marine occupations in the Caribbean brought news of even more exotic destinations, including Haiti and Santo Domingo, where Wilson sent troops in 1915 and 1916, respectively. Haiti had been terra incognita to most Americans, though it was only six hundred miles away. As the first black republic, founded in 1804 after Toussaint L'Ouverture's revolt in 1791, it had been seen as a frightful omen by the slave states. Southerners spoke with dread of a "second Haiti," much as modern administrations talk of a "second Cuba," and the most recalcitrant of the slaveowners pointed to the chaos and bloodshed of the revolt as proof that blacks were bestial and incapable of self-government. Since the Civil War, Haiti had suggested the mysteries of voodoo, and little else.

Haiti became known to a mass audience in the late 1920s and early 1930s, however, through the exploits of a folk hero named Faustin Wirkus, "a blond, tough, Pennsylvania former miner-boy in American Marine Corps uniform." Wirkus had arrived in Port-au-Prince aboard the USS *Tennessee* in August 1915. "Join the Marines and See the World," Wirkus wrote in his autobiography, published in New York in 1931. "It seemed to be my only chance to get away from the Dupont section of the Pittston coal mining district, in Pennsylvania, where I was born. . . . There was supposed to be something going on in Haiti—wherever that was—which called for the 'Marines to land, and take the situation in hand.' . . . A lot of my companions, I know, thought

**THE KING GOES ABOUT
HIS BUSINESS**

Three modes of travel
for a Marine on duty
in Haiti.

••••••

FAUSTIN WIRKUS IN HAITI.
"WHEN A MAN HAS STINTED
AND ECONOMIZED ALL HIS LIFE
ON A NEW ENGLAND HILLSIDE
AMID STONES AND STUMPS,
THE JUNGLE TAKES THE LOAD
OFF HIS SOUL AND SETS HIM FREE
IN A UNIVERSE OF NEW
AND UNTESTED DIMENSIONS."
—GEORGE A. MILLER, 1919.

"WIRKUS AND LA REINE JULIE: THE

FIRST DEPUTY QUEEN UNDER TI

MEMENNE, DRESSED IN CLOTHES

WIRKUS BROUGHT HER FROM THE

STATES."

that Haiti was in the Samoan group; others thought it was merely 'somewhere south of Suez.' "

The rookie marine was invalided out in 1916 with a broken arm but chose to go back three years later to join the Haitian *gendarmerie*. He was posted to La Gonave, the island province across the bay from Port-au-Prince, which had a reputation as "a God-forsaken hole inhabited by savages." The island had its own kind of autonomous monarchy, with a queen called Ti Memenne and a "first deputy queen," La Reine Julie. Wirkus was the first white man many of the islanders had seen, and they crowned him king. As monarch, he recalled, he was known "for being fair and an 'easy boss,' though exacting and dangerous to lie to or disobey." He brought Deputy Queen Julie clothes from the United States, and dressed her as a flapper for a visiting photographer. When visitors arrived from the U.S. military, Wirkus would welcome any ladies in the party "by having them installed as honorary queen for the night and sit by me to watch the natives dance."

Back home, his story, written up by William B. Seabrook, an authority on voodoo, proved a sensation. "A surprising number of people . . . were interested in voodoo," Seabrook said, "but taking the immense American public by and large, they formed a very small minority compared with the number of people who were interested in Wirkus. . . . At least ten million people had heard of Wirkus and La Gonave, had seen his photograph." Major magazines such as the *Literary Digest* and *Collier's*, as well as the big Sunday newspaper syndicates, carried features on the "White King of La Gonave." His story, Scabrook wrote, was an American myth as potent as that of Horatio Alger. It "contained the essence of the dreams of small boys and grown-up men stifled by a too-close-pressing strait-jacket of civilization-limitation."

Wirkus stayed on his island as king until March 1928, when Haiti's president, Louis Borno, and the U.S. high commissioner, General John H. Russell, paid a call. Wirkus was relieved of his post, and Borno declared, "Haiti is a republic. I am its president. It is unthinkable that there should be a kingdom within a republic or a 'king.'" Wirkus took the boat home to write a highly successful memoir of his royal years.

-- -- --

The marines withdrew from Nicaragua in August 1925. But the troops were back within the year after renewed political upheavals: the collapse of an unstable coalition government; a Conservative coup; the reinstallation of the former mine treasurer Adolfo Díaz as president; and finally the declaration of

"THE TROUBLE IS AS CLOSE TO HIM
AS HIS OWN COAT-TAILS."
—*COLUMBUS DISPATCH*, 1927.
"FOR THE MOMENT, THE QUESTION
OF MEXICAN INTERFERENCE IN
CENTRAL AMERICAN COUNTRIES,
PRESUMABLY FOR THE PURPOSE OF
FOSTERING RADICAL PROPAGANDA
AND BOLSHEVIST PHILOSOPHY, HAS
SWEPT OFF THE STAGE OTHER
QUESTIONS PENDING BETWEEN
MEXICO AND THE UNITED STATES."
—*NEW YORK TIMES*,
NOVEMBER 18, 1926.

a provisional government by the Liberals on the Atlantic Coast. The situation was chaotic, and when the marines went back in, the action was unpopular at home.

The pundit Walter Lippmann wrote a scalding commentary in the *New York World* at the end of 1926. Nicaragua was "not an independent republic," Lippman wrote, and "the direction of its domestic and foreign affairs are determined not in Nicaragua but in Wall Street." Even so, Lippmann seemed to anticipate that not even his Olympian reputation could penetrate his readers' mental block about American conduct. "We continue to think of ourselves as a kind of great, peaceful Switzerland," Lippmann lamented, "whereas we are in fact a great, expanding world power. . . . Our imperialism is more or less unconscious."

Eager to rally public support for his unpopular Nicaragua policy, President Coolidge declared that the problem was outside interference. The culprits this time were the Soviet Union and, closer to home, Mexico, which was then in bitter dispute with Washington over plans to nationalize foreign oil companies. Coolidge announced that he had "conclusive evidence" of arms shipments to the Nicaraguan Liberals from Mexican ports. Secretary of State Frank B. Kellogg then presented the Senate Foreign Relations Committee with a paper titled "Bolshevist Aims and Policies in Latin America," alleging a Nicaraguan-Mexican-Soviet conspiracy to impose a "Mexican-fostered Bolshevist hegemony" within striking distance of the Panama Canal.

The cartoonists of the day went to town with the image. They showed Mexico dispensing "Bolshevik Red Eye," or chasing Nicaragua—usually depicted as a barefoot ragamuffin—with a goat labeled "Bolshevik propaganda." But the Russian Information Bureau retorted, "The Soviet Government has no more interest in factional political squabbles in Nicaragua than it has in the mountains of the moon," and Lippmann scoffed, "The thing which the ignoramuses call Bolshevism is in essence nationalism, and the whole world is in ferment with it."

For Díaz in Nicaragua, things were going from bad to worse. Liberal troops controlled most of the Atlantic half of the country, and were closing in on major cities on the Pacific side. Their advances in the North owed a good deal to the efforts of troops under a charismatic young commander named Augusto César Sandino, who, like most of his Liberal peers, had taken the title of general. Sandino's persistence and discipline convinced the marines that he must be receiving outside support—a charge that in later years would be leveled at any persistent guerrilla movement. As evidence, Colonal Louis Mason Gulick (who later gave his name to the huge U.S. military base in Panama) pointed to the fact that "the bandits wore khaki uniforms, instead of their former nondescript rags."

The marines' role was to act as a shield for the Nicaraguan government. But Díaz's demoralized troops were battle-shy, and the United States public grew fearful that American soldiers would end up in the thick of the hostilities. In response to these anxieties, Coolidge sent special envoy Henry L. Stimson, who had made his reputation as secretary of war under Taft, to

Managua to resolve the conflict. Nicaragua, previously seen as a squalid backwater, was now a diplomatic flash point, and a certain romance attached to that. In a volume published in 1928, travel writer Arthur Ruhl excoriated "the curious short-sightedness of the occasional young 'career diplomat' who fancies that the Caribbean posts are somehow beneath his talents, and that Managua, in particular, is a cruel and unusual punishment." In fact, Ruhl believed, "the chance the younger men have to do something real are quite different. . . . With local government more or less a family affair, he can go directly to the president and get things done which, in Europe, might take months of negotiation. . . . It is quite big enough a post to be taken seriously, even by the most gilded of our young Talleyrands—and even though at some official function the local caterers may commit the incredible crime of serving red and white wine in the same glass."

••••••

U.S. MARINES IN NICARAGUA.
"AN EXCHANGE OF PLEASANTRIES IS
MORE FAVORABLE TO LASTING
FRIENDSHIP BETWEEN NATIONS
THAN PONDEROUS
PRONOUNCEMENTS OF POLICIES OR
PLANS."
KENT COOPER, GENERAL
MANAGER OF THE ASSOCIATED
PRESS, 1928 SPEECH ON U.S.-
CENTRAL AMERICAN RELATIONS.

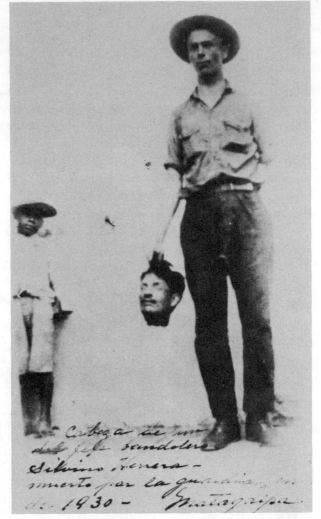

◆━━━━━━

Under a blackthorn tree in the town of Tipitapa, on May 4, 1927, Stimson brought the warring factions together. It took less than half an hour, he wrote, for them to reach an understanding: in exchange for U.S.-supervised elections the following year, and the creation of a "nonpartisan" National Guard of the sort being formed in the Dominican Republic and Haiti, the Liberals would lay down their arms. Their negotiator was José María Moncada, a man who had once acknowledged, "We Nicaraguans are accustomed to designate the State Department as the arbiter of our fights and differences."

Sandino, the only Liberal commander to reject the pact, withdrew to the mountains of Jinotega, near the Honduran border. Within two months, he gave an impressive show of strength by laying siege to the town of Ocotal, and was dislodged only by the Marine Air Corps, who gave the first display of aerial dive-bombing in military history (the distinction is often mistakenly granted to the fascists' attack on the town of Guernica during the Spanish Civil War, immortalized in Picasso's 1937 painting). Sandino recognized that he was helpless against this kind of military force, and retired to wage a guerrilla campaign from a mountain stronghold called El Chipote.

The *New York Times*, then as now, set the tone for what Americans learned. Its correspondent, Harold N. Denny, later wrote a book critical of U.S. policy. For the moment, however, he portrayed the war as a black-and-white struggle: on one side, savagery and disorder; on the other, technology and progress. His disdain for Nicaraguans was undisguised: they were "charming, but in many ways so futile." He called Sandino "perhaps a patriot, probably unbalanced, but certainly a poseur." There was no denying that Sandino's men fought well, but Denny thought the explanation was racial: "The Nicaraguans are better fighters than the Haitians, being of Indian blood, and as warriors similar to the aborigines who resisted the advance of civilization in this country." Sandino's troops, he commented in one dispatch, were "men who could kill with ferocity unknown to any white soldier."

On the U.S. side, he appreciated the experimental quality of the war. "From a tactical standpoint," he wrote in January 1928, "the present activities furnish the first practical laboratory for the development of post-war aviation in coordination with ground troops." Denny was flown around the country by marine aircraft. The "obliging warriors against Sandino," he reported, were "rugged, hearty, and in good spirits." The marines were also learning the art of press relations in a combat zone, and their own publicity played heavily on the image of the brave, clean-limbed troops and their shining battery of modern air power: seven Loening flying boats, six Vought Corsairs, and five Fokker trimotor bombers.

The hunt for Sandino's remote headquarters at El Chipote was rather like the search that Frances FitzGerald describes in *Fire in the Lake* for a "reverse Pentagon" in the jungles of Cambodia, which, if found and destroyed, would alter the course of the Vietnam War. In Nicaragua, after a nightmarish search, facing insects, ambushes, and the floods and mists of the rainy season, the

"A MOVING-PICTURE THEATER EXHIBITS RECENT RELEASES. THERE ARE TENNIS, HANDBALL, AND BASKETBALL COURTS, AND THERE IS A RECREATION HALL WITH A PLAYER PIANO, A PHONOGRAPH, AND A LIBRARY OF 1,000 BOOKS, FROM WHICH SELECTIONS ARE SENT REGULARLY TO THE OUTPOSTS IN THE HILLS."
—HAROLD DENNY, DESCRIBING THE MARINE HEADQUARTERS IN NICARAGUA, 1928.

Leathernecks finally located Sandino's base camp in January 1928 and attacked it with wave upon wave of aircraft and ground troops. Denny called the aerial bombing of El Chipote "one of the most exciting day's works since the Sandino operations started," and told his readers that Sandino was dead or grievously wounded. However, when the marines reached the peak, they found nothing but a collection of straw dummies wearing the red-and-black neckerchieves of the rebel army.

But on February 3, journalist Carleton Beals tracked down Sandino in the town of San Rafael del Norte and became the first and only American correspondent to interview him. He told Sandino's story in six weekly installments in the *Nation,* causing a sensation in the United States and Europe. Even before Beals, the U.S. government had complained bitterly of a pro-Sandino bias in the press. Stimson had been angered in 1927 by the "comparative superiority of facility enjoyed by revolutionist propaganda in reaching America," but thought he had the explanation: the Sandinistas were strong in the east of the country, which gave them access to the Caribbean ports and so to the American press. In fact, most of the copy from Managua came from the wire services, and their resident correspondents could hardly have been accused of "revolutionist" sympathies. United Press's Clifford W. Ham had also served, in 1917–28, as the U.S.-appointed collector general of customs, at a salary of $10,000. And Colonel Irving A. Lindberg of the rival Associated Press was his deputy and successor.

•• •• ••

Discontent at home came less from press accounts than from the rising count of marines killed in Nicaragua, which invariably made the front pages. The *New York Times* carried a number of eloquent letters from their parents. Some expressed moral opposition to the war, like John S. Hemphill of St. Louis, Missouri, who condemned the "disgraceful war against this little nation. . . . What we are doing is no less than murder for the sole purpose of keeping in power a puppet president and acting as a collector for Wall Street." Others advanced an argument that became familiar in later years—the fear of the quagmire, of being nickel-and-dimed into an undeclared war. N. H. Dowdell of Carbondale, Illinois, wrote, "We ought to go down there and clean up that situation or get out of there and stay out. There's no use of sending a handful of our boys down there to get butchered. If it's war, let us call it that and successfully conclude it." The problem, however, was not a shortage of troops. It was that the six thousand marines in Nicaragua were not equipped to defeat a guerrilla force one-tenth as strong that was fighting on its own terrain. Nicaragua was the first place the United States encountered that particular dilemma.

The Marine Corps tried to placate its opponents by sending home a steady stream of reassuring propaganda images. While the foot-soldiers often recorded their resentment and demoralization in their diaries and letters home, official photographers recorded "Hi, Mom" shots of marines at play in a

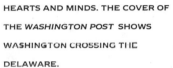

HEARTS AND MINDS. THE COVER OF
THE *WASHINGTON POST* SHOWS
WASHINGTON CROSSING THE
DELAWARE.

tropical paradise: playing baseball, taking local children for rides in motor-cycle sidecars, or, in posed shots, reading to them from their hometown news-papers. It was an imaginary world in which you could get a shoeshine with a cluster of tiny green parakeets perched on your shoulder, or spend a day off riding beneath an avenue of palm trees in a rustic pony trap.

-- -- --

The 1928 elections duly took place, with Brigadier General Frank R. McCoy acting as president of the Central Electoral Board, and an American, whether civilian or military, in charge of each polling place. The winner was José María Moncada, the Liberals' representative at the Tipitapa talks the previous year. But the war dragged on for four more years, and never became popular. Will Rogers paid a morale-boosting visit to the troops in 1932, but

"BALLOT BOXES TO BE USED
IN THE NICARAGUAN ELECTION
NOVEMBER 4 BEING TRANSPORTED
ON MULES FROM MATAGALPA
TO REMOTE PRECINCTS WHERE
THERE ARE NO ROADS," 1928.

WILL ROGERS JOKES WITH ENLISTED
MEN AT MANAGUA, NICARAGUA,
OCTOBER 1932.

he showed little stomach for the war. Listening to the keynote speech by Senator Simeon D. Fess at the 1932 Republican Convention, Rogers commented sardonically: "He brought up Nicaragua, but he left our marines down there. He said that he would protect American lives down there, even if we had to send some there to protect." It was only in January 1933 that the last of the marines pulled out, leaving behind a grinding stalemate—and Sandino still in control of large stretches of the North.

-- -- --

Nothing took the minds of Americans, or angry Latin Americans, off the war in Nicaragua more successfully than a spectacular flying tour of the region by Charles Lindbergh between December 1927 and February 1928, at the height of the controversy over Sandino. Lindbergh was the American hero of the hour. He had followed up his epic solo trans-Atlantic flight in May 1927 with a forty-eight-state cross-country tour of the United States, and in December he set off on a fourteen-country Pan-American journey in the *Spirit of St. Louis*. His final stop, and the climax of the tour, was Havana, where his arrival was timed to coincide with the Sixth Pan-American Conference, which was expected to be the scene of a stormy debate on U.S. policies in Mexico, Nicaragua, and the Caribbean.

"LINDBERGH ADDS NEW CHAPTER TO HIS SAGA

PAN-AMERICAN GOOD-WILL TOUR

SIXTEEN COUNTRIES
9,390 MILES

THIRTEEN LATIN NATIONS
TWO AMERICAN TERRITORIES
ONE ENGLISH COLONY

FLYING TIME
116 HOURS
30 MINUTES

DECEMBER 13, 1927, TO
FEBRUARY 13, 1928."

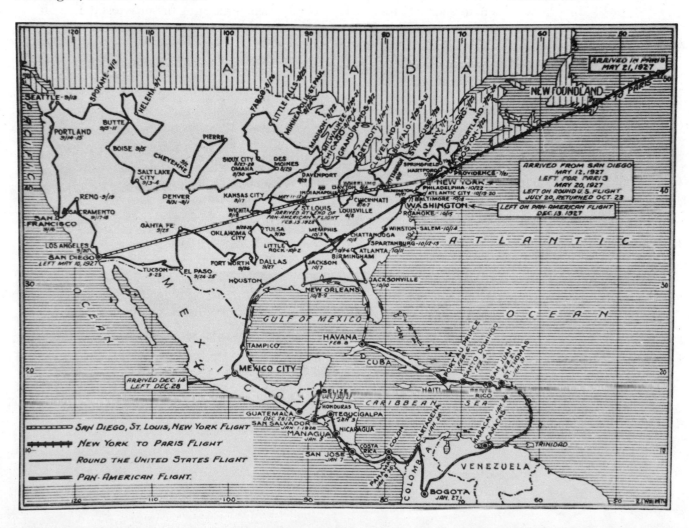

Lindbergh contracted to write the story of his flight exclusively for the New York Times, and did so, he informed his readers, while holding the plane steady with his other hand—a fitting image for "America's young Viking of the air." January 1928, with the marines fighting Sandino, the mythic figure of Lindbergh dominating the front pages, and U.S. diplomats under fire in Havana, was one of those rare moments in history when a series of dramatic firsts—in this case, military, technological, and journalistic—can, if skillfully orchestrated for public consumption, be made greater than the sum of its parts. The role of reporters and photographers in the Lindbergh episode, especially those from the Times, was crucial. The paper dispatched staff reporters by air, boat, railroad, and mule to each of Lindbergh's stops, in an effort that was unprecedented for foreign-news coverage in peacetime. Harold Denny, in fact, whose stories about Sandino were so influential, had not traveled to Managua to cover the war at all; he had gone there to cover Lindbergh, and stayed on.

In Mexico, Lindbergh's first stop, the flier's host was a new U.S. ambassador, Dwight Morrow. Morrow's appointment heralded a new sensitivity to Latin American relations that for the moment was called Good Will, and within five years, under President Franklin Delano Roosevelt, would come to be known as the Good Neighbor Policy. The journalists' mood was apparent as soon as Lindbergh touched down, prompting the heaviest daily volume of wire copy ever filed from Latin America. Even in a less cynical age than our own, the headlines must have alerted the most casual reader to the press's willingness to help the Coolidge administration extract political mileage from

Lindbergh. "Country Forgets Its 'Crises' in Universal Acclaim for Messenger of Good Will," announced the *Times*. The young colonel, said the story, "seems destined to make men of alien race forget their differences in a common admiration of a splendid manhood."

Carleton Beals, who was stringing for AP at the time, was on hand to cover Lindbergh's arrival in Mexico. The pilot touched down several hours late. As Ambassador Morrow hustled the colonel away for his exclusive interview with the *Times*, Beals, yelling to make himself heard above a crush of reporters, asked the reason for the delay. Lindbergh replied that he had become hopelessly lost: the railroad stations did not have their names painted on the roofs as they did back home, and, "Besides, I got my maps from the War Department in Washington, and they aren't any good." Beals used Lindbergh's comments as a colorful lead, only to learn later that his editors had killed the story. Elsewhere in Central America, Lindbergh was met by demonstrators and leaflets protesting U.S. policy in Nicaragua, which the press studiously ignored. The tone of press coverage was to be one of uninterrupted patriotic euphoria; in recent memory, the only parallels may be the coverage of the Bicentennial in 1976 or Liberty Weekend in 1986.

As Lindbergh moved south, the marines were working their way north, toward Sandino's base camp, engaged in their heaviest fighting since World War I. Marine commander Admiral David Foote Sellers warned of the dangers of flying low "over the part of Nicaragua infested by the bandit Sandino and his followers." Denny agreed about the risk, but doubted that Sandino would make Lindbergh a special target, since, "being an ignorant peon, it is possible that he has never heard of the flier or the *Spirit of St. Louis*." As it turned out, Lindbergh reached Managua without incident on January 5, and Denny greeted his arrival with enthusiasm. "Fiery Nicaragua saw a hero today such as it never dreamed could exist," he began. Lindbergh appeared as "a superman and a demigod to these warm-souled people of the Tropics."

Outspoken critics of the war, like Representative Huddleston of Alabama, saw the hypocrisy in this. "Our ambassador of peace wings his way through the air," Huddleston complained, "while our ambassadors of death struggle in the jungles of Nicaragua." But the *Times* front page saw no irony. Its left-hand lead read, "Lindbergh Honored as Envoy of Peace by Díaz Congress: Factions Forget Enmities." In the center of the page was Lindbergh's own daily dispatch, headlined, "Friendship for the United States Impresses Lindbergh." And in the right-hand column, the main news story: "Gen. Lejeune Going to Nicaragua with Marine Units." The Coolidge administration was taking advantage of public enthusiasm for Lindbergh to send in an additional thousand troops. There is also little doubt that the marines, making their own experiments with air power as the cutting edge of foreign policy, benefited from the romance of Lindbergh's conquest of the skies. Civilian air transport, too, was beginning to infatuate the U.S. public. Just three months earlier, in October 1927, Pan-American Airways had made its inaugural flight, the ninety-mile crossing from Key West, Florida, to Havana.

Although the Lindbergh flight was a popular piece of damage control, the January 1928 Pan-American Conference in Havana could hardly have been more poorly timed. Though the U.S. press tried to play the issue down, the violent search for Sandino brought to a head all the Latin Americans' festering resentment over marine occupations and landings in the Caribbean. Nor could the press, writing in an age before superpower summits, ignore the importance of the event. Coolidge's trip to Havana, only the fourth time a sitting president had traveled abroad, merely emphasized the sense of urgency. When he approached the podium to give his address, he faced a sullen gathering. Led by the delegate from El Salvador, the Latin American countries later resolved, "No state has a right to intervene in the internal affairs of another."

Coolidge's secretary of state, Charles Evans Hughes, fought hard to save the United States from diplomatic isolation, and succeeded in splitting the Latin American vote with a resolution of his own. Hughes insisted that the United States had a perfect right, "I will not say to intervene, but to interpose in a temporary manner to protect the lives and interests of its nationals." His trump card was the outspoken support of Cuba (the host) and both the Díaz and Moncada factions in Nicaragua (the supposed victim). The Cuban dictator, General Gerardo Machado, announced, "The Monroe Doctrine is, and ought to remain, the common defensive policy for the territorial integrity of America." Even at this late date, and with Machado in power (in Cuba

UNCLE SAM: "IT'S THE WIND,

RUSTLING THE PALMS."

—JERRY DOYLE,

PHILADELPHIA RECORD, 1927.

he was commonly known as *El Carnicero,* "the butcher"), Hughes was able to hold up U.S. conduct in Cuba as proof that its conduct in Nicaragua gave Latin Americans nothing to fear. By a happy coincidence, the thirtieth anniversary of the explosion of the *Maine* occurred during the conference, and at a memorial ceremony, Ambassador Harry P. Fletcher, a veteran of the Spanish-American War, vowed that the United States stood ready, "as she was here in Cuba in 1898, to champion and support the cause of democracy and freedom and independence in this hemisphere."

That view had few takers. Yet the U.S. press was much less interested in reporting Coolidge's isolation than in muting, ignoring, or discrediting the hostility of the international community. Taking the lead again, the *Times* suspected Russians from Mexico of "seeking to inject a Bolshevik virus into the proceedings of the conference." The newspaper surveyed European press comment, and although it found only one instance of praise—from the official Italian Fascist paper, *Tribuna,* which hailed the "majesty of utterances and breadth of vision shown by President Coolidge"—this was enough to earn the headline "Coolidge Views Approved." The stories again depicted Cuba as a land of American firsts, this time because Coolidge's Havana speech was the first foreign broadcast to be transmitted nationwide, over NBC.

When Lindbergh touched down in Havana, just as the row over intervention was reaching its climax, he swept the conference off the front pages altogether, to the satisfaction of the U.S. representatives. The delegates declared a recess in his honor, and Lindbergh spent the day treating Machado and the other asembled dignitaries to free joyrides over Havana. The conference migrated from the news section to the social pages, and a serious diplomatic embarrassment was turned into a celebration of the life-styles of the rich and famous. "The whole atmosphere of Havana suggests that the gala season is in full swing," wrote one *Times* reporter. "Gray gloves are easy to obtain, but [there is not] a pair of gray spats to be found in all Havana." The usual American colony of ten thousand had doubled, attracted by the horse races and "the appeal of a winter vacation in the balmy semi-tropical climate." The women's costumes were particularly noteworthy: for Coolidge's big speech, "The boxes, balconies, and floor were occupied by well-dressed people. American women there said that they had never seen in Europe or elsewhere a better-dressed assemblage of their own sex. They praised their Cuban sisters, who were present in large numbers, as having marked taste in costume and noted that the gowns for the most part were the latest Paris creations."

In fairness, not all the *Times*'s coverage of the region was so frivolous. Once the euphoria over Lindbergh had died down, some of the reporters who briefly stayed behind attempted a more thoughtful analysis of the issues that had dominated the conference. Clarence K. Streit, who had covered Lindbergh's two-day stopover in Haiti, wrote an unusually perceptive commentary that came to grips, like few reports of the time, with the feelings of the local population. Perhaps more important, he understood that U.S. policies, however well-intentioned, had damaging long-term effects on the country's political life.

The accomplishments of the thirteen-year Marine occupation, Streit acknowledged, were "impressive and manifold . . . the establishment of order, sound finances, numerous public works, sanitation, rural farm schools . . . the appurtenances for stimulating productivity for which America is known." Why, then, should so many Latin Americans call us imperialists? The answer, Streit thought, was that, "finding everything in Haiti to be done, our advisers in Haiti plunged with characteristic American energy into the job of getting everything done as quickly as possible. With our national proneness to emphasize material accomplishments and speed, they have tended to neglect the human and political side of the Haitian problem. It is a system adapted more to speeding material work than to giving practice in self-government. It has the further disadvantage of hitching our chariot very close to that of one man, President Borno, whose policy of repressing opposition has especially inflamed sentiment against not only him but us."

•• -- ••

There were signs, as the year went on, that some of these ideas might be filtering through to high places. In November, the Republican Herbert Hoover was elected president on a wave of national prosperity, and he immediately announced his desire to "get away from it all" by taking a seven-week "Good Will cruise" to Central and South America. Hoover's image was that of a technically competent, hands-on chief executive, a skilled engineer who had made his reputation in postwar European relief work and had traveled widely in Asia and Africa. His trip south signaled a readiness to improve U.S.–Latin American relations, continuing on the course begun by Dwight Morrow, Coolidge's envoy to Mexico.

But in the haste to turn over a new leaf, there was a characteristic desire to reaffirm American innocence and good intentions: the past had been a misunderstanding; the future would begin with a clean slate. In essence, it was the same message that Hughes had delivered to the Havana conference ten months earlier: Latin Americans had to understand that there was a difference between "intervening" and "interposing."

Hoover's message was relayed to the public by the large group of reporters and photographers who accompanied the president and his wife aboard the USS *Maryland*. Their dispatches made it apparent that they still viewed Central America through old, familiar lenses. As the *Maryland* approached the Nicaraguan port of Corinto, Richard J. Beamish of the *Philadelphia Inquirer* described the view from the ship's rails: "Central America, land of Richard Harding Davis romances, setting for many a tale of derring-do, of bucko and buccaneer, emerged like a stage set cut from cardboard with its volcanic, sharp-angled backdrop."

News reports from the vessel were effectively censored by George Barr Baker, a California newspaperman who had formerly been in charge of pub-

•••••

"DURING THEIR WEEKS OF LIVING
WITH THE NATIVES, THE SOLDIERS
OF THE SEA LEARNED THAT THE
DEMARCATION POINT BETWEEN A
LIBERAL AND A CONSERVATIVE
BEGAN WITH BIRTH AND COULD END
ONLY WITH DEATH—A BLOOD FEUD
OF CENTURIES' STANDING."
—FROM THE OFFICIAL REPORT OF
HOOVER'S GOODWILL TOUR.

licity for the Republican National Committee. "Nothing is accepted for trans-
mission except after his 'OK,' " one reporter noted. "He is unwilling to have
this appear as censorship in any form, but naturally nothing that Mr. Hoover
could object to is sent out." Deference to the wishes of the president was an
iron rule of reporting in 1928, and the stories from the ship were relentlessly
upbeat. "That intervention is not now, never was, and never will be a set
policy of the United States is one of the most important facts President-elect
Hoover has made clear," wrote the man from the *Times*. "The result is that
for the first time in a generation, Latin America really understands the attitude of the United States toward Nicaragua, Haiti, and Santo Domingo."

Large crowds were on hand to see Hoover wherever he stopped, as were
posses of photographers to record every display of enthusiasm. Hoover's

speeches brimmed with optimism and Good Will and his distinctive philosophy of "American individualism." As he had asserted in his 1922 book of that title, the notion that men were equal "was part of the clap-trap of the French revolution." The answer was individualism, with its potential for injustice tempered by equality of opportunity. That was the key to the United States's success, and if Central Americans would mimic it, they could look forward to the same results.

Hoover was struck by the "encouraging" panorama of Nicaraguan politics in the wake of the U.S.-supervised 1928 elections, whose architect, Henry L. Stimson, would shortly be named secretary of state. As an engineer, Hoover was also interested in reviving talks about a Nicaraguan canal route, a proposal that was warmly endorsed by the newly elected president, José María Moncada, and his Conservative predecessor, Adolfo Díaz. Hoover also spelled out the direction of U.S. policy in the postelection period. Its centerpiece would be a phased withdrawal of the 5,500-strong Marine force, and the inauguration, on January 1, 1929, of a Nicaraguan military academy, staffed by U.S. officers, "modeled along the lines of West Point," to train a National Guard capable of policing the country even-handedly.

The Hoover tour helped to strengthen a definite though limited shift in attitudes toward Central America and the Caribbean that had already taken place among academic policy elites in the United States. According to conventional wisdom, wrote Raymond Leslie Buell, research director for the Foreign Policy Association, in 1930, the region was "semi-civilized." However, "A summer's journey through Central America had convinced me that this picture is distorted." The region was now governed by "presidents at least tolerably acceptable to articulate opinion," although of course, he added in a cautionary aside, "it should be remembered . . . that Central America is in the tropics and is inhabited by a population predominantly Indian."

But the flush lasted only nine months. October 1929 brought the Wall Street crash, and the president's name became forever associated with Hoovervilles, the squatter settlements of the jobless that blighted American cities during the Depression. Hoover never faced up to the domestic economic reasons for the crash, which he continued to blame on outside accidents—revolution in China, overproduction of cocoa in Ecuador. There was a similar fallacy in Hoover's view of the linkages between the U.S. economy and those of its neighbors. He had recommended that the region's leaders mimic the American system; they had done so eagerly, but the outcome was neither stable democracy nor any noticeable improvement in living standards. To make matters worse, when the U.S. economy failed, the real linkages were all too clear. After 1929, the effects of the Depression ripped through the marginal, unprotected economies of Central America and the Caribbean with devastating results. No countries suffered more than El Salvador, where the collapse of coffee prices on the world market sparked a revolt in 1932, in which the government killed thousands, and Cuba, whose economy was hostage to the price of sugar.

"FIRST PHOTOGRAPH FLOWN FROM HAVANA BY SPECIAL PLANES FOR THE ASSOCIATED PRESS SHOWING LOYAL SOLDIERS OF THE [RAMÓN] GRAU SAN MARTÍN REGIME FIRING ON THE ILL-FATED ATARES CASTLE, FROM BEHIND BARRICADES."
—AP WIRE SERVICE, NOVEMBER 1933.

THREE

······

GOOD
NEIGHBORS

1933–47

ENDURING PEACE CANNOT BE BOUGHT AT THE COST OF
OTHER PEOPLE'S FREEDOM.
—FRANKLIN DELANO ROOSEVELT

H oover was the first
to use the phrase "good neighbor," but Franklin D.
Roosevelt, his successor, made it his own. At his
inauguration on March 4, 1933, he spelled out his
new approach: "In the field of world policy, I
would dedicate this nation to the policy of the Good
Neighbor, the neighbor who resolutely respects
himself, and, because he does so, respects the
rights of others; the neighbor who respects his ob-
ligations and respects the sanctity of agreements in
and with a world of neighbors. We now realize as
we have never realized before our interdepen-
dence on each other; that we cannot merely take,
but must also give."

Roosevelt's election in 1932 was a repudiation
of Hoover and all that he stood for. And FDR's first
foreign-policy challenge was to deal with the consequences of the Hoover era in the United States's
closest neighbor, Cuba. By 1933, the island was a
shambles. The Depression had brought the collapse of world sugar prices, from twenty-two cents
a pound to half a cent. Banks were foreclosing on
Cuban farmers; starving plantation workers roamed

the country in search of casual labor at twenty cents a day. By July there were nationwide strikes and riots, to which Machado, "the butcher," responded with wholesale killings. Roosevelt sent the cruiser *Richmond*, the battleship *Mississippi*, and more than twenty other warships into Cuban harbors, and dispatched Sumner Welles as a special envoy to Havana. Under his prodding, Machado quit. But the first provisional government lasted only seventeen days; a second one was installed by noncommissioned officers, but Roosevelt refused to recognize it because of its leftist tinge; then came a countercoup by Machado loyalists, who would not accept a regime "guided by children, or insane or communist people." They were finally rousted out of their strongholds by troops under an ambitious young sergeant, Fulgencio Batista. The Associated Press, for the first time, used a special plane to rush photographs of the fighting to New York. The first one showed Batista troops laying siege to rebel positions in Atares Castle. The victorious Batista persuaded the Roosevelt administration that he was the only man capable of restoring order, and Roosevelt in turn declared his new approach to Latin America a success, because he had ridden out the crisis without landing the marines. In 1934, Washington allowed the repeal of the outmoded Platt amendment, which had so gravely limited Cuban independence. (The United States did, however, retain its control of the Guantánamo naval base.)

In its elevated moral tone, and its belief in the natural community of interests of the New World under U.S. leadership, the Good Neighbor Policy had much in common with Woodrow Wilson's notion of Pan-Americanism. As Wilson's assistant secretary of the navy, FDR had visited Haiti, Santo Domingo, and Cuba. (Teddy, his wife's uncle, had held the same post twenty years before, on the eve of the Spanish-American War.) FDR had been cheered by the sight of "his" marines bringing benevolent order to the chaos of the Caribbean, and assumed that the United States was naturally bound to control the destinies of the region as "a guardian and big brother." The region stayed close to his heart. In 1920, he reminisced, "You know, I had something to do with the running of a couple of little republics. The facts are that I wrote Haiti's Constitution myself, and, if I do say it, I think it's a pretty good Constitution."

Roosevelt as president had a less simplistic view of events. He returned to Port-au-Prince in 1934 to tell the Haitians, in his best Harvard French, that the Marines would soon be leaving. They had already ended their unpopular occupation of Nicaragua, two months before his inauguration. Even so, wrote Richard Hofstadter, his desire to bring an end to instability in the region was tied up with the desire to expand U.S. trade. It was "characteristic," Hofstadter noted, "the quick sympathy with oppressed colonials, the ideal of liberation and welfare, and yet the calculating interest in American advantage."

The idea of being a Good Neighbor caught on in the country at large, especially in FDR's second and third terms. A whole cottage industry of Good Neighborism flourished: there were state-based Good Neighbor Committees and Good Neighbor Leagues and Good Neighbor Commissions, all working to improve cultural ties and publishing guides for newly arrived refugees and émigrés. The phrase entered the broader popular culture too: Mrs. Eleanor Pearson did well with her novel *The Good Neighbor Murder*; Jack Levin's play *The Good Neighbor* opened on Broadway in 1941, where it was followed within two years by Robert Ray's three-act comedy *Good Neighbors*.

Yet the main impact of the Good Neighbor Policy seemed to be a reaffirmation of the United States's faith in its own virtue. In school textbooks issued after 1933, for example, the word "imperialism," once used freely to describe U.S. conduct in the Caribbean and Central America, became the monopoly of the European powers. Good Neighborism seemed to have rather less to do with any improvement in Americans' opinion of Latins. A poll conducted in December 1940 by the Office of Public Opinion Research offered respondents a choice of nineteen adjectives with which to describe Central and South Americans. "Dark-skinned" was the easy winner, picked by 80 percent of respondents. Next, bunched together between 40 percent and 50 percent, came "quick-tempered," "emotional," "religious," "backward," "lazy," "ignorant," and "suspicious." Right at the bottom, selected by just 5 percent of those questioned, came "efficient." Above that, in order, were "progressive," "generous," "brave," "honest," "intelligent," and "shrewd"—none of which were chosen by more than 16 percent.

In essence, Roosevelt's policies were a continuation of Hoover's, guaranteeing the stability of these "ignorant, quick-tempered" neighbors through a set of indirect controls. The main instrument was the military: in Nicaragua and Santo Domingo, the National Guard left behind by the marines; in Haiti, the *gendarmerie;* elsewhere, the established armed forces. The indigenous constabularies were intended to stand aloof from local factional rivalries and avoid the need for messy direct involvement by the marines, which was always an unpopular business—opposed on nationalist grounds by Latin Americans, on moral grounds by U.S. liberals, and on fiscal grounds by U.S. conservatives. But where direct intervention was required, the marines would always leave with parting instructions to the local troops on democratic values, adherence to the constitution, and what today would be called human rights.

The military was the springboard to power for a whole new generation of dictators, who were already firmly in control by the time FDR reached the White House. They justified their draconian rule by pointing to the ravages of the Depression, and then used their powers to corner the most profitable sectors of the economy. Each of the dictators had his own distinctive personality. Tiburcio Carías Andino, who ruled Honduras from 1932 to 1948, was probably the most lethargic and (relatively) benign; Jorge Ubico of Guatemala (1931–44), who surrounded himself with busts and portraits of Napoleon, the most rigid; Maximiliano Hernández Martínez of El Salvador, brought to power in 1931 by a coup led by officers whom the U.S. minister in San Salvador described as "little more than half-witted," the most murderous and eccentric. The prize for totalitarianism and sheer megalomania would without a doubt have gone to Rafael Leonidas Trujillo of the Dominican Republic, a streetwise lieutenant in the National Guard who rose to prominence through his skill at flattering the marines. He won the 1930 presidential election with more votes than there were registered voters. Trujillo ran the country, either directly or as the power behind the throne, until his death in 1961.

Unrivaled, however, as the shrewdest and most pro-American of the dictators was Nicaragua's Anastasio Somoza García. Somoza had won the hearts of U.S. Minister Matthew Hanna and his wife with his slangy, B-movie English, his eagerness to please, and his light steps on the dance floor. Henry Stimson was especially taken: "Somoza is a very frank, friendly, likable young Liberal," he told Washington, "and his attitude impresses me more favorably than almost any other." In January 1933, two months before Roosevelt reached the White House, Somoza had become the first Nicaraguan commander of the National Guard and was well on the way to turning it into the private army that controlled Nicaragua on behalf of his family until 1979.

Hanna's replacement, Arthur Bliss Lane, was stricken with doubts about the Frankenstein's monster that had been turned loose. In 1935, he told his superiors with some alarm, "The people who created the National Guard had no adequate understanding of the psychology of the people here. Otherwise they would not have bequeathed Nicaragua with an instrument to blast constitutional procedure off the map." But Lane's sensible advice fell on deaf ears. Washington stood by passively in February 1934, when Somoza lured Sandino to Managua with a promise of peace talks and had him murdered; in June 1936, when he overthrew the elected president, Juan Bautista Sacasa; and on New Year's Day 1937, when he installed himself as president. To block his ascent, Secretary of State Cordell Hull reasoned, would be to intervene in Nicaragua's internal affairs, and that would be a betrayal of the principles of the Good Neighbor Policy.

•• •• ••

"The motor car, radio and newspaper syndicate, let alone cables and modern steamships, are shrinking the world faster than many stay-at-home people think," wrote travel writer Arthur Ruhl in 1931. Despite political upheavals, "all sorts of things from automobiles and concrete-mixers to breakfast foods and syndicated Sunday photographers continue their peaceful penetration. . . . Parties of Yankee trippers drop into the capitals weekly," Ruhl observed, "from their Caribbean cruises or their trips from San Francisco to New York by way of the Canal, and one can leave the Guatemala banana-country at luncheon-time on a Saturday and have his Tuesday's breakfast in New Orleans."

Until about 1930, tourism in Central America had been a rarity, and the odd traveler's tale that emerged was the stuff of cliché. A typical example of the genre was the 1925 *A Gringo in Mañana Land,* by one Harry L. Foster, with a set of chapter titles that included "Those Dark-Eyed Señoritas!" and "Those Chronic Insurrections!" Now, however, the United States's first strides in international airline and road travel opened up Central America to large-scale tourism, while Good Neighbor sentiment encouraged travelers to believe that the local inhabitants were really their brothers and sisters (or at least their country cousins) under the skin. That belief could easily be made

AMERICA'S LUXURY LINERS
to HAVANA

THESE gorgeous debutantes are the latest ships to fly the American flag . . . up to the minute and beyond. The fastest and finest liners in the Havana run . . . vibrationless motion . . . turbo-electric drive . . . Twice the deck space that used to be thought enough. New chefs . . . already getting compliments three times a day.

Sail on the new "Morro Castle" or "Oriente" for one of those marvelous Ward Line All-Expense Tours, including hotel accommodations and four sightseeing trips . . . Motor drive to Morro Castle and Cabanas Fortress . . . Havana at night . . . Jai Alai, the Casino Nacional, the Malecon, alight and laughing . . . The countryside . . . The Tropical Gardens, the plantations, the Avenue of Palms . . . Everything included in these new low rates.

9 Days—$145 up 10 Days—$150 up
INCLUDING ALL EXPENSES
Tours of 13 to 17 Days Available
Sailings every Wednesday and Saturday

For Literature and Reservations address General Passenger Dept., Foot of Wall Street, Uptown Ticket Office, 545 Fifth Avenue, New York, or Any Authorized Tourist Agent.

WARD LINE

"INDEED, OWING TO THE DELIGHTFUL WINTER CLIMATE AND THE EXCELLENT TRAVEL FACILITIES FROM THE UNITED STATES, THE TOURIST BUSINESS HAS BECOME ONE OF THE CHIEF INDUSTRIES OF HAVANA, ESPECIALLY, I MIGHT ADD, SINCE THE ADOPTION OF THE EIGHTEENTH AMENDMENT TO OUR CONSTITUTION."
—*CARPENTER'S WORLD TRAVELS*, 1925.

A BIG SHIP IN MANAGUA. "HERE WAS A TYPICAL AMERICAN PROBLEM TACKLED IN A TYPICAL AMERICAN WAY, AND YET IT HAD ITS ROMANTIC ELEMENTS LIKE THE COVERED-WAGON DAYS OF PIONEERING OR THE ADVENTUROUS FEATS OF THE IRON-HORSE PHASE OF RAILROADING, WHEN THE TRACKS WERE LAID FROM THE MISSISSIPPI TO THE PACIFIC."
—HUDSON STRODE, *SOUTH BY THUNDERBIRD*, 1937.

into a self-fulfilling prophecy if the traveler made a point of choosing his companions from the small local business class that sent its sons and daughters to college in the United States and was desperately bent on aping American manners. Ruhl, for one, insisted that there was nothing alien here to alarm the tourist. "A Saturday-night dance at the San José de Costa Rica Golf Club," he reported, "is exactly like a Saturday-night dance at any well-regulated country club in the United States. At a Friday-afternoon dance at the beautiful country club of El Salvador, with people taking tea on the terrace, a marimba orchestra playing, and the volcano on the left curving down to the distant town, you might fancy yourself in Honolulu, or the Riviera, or Southern California, or where you will—in any case, a world away from the Central America of O. Henry or our newspaper cartoons."

Havana, of course, had been a major tourist destination since the Spanish-American War. With Prohibition, its tourist industry went through the roof. In a series of "don'ts" for visitors that suggested one of the main motives of holidays there, the English-language *Times of Cuba* cautioned against the dangers of the local sugar industry and its alcoholic by-products. "Don't try to consume it all the first few days," it advised. "Remember that Cuban distilleries work night and day." During the Prohibition years, Havana was customarily included in guidebooks to Florida, just as if it were part of the U.S. mainland. It was, after all, just a seven-hour boat ride from Key West. In 1925, P&O Lines charged $17.50 for the crossing, or $30.00 for the round trip, including a berth and meals. From New York, Havana was a three-day cruise from Pier 14 on the East River. By 1927, the adventurous could even fly there if they were prepared to fork over $75.00 for the short hop from Miami.

Cuba, the land of the mambo and the rumba, became a national metaphor for romance, escapism, and sex. MGM released the film *Cuban Love Story* in 1932. "Cuban Moonlight," one of many similarly titled hit songs of the early 1930s, lifted its melody from "Lamento Borincano," by the Puerto Rican composer Rafael Hernández, replacing the original lyrics, which lamented the depressed economic condition of Puerto Rican peasants, with romantic fantasy for American holidaymakers: " 'Twas on a night in Cuba we first met. Mem'ries of that night I can't forget."

The Key West–Havana route saw the inaugural flight of Pan-American Airways in October 1927, a company founded by Juan Terry Trippe. A former World War I naval pilot who had founded a collegiate flying club at Yale, Trippe was worried that the United States was lagging behind Europe in international air transport. As early as 1919, German investors had established a regular airline service in Colombia, and Trippe feared the United States might lose its control of Latin American trade if it did not move rapidly to dominate the airways. In 1929, Trippe included Puerto Rico on his itinerary, and added the airmail route from Miami down through the Mexican state of Yucatán to Panama, by way of the Central American capitals. Lindbergh, who was now acting as the new company's technical adviser, made the first Central American flight. The State Department was watching these developments closely. It granted Pan-Am a monopoly on the lucrative new access routes to Panama and provided for government subsidies for the mail run. In some strategic areas, it seemed, marketplace competition was not to be trusted. As the State Department argued, "It is certainly desirable and perhaps essential that the United States should, in so far as possible, control aviation in the Caribbean nations."

Traveling south by the Pan-Am Clipper became one of the great adventures of the age; and Miami, one of the great modern transportation hubs. Traveler Hudson Strode, who described his Pan-Am adventures in his 1937 book *South by Thunderbird*, was one of many awed by the new Pan-American Dinner Key Air Terminal in Miami, with its art-deco hangars, its flying-boat docks, and its giant replica of the globe in the lobby.

The advances in air travel were paralleled by the first efforts to build the Pan-American Highway, which would eventually run from Alaska to Tierra del Fuego, at the southern tip of Chile. The idea had initially been raised in 1923, at the Fifth Pan-American Conference in Santiago, Chile, and the U.S. automobile industry latched on quickly. By the mid-1920s, the domestic car market was saturated; as an industry spokesman noted, the two-car family had ceased to be an oddity. When U.S. automobile and truck manufacturers tried to break into the European market, they came up against stiff competition from the low- and mid-priced vehicles being turned out by the giant local companies like Morris, Fiat, Austin, and Citroën. Africa and Asia offered no prospects. "Within striking distance to the south, however," wrote Edwin Warley James, chief of the Inter-American Regional Office of the U.S. Public Roads Administration, "with good, hard land connecting all the way, was another continent—Latin America. It was huge, it was almost virgin territory for motor vehicles, free from home competition; but it had few roads." It was

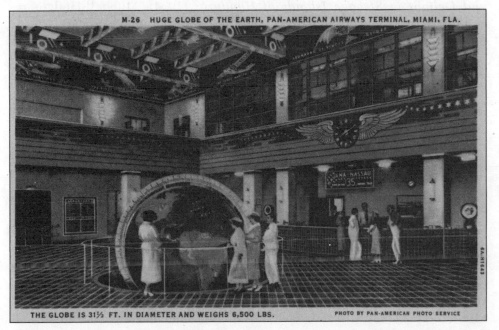

M-26 HUGE GLOBE OF THE EARTH, PAN-AMERICAN AIRWAYS TERMINAL, MIAMI, FLA.

THE GLOBE IS 31½ FT. IN DIAMETER AND WEIGHS 6,500 LBS.   PHOTO BY PAN-AMERICAN PHOTO SERVICE

"IN THE CENTER OF THE GREAT LOBBY OF THE PAN-AMERICAN AIR TERMINAL AT MIAMI . . . A REPLICA OF THE WORLD REVOLVED. . . . HERE THE WORLD, BROUGHT WITHIN A CONCEIVABLE INTIMATE SPACE AND ROBBED OF ITS VAST IMMENSITIES, SEEMED SYMBOLICAL OF THE MAGIC OF AVIATION, WHICH HAS ELIMINATED TIME AND DISTANCE, THOSE CHIEF OBSTACLES TO COMMERCE AND COMPREHENSION."
—HUDSON STRODE.

another challenge, then, to Yankee ingenuity, and the response was characteristic: if there were no roads, build them.

In two missions, in 1930 and 1931, a team of drivers from the Automobile
Club of Southern California explored a 2,800-mile route. The first year took
them as far south as Mexico City; on the second expedition, they reached San
Salvador. "Link by link," they announced, "this chain of international good
will and understanding is in the making." Avoiding the rainy season, they
drove in a convoy of six Ford pickups, blasting away solid rock in places and
hauling their cars around impassable bends with a block and tackle. "Except-
ing in the Valley of Mexico and in the vicinity of a few of the larger cities of
both Mexico and Central America," they wrote in their report, "we had followed trails little used except by pack trains and ox-carts."

Section by section, the road took shape during the 1930s and 1940s. It was
not until 1948 that anyone was bold enough to drive the entire route from the
Rio Grande to Panama City. Roger Stephens, an American, was the first to do
so, taking thirty-two days to cover the 3,231 miles. He reported meticulously
that the undertaking had cost him $140.14.

-- -- --

With the growth of transportation routes, the late 1920s and early 1930s were
boom years for travel-writing, and even the remoter parts of Central America
became objects of fascination for an entire new breed of middle-brow anthro-
pologists and explorers, like the British adventurer F. A. Mitchell-Hedges.
Together with his constant companion, Lady Richmond Brown (known more
familiarly as Mabs), Mitchell-Hedges churned out a series of books with lurid
titles for armchair travelers. The first of these was *Battles with Giant Fish*
(1928), which was followed by *Land of Wonder and Fear* (1931) and *Danger
and Delight in Strange Islands of Honduras* (1934). Mitchell-Hedges recounted "the sheer ruthlessness and barbarism of the true wilds"; his
encounters with "primitive and degenerate Indian tribes"; and his poker-
playing sessions with the Nicaraguan Conservative warlord Emiliano Cha-
morro and the veteran New Orleans soldier of fortune Lee Christmas.

The explorer had himself photographed—beaming genially, with an enormous pipe clamped between his teeth—at one Central American site after
another: descending into the crater of the Masaya volcano, the same one that
had so captivated John Lloyd Stephens almost a century earlier; caught up in
a Honduran "revolution"; perched on the domed roof of the great ruined
cathedral of San Francisco in Antigua, Guatemala; towering over a group of
Tzutuhil Indians; lying (in the position of the victim) on the great sacrificial
altar stone at the Mayan site of Quiriguá, which was excavated and maintained by the United Fruit Company.

Though there is something of Bulldog Drummond or Indiana Jones in the
intrepid figure of Mitchell-Hedges, he is more than a comic curiosity. His
Central American journeys were sponsored by the Museum of the American
Indian in New York and underwritten by the Hearst Newspaper Group, and
Mitchell-Hedges uncovered several of the more notable sites of the ancient

LADY RICHMOND BROWN AND
F. A. MITCHELL-HEDGES WITH
THE QUICHÉ SACRIFICIAL STONE:
"THE FACT THAT WE HAVE LIVED
FOR YEARS AMONG INDIAN TRIBES
STOOD US IN GOOD STEAD. WE HAVE
GROWN TO UNDERSTAND THEIR
TEMPERAMENTS, AND BY
DIPLOMACY WE GAINED THE
CONFIDENCE OF THE NATIVES. THEY
BECAME VERY FRIENDLY TOWARD
US, AND BY PATIENT DELVING WE
UNEARTHED A WEALTH OF
SURPRISING INFORMATION."

Mayans, such as Lubaantum in Belize. His writings helped to introduce readers to the treasures of pre-Columbian civilization, in a period when antiquity was the rage and readers were riveted by the excavations of the tomb of King Tutankhamen in Egypt. The ruined cities of the Maya, set among the ravishing landscapes of Guatemala, were a more convenient destination for the adventurous holidaymakers than the pyramids of the Nile.

By 1936, a travel guide issued in Washington by the Pan-American Union would exclaim, "As a tourist Mecca Guatemala City stands among the most popular in the Americas." U.S. travelers to Guatemala could register as temporary, twenty-day members of the splendid American Club. Dating from 1896, it had since "grown and prospered until today it has one of the finest homes to be found in Central America, a structure representing a large investment on the part of its members."

The Pan-American Union produced a whole series of glossy little illustrated guides to entice tourists and investors to the region's capitals. In these pages, even the most grotesque behavior of the local dictators was submerged in a warm bath of Good Neighborly feelings. In 1938, the union published a revised edition of its guide to Santo Domingo, which it had to retitle, since the Dominican dictator had just renamed his capital Ciudad Trujillo. It was a typical gesture by a man who left his stamp on everything: on a home for the aged, a plaque reading, "Trujillo is the only one who gives us shelter"; on village water pumps, the inscription, "Trujillo alone gives us water to drink"; on the town market in Santiago, "This structure will bear witness through the centuries of the grandeur of the Era of Trujillo." Authors clamored to take part in official poetry and biography contests. The 1938 winner was Gilberto Sánchez Lustrino's *Trujillo: Builder of a Nationality.* One of numerous biographies by A. R. Nanita, which were left in Dominican hotel rooms like so many Gideon Bibles, compared Trujillo to Christ: "Two thousand years ago Jesus preached his doctrine of Justice and Peace . . . ten years ago Trujillo submitted his luminous project creating the League of American Nations."

The league, like many of Trujillo's plans, remained on the drawing board. The most grandiose scheme was a colossal memorial lighthouse containing the tomb of Columbus, to celebrate his landfall in the Western Hemisphere in 1492. The international design competition for the lighthouse involved 450 architects from forty-eight countries; the winner was an Englishman from Manchester named J. L. Gleave. He planned a giant recumbent cross with beacon lights for ships and aircraft. "The great mass shoots forward, westward," he wrote. "Civilization always travels westward, as did Columbus. When it reaches the tomb it turns also north and south to both the Americas, and from it radiate, fan-shaped, twenty-one roads, one for each of the Pan-American Republics."

This kind of travesty of the Good Neighbor ideal is usually thought of as something that emerged from the megalomaniacal imagination of the dictators themselves. But during World War II especially, faced with the common enemy of Nazism, U.S. government officials and private interests did everything to encourage them. A 1941 edition of *Caminos del Aire*, Pan-American Airways' Spanish-language magazine, was dedicated to that "intelligent and cultured statesman," Anastasio Somoza. In terms the dictator himself could not have outdone, it hailed him as "Heroic champion of peace and pure idealist, whose goals, since he took charge of his country's Executive Power, have been to channel the destiny of Nicaragua along the paths of progress; exemplary commander of a people dedicated to work; firmly upholder of Inter-American ideals . . . [he] enjoys the confidence and esteem of his people and the admiration of the inhabitants of all the nations of America."

•••••••

COLUMBUS MEMORIAL LIGHTHOUSE,

CIUDAD TRUJILLO, DOMINICAN

REPUBLIC. SAID ARCHITECT J. L.

GLEAVE, "THE GREAT MASS SHOOTS

FORWARD, WESTWARD.

CIVILIZATION ALWAYS TRAVELS

WESTWARD, AS DID COLUMBUS."

"A GROUP OF RECENT GRADUATES
OF THE ENGLISH-AMERICAN
SCHOOL. GUATEMALA CITY," 1936.

-- -- --

During World War II, Hollywood also got into the Good Neighbor act in a big way. The Hays office, which controlled film censorship, appointed a Latin American expert to advise Hollywood on avoiding prewar Latin stereotypes. At the same time, the State Department's Office of the Coordinator of Inter-American Affairs, headed by Nelson Rockefeller, opened a special Motion Picture Section, whose director, John Hay Whitney, spoke explicitly about his political goals: "The menace of Nazism and its allied doctrines, its techniques and tactics, must be understood from Hudson Bay to Punto Arenas. Wherever the motion picture can do a basic job of spreading the gospel of the Americas' common stake in this struggle, there that job must and shall be done." As their cultural ambassador, Whitney and Rockefeller hired Walt Disney to "show the truth about the American way" and be "the first Hollywood producer of motion pictures specifically intended to carry a message of democracy and friendship below the Rio Grande." Disney responded with two films that looked at America's neighbors through the eyes of Donald Duck: *Saludos Amigos!* (1943) and *The Three Caballeros* (1945). Latin America was represented by a feisty green parrot in a sombrero named José Carioca. ("Disney's famous cuteness," commented the writer James Agee, when he saw these films, "however richly it may mirror our national infantilism, is hard on my stomach.")

The Rockefeller office also declared its intention to "create 'Pan Americana,' a noble female figure, bearing a torch and a cross, subtly suggesting both the Virgin Mary and the Goddess of Liberty." What it got instead was

Carmen Miranda, who replaced one stereotype, the shiftless, violent Latin male, with another, the oversexed, featherbrained female song-and-dance act. During the war years, Miranda made a series of successful movies for Twentieth Century–Fox, notably *Weekend in Havana* and *That Night in Rio*. Then came the climax of the cycle, a lavish Busby Berkeley musical called *The Gang's All Here*. The film introduced a new dance, the Uncle Sam-ba, but its high point was a spectacular production number, and though Miranda was Brazilian, its key image was the banana—an inescapable Central American cliché. Two dozen female dancers, carrying six-foot-tall yellow bananas, form elaborate patterns while waving their fruit rhythmically over another group of dancers holding giant strawberries between their legs. "These peripatetic phallic symbols," writes UCLA film historian Allen L. Woll, "led President Getulio Vargas to censor the film in Miranda's native Brazil."

•• •• ••

The 1939 World's Fair in New York City may well have been the boldest symbolic expression of Roosevelt's vision of a future world of Good Neighbors. The centerpiece was a towering needle called the Trylon, and, next to it, the enormous globe of the Perisphere, which housed a model of the utopian city of the future, Democracity. Heads of state and foreign dignitaries made a beeline for the fairgrounds in Flushing Meadows, and none of them caused a bigger splash than Nicaragua's Anastasio Somoza, who arrived in May. As far as anyone in Washington could recall, it was the most extravagant military reception the city had ever given a foreign leader. In fact, it was also a dress rehearsal for the visit of King George VI and Queen Elizabeth, but that did nothing to deflate Somoza, who reveled in the military salutes, his night in the White House, and his ride to Mount Vernon in an open carriage with FDR.

Most budding Latin Americanists commit two phrases to memory within their first few weeks of study. One is the lament by "the Liberator," Simón Bolívar, "The United States seems destined to plague us with miseries in the name of liberty." The other is the exchange FDR is alleged to have had on the eve of Somoza's visit. "Somoza?" the president asks his secretary of state, Cordell Hull. "Isn't that fellow supposed to be a son of a bitch?" To which Hull replies, "Yes, but he's our son of a bitch." In other versions, Roosevelt makes the comment himself after reading a State Department briefing paper. Others claim the reference was not to Somoza at all but to the Dominican

ANASTASIO SOMOZA GARCÍA
ARRIVES IN WASHINGTON,
MAY 1939.
"EVER SINCE I BEGAN MY POLITICAL
LIFE, I HAVE APPRECIATED THE
IMPORTANCE TO NICARAGUA OF
CULTIVATING CORDIAL RELATIONS
WITH THE UNITED STATES."

tyrant Trujillo, who visited FDR two months later, accompanied by his nine-year-old son, Ramfis, whom he had just promoted to the rank of brigadier general. Both stories may be true; equally, both may be apocryphal. But as with any good piece of apocrypha, it is the essential truth that counts.

U.S. taxpayers footed the bill for Somoza's travel from New Orleans via Washington to the World's Fair and back. To show his gratitude, Somoza presented his host with an inlaid table of Nicaraguan hardwoods and gold that bore the portrait of Teddy Roosevelt and a map of the Panama Canal, flanked by a portrait of Franklin Roosevelt and the route of a Nicaragua canal (which, he declared in an address to the Senate, was needed for the defense of the continent). Aware of FDR's reputation as an avid collector, Somoza also threw in a set of Nicaraguan stamps, and, on his return, had a series printed to commemorate the visit. The most expensive, one *córdoba*, showed the dictator, in dress uniform, next to the Trylon and Perisphere.

Somoza's encounter with FDR marked Nicaragua for years. In his office, Somoza took down the composite picture of himself and Adolf Hitler and put up four portraits of Roosevelt. His supposed intimacy with the great democrat was unique political capital, and gave him credentials he could use to intimidate opponents. It also changed the face of Managua. Somoza renamed the city's main thoroughfare the Avenida Roosevelt, and, on the hill beneath the presidential palace, he built a huge monument to his "friend," with a plaque inscribed, "From Somoza to Roosevelt." He was photographed there in 1944 by *National Geographic,* celebrating Flag Day with Roosevelt's affable, mild-mannered ambassador, James Bolton Stewart. (Somoza, who was fond of a good English pun, would sometimes introduce him as "my steward.") One

"NICARAGUA CELEBRATES FLAG DAY ON THE SAME DAY AS THE UNITED STATES. HERE GENERAL ANASTASIO SOMOZA, PRESIDENT OF THE REPUBLIC, SHAKES HANDS WITH UNITED STATES AMBASSADOR JAMES B. STEWART, IN AN EXPRESSION OF THE WARM FRIENDSHIP THAT UNITES THE TWO COUNTRIES."
—*NATIONAL GEOGRAPHIC,* 1944.

Easter weekend, reported William Krehm, a correspondent for *Time*, a Somoza freighter was unloading cement at the wharf of the dictator's Pacific Coast estate, Montelimar. The stevedores were on holiday, so Stewart rolled up his shirtsleeves and pitched in. "Frankly," one opposition journalist commented on the spectacle, "there are moments when Somoza satisfies me completely—when he humiliates the representatives of the country to which Nicaragua owes her humiliation."

Somoza was not alone in invoking Roosevelt to his own advantage. Several of his fellow dictators pointed to FDR's unprecedented decision to seek a third and fourth term to justify their own indefinite stays in power. Carías of Honduras issued a circular to government employees in January 1944 that announced, "As partners of the great nation of the North in the armed struggle, we can participate without fear in the civil contest approaching in the United States for the election of a citizen to guide its destinies during the next four years. We therefore proclaim as sole candidate . . . the illustrious patriot Franklin Delano Roosevelt." At the time, Honduran consulates in Europe were doing a brisk trade selling passports to Nazi agents. And in June 1943, when the editor of the opposition newspaper *El Cronista* called for democracy and published attacks on Carías, he was summoned to the U.S. embassy, where the first secretary said he thought criticism of the dictator was damaging to the war effort, and wondered whether "we do not need strong men at a time like this." Soon afterward, Carías closed the paper down.

The backdrop to all this, of course, was the very real fear that North America was vulnerable to a new external enemy, Nazism. In that atmosphere, it was easy to turn a blind eye to the shortcomings of local leaders and (for neither the first time nor the last) opt for a short-term stability while ignoring its long-term consequences.

In the prewar years, with the bloom still on the New Deal at home, Hitler and Mussolini in power, and Franco soon to join them, some reporters understood that the United States had made a Faustian bargain in Central America in the name of stability. Frank L. Kluckhohn paid a visit to what he called "the American Balkans" in 1937 for the *New York Times Magazine*. "In Central America today," he concluded, "there is little tranquillity save that sullen quiet that comes with repression." The isthmus was "a dictatorship belt," Kluckhohn reported, ruled by "would-be Fascist chieftains . . . midget Hitlers and Mussolinis" who had brought "superficial peace and order to lands where revolution and disturbance have long been bywords."

Their emulation of the European fascists was quite explicit. In 1936, Somoza had used a gang of shock troops called the *camisas azules* (blueshirts) to bludgeon his way to the presidency. El Salvador was the first country in the world to recognize Franco in Spain, ahead of even Italy and Germany, which had underwritten his overthrow of the Republic. The Salvadoran dictator, Maximiliano Hernández Martínez, brought in a German to rule his military college and barred all immigration by Arabs, Hindus, Chinese, and blacks. What mainly concerned the Roosevelt administration, however, was the prospect of a fifth column in Panama. As far back as 1934, Cordell Hull

U.S. ARMY PLANES
OVER PANAMA, 1940.
"THE INEVITABLE EFFECT OF OUR
BUILDING THE CANAL MUST BE TO
REQUIRE US TO POLICE THE
SURROUNDING PREMISES."
—ELIHU ROOT,
SECRETARY OF STATE
UNDER TEDDY ROOSEVELT, 1905.

had warned FDR of the arrival there of an unusual number of Japanese, some of whom had been expelled from the Philippines as spies. On a 1936 visit, Hull was shocked to discover that "Axis penetration had made rapid, alarming headway under various guises."

The concern about Panama became acute in 1940, when a charismatic young politician named Arnulfo Arias—who many voters thought resembled Errol Flynn—won a presidential election in a landslide. Once in office, he used a fascist-tinged nationalism to play cleverly on local anti-U.S. feelings. Arias had formerly been Panama's envoy to Italy, and in 1937 he had been granted a personal audience with Hitler. The U.S. embassy reported that Arias had "referred to the desirability of improving the nation's racial strains by selected immigration," and that he had rejected "as biologically without justification the 'demagogic concept' that 'all men are born free and equal.'"

In October 1941, the second-in-command of the Panamanian National Guard asked U.S. Ambassador Edwin C. Wilson whether Washington would look favorably on a military coup. Choosing his words carefully, Wilson replied that, under the Good Neighbor Policy, this was entirely a Panamanian affair; the United States could not interfere. The coup went ahead. Henry Stimson, who by this time was again secretary of war, said it was "a great relief to us, because Arias had been very troublesome and very pro-Nazi." State Department official Adolf Berle noted, "I don't like revolutions on principle," but added that this one was "probably all to the good."

Dictators like Somoza saw now that the winds of the Good Neighbor Policy could blow both ways. And within two months of the coup against Arias, Japan attacked Pearl Harbor and the United States entered the war, leaving no room for ambiguity about the loyalties of Panama's neighbors. The threat of Axis military activity in the region was certainly real, as was the public fear that Hitler would invade the United States if he emerged victorious in Europe. In the early part of 1942, Nazi submarines sank more tonnage in the Caribbean than in the whole of the Atlantic. (Forty-one years later President Ronald Reagan would remind Congress of this fact when he appealed for aid to the Nicaraguan contras, though he had in mind a different external menace to the Caribbean sea-lanes.) To meet the threat, the United States added to its defense perimeter by building two large military airfields and a naval base in Nicaragua to back up the military nerve centers of Puerto Rico, Panama, and Guantánamo. It had also acquired a string of Caribbean island bases from Britain in 1940, notably Trinidad, in exchange for some antiquated warships. Out of deference to the large number of U.S. servicemen stationed in the British islands after 1941, "The Star-Spangled Banner" was now played together with "God Save the King" at the end of dances and movies.

After Pearl Harbor, each of the dictators rushed to declare war on the Axis powers they had once embraced. Somoza proclaimed, "I consider every Nicaraguan aviator and soldier as a potential fighting man for the U.S." Japanese immigrants in Central America were rounded up and held in internment camps, as they were in the western United States. After a Nazi submarine attacked the U.S. cargo ship *San Pablo* at Puerto Limón on the Caribbean coast, killing thirty-three sailors, Costa Rican crowds ransacked German-owned property. News photographs show them carrying placards that read, "Now it's not just Hitler, it's all Germans." For Somoza, the change in political loyalties was good business. He added to his personal fortune by confiscating all German-owned farms, as did Jorge Ubico in Guatemala. By 1944, Somoza was the richest man in Central America, and oppositionists were able to construct a list of his holdings that included every letter in the alphabet—including X, for companies concealed from the public.

The war was a boom time for Central American landowners and exporters of strategic raw materials and goods that were rationed in the United States. Where the troops and bases went, the dollars followed. Coffee exports, which earned the region three-quarters of its foreign currency, swung from Europe to the United States like a needle to magnetic north. Between 1930 and 1934, 75 percent of Central American coffee had gone to Europe, and just 20 percent to the United States. Between 1940 and 1944, the U.S. share leapt to 87 percent.

In 1943, the United Fruit Company opened a Middle American Information Bureau to foster public awareness of the region and encourage "mutual knowledge and mutual understanding." The bureau put out a steady stream

UNEXPLODED NAZI TORPEDO, ARUBA, 1942. "THE DUTCH ISLANDS . . . ARE NOW GARRISONED BY BRITISH TROOPS. NOR IS OUR NAVY IDLE. THE ISLANDS ARE ONLY 620 MILES FROM THE CANAL, AND THEIR PROXIMITY TO THE VENEZUELAN COAST GIVES THEM STRATEGIC VALUE." —JOHN GUNTHER, *INSIDE LATIN AMERICA*, 1941.

HELP BRITAIN FINISH THE JOB!

HELP BRITAIN FINISH THE JOB!

HELP BRITAIN FINISH THE JOB!

PORT-OF-SPAIN, TRINIDAD, 1942. "SWAP OF DESTROYERS FOR BASES MAKES U.S. DREAM COME TRUE; NATION'S EASTERN FLANK THUS MADE ALMOST IMPREGNABLE." —*NEWSWEEK* HEADLINE.

"TORPEDO BOATS IN THE RAW ARE THESE MAHOGANY PLANKS DRYING IN THE BLUEFIELDS SUN: CURVED MARKS SHOW THAT THE WOOD HAS BEEN CUT BY A CIRCULAR SAW. MOST MAHOGANY IS EXPORTED FROM NICARAGUA IN ENTIRE LOGS. MAHOGANY IS VALUABLE IN MAKING PT BOATS, AIRCRAFT PLYWOOD, AND OTHER WAR ESSENTIALS BECAUSE OF ITS STRENGTH, RESISTANCE TO ROT, AND SMOOTH GRAIN." —*NATIONAL GEOGRAPHIC*, 1944.

Have a Coca-Cola = ¿Qué Hay, Amigo?

(WHAT GIVES, PAL?)

...or making pals in Panama

Down Panama way, American ideas of friendliness and good neighborliness are nothing new. Folks there understand and like our love of sports, our humor and our everyday customs. *Have a "Coke"*, says the American soldier, and the natives know he is saying *We are friends* ... the same friendly invitation as when you offer Coca-Cola from your own refrigerator at home. Everywhere Coca-Cola stands for *the pause that refreshes*,—has become the high-sign of kindly-minded people the world over.

*   *   *

In news stories, books and magazines, you read how much our fighting men cherish Coca-Cola whenever they get it. Yes, more than just a delicious and refreshing drink, "Coke" reminds them of happy times at home. Luckily, they find Coca-Cola — bottled on the spot — in over 35 allied and neutral countries 'round the globe.

Coca-Cola
-the global
high-sign

It's natural for popular names to acquire friendly abbreviations. That's why you hear Coca-Cola called "Coke".

COPYRIGHT 1944, THE COCA-COLA COMPANY

of pamphlets on Central American hardwoods, cocoa, tropical oils, and spices, all aimed at the lay reader and the housewife, with titles such as "Fifty Questions about Middle America for North American Women" and "Middle America and a Woman's World." "Since the Japanese invasion of Malaya, the Netherlands Indies, and many other highly productive tropics of the Far East," one of these pamphlets explained, "we in the United States are particularly dependent on Middle America for our supplies of . . . bananas, rubber, coffee (rationed), abacá [hemp], cacao, and sugar (rationed)." Mahogany from Nicaragua's Atlantic coast was vital for defense industries, being used to make airplane fuselages, torpedo boats, and patterns for metal parts.

United Fruit publicity materials, government literature, and even school textbooks promised a bright new dawn for the countries of Central America and the Caribbean once the war was over. In one typically optimistic 1943 school text, *Nicaragua in Story and Pictures,* the Panama Canal is celebrated as an economic panacea. The final illustration shows a DC-3 Clipper skimming over a landscape of lakes and volcanoes. The accompanying text reads, "Our Panama Canal has changed the bright blue Caribbean Sea into a great highway connecting Nicaragua with North and South America, Europe, and the Far East. As a result, the country is changing rapidly. More machines and factory tools are being imported. More tractors and plows will find their way to many farms. And railroads will become longer so as to move away the larger quantities of coffee, bananas, and other crops. Nicaragua can look forward to a bright and prosperous future."

•• •• ••

FDR's January 1941 "Four Freedoms" speech was a high-water mark of this ambitious talk of peace, freedom, and prosperity. The president warned Congress that the prelude to any totalitarian assault on the United States would be the establishment of strategic bases in Latin America, and promised that "enduring peace cannot be bought at the cost of other people's freedom." Opponents of the Central American dictators, who were listening intently, thought Roosevelt was referring to them. In November 1942, a group of exiles founded the Central American Democratic Union in Mexico City. And in 1944, Nicaraguan and Dominican refugees joined the exiled Costa Rican politician José Figueres to form the Caribbean Legion, which announced that it intended to rid the region of the scourge of tyranny—by force if necessary. With the blessing of democrats like Luis Muñoz Marín of Puerto Rico and Rómulo Betancourt of Venezuela, the legion declared that its main targets were Somoza, Trujillo, and Batista.

No country was immune from the summer-long revolts of the "Generation of '44." In the new climate of tolerance for pluralism, even Cuba's Batista made no move when his handpicked candidate lost an election to Ramón Grau San Martín, the man the Roosevelt administration had refused to recognize back in 1933 because of suspected "communistic tendencies."

Some of the despots managed to survive. Carías rode out the storm after

GENERAL JORGE UBICO ARRIVES IN
NEW ORLEANS AFTER HIS
OVERTHROW, 1944. "THE
PRESIDENT'S RULE OF CONDUCT IS
NEVER TO GIVE GROUNDS FOR
HOPE, AND EVERYONE MUST BE
KICKED AND BEATEN UNTIL THEY
REALIZE THE FACT."
—MIGUEL ÁNGEL ASTURIAS,
EL SEÑOR PRESIDENTE.

GENERAL MAXIMILIANO
HERNÁNDEZ MARTÍNEZ AND
FAMILY, 1944.
"YOU WOULD NEVER HAVE
SUSPECTED THIS LEAN, LOOSE-
SLUNG, DROOP-MOUTHED
VEGETARIAN OF BEING A SINISTER
KILLER. HE CREATED THE
IMPRESSION OF A BENIGN,
BONELESS GRANDPA."
—WILLIAM KREHM.

his troops gunned down two hundred protesters, mainly women, in the streets of Honduras's second city, San Pedro Sula, in July. The same month brought mass demonstrations in Nicaragua in protest against Somoza's attempt to tamper with the constitution and extend his term in office. July also saw the collapse of the Guatemalan government in the face of unprecedented street protests by middle-class marchers. The regime of General Ubico had received mixed reviews in the American press. Though *Time* had condemned it as "one of the world's most flagrant tyrannies," an article in *Reader's Digest* as recently as that February had lauded the "hard-headed Ubico" as "just the kind of ruler for free America." But he could not withstand the unrest, which brought the most sweeping changes in the region. Elections in December brought to power the schoolteacher Juan José Arévalo, an admirer of Abraham Lincoln and the New Deal and an opponent of communism, who promised a modern capitalist economy that would bring Guatemala into the twentieth century. The U.S. reaction was positive. Diplomat Spruille Braden announced that Washington was "happy to see that Guatemala now occupies the high place of one of the hemisphere's democracies."

Despite its rhetorical commitment to democracy, Washington's attitude to the new pluralism was ambivalent, and Roosevelt's image was badly tarnished by U.S. diplomacy in El Salvador, where the dictator Martínez had been the first victim of the Generation of '44. Martínez was bundled out of office, and out of El Salvador, on May 9 by an alliance of students, young army officers, and middle-class professionals that had its counterpart in each country. He never returned to El Salvador, but holed up next door in Honduras, where he was eventually murdered in 1966 after a domestic quarrel with the chauffeur on his hacienda.

El Salvador's democratic interlude turned out to be brief, however. The interim government that replaced Martínez was toppled within five months by Colonel Osmín Aguirre, the dictator's former chief-of-police, whose only visible sources of support were the armed forces and the coffee barons. When the United States recognized him—ironically as part of an effort to line up a united bloc of Latin American votes against "fascist" Argentina at the February 1945 Chapultepec Conference—it threw away much of the goodwill that Roosevelt had generated. In El Salvador, reported *Time*'s William Krehm, "leaflets circulated with a picture of Roosevelt against a swastika background and the text: 'Roosevelt sheds his mask.' By every mail the United States embassy received photos of Roosevelt previously used as toilet paper."

•• •• ••

A large part of the problem was a kind of recurrent historical amnesia that seemed to seize hold each time the unrest passed. When there was no crisis, or when the crisis did not directly involve the United States, it was as if the country in question had simply ceased to exist. For a long time, El Salvador had been especially prone to this syndrome. Thanks in large measure to the

pioneering journalism of Krehm, who was eventually pulled from the Central America beat after complaints from the State Department, intermittent stories did filter through about Martínez's more notorious eccentricities—covering the street lamps of San Salvador with colored cellophane to ward off disease; arguing that an ant's life was worth more than a man's, because the ant did not have the benefit of reincarnation.

Otherwise, El Salvador was terra incognita, subject to an almost total news blackout. At best it was portrayed as a kind of folkloric Shangri-La. In a 1939 promotional film made for the Hills Brothers coffee company, a Clipper comes in to land against a background of cloud-capped volcanoes; the camera cuts to a shot of dancing women in long braids and brightly colored, traditional Indian costumes. The narrator begins: "High in the mountains of Central America lies the republic of El Salvador, and here, at the beginning of the new coffee season, we find gaiety and laughter, as, to the soft sweet strains of the melodious marimba band, fiesta holds sway."

In much the same vein was a report in the November 1944 issue of *National Geographic*, which sent its area specialist Luis Marden down to do a piece titled "Where Coffee Is King." Marden was writing at a time of immense upheavals: in May, Martínez had fled El Salvador after thirteen years in power; the country was racked by a succession crisis that ended in October with Aguirre's coup. But Marden presented an idyll with not a word of politics. The habit of tying a prisoner's thumbs behind his back, which later

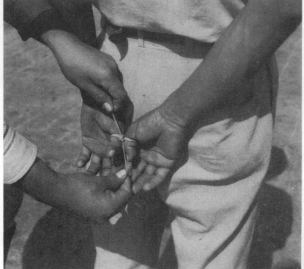

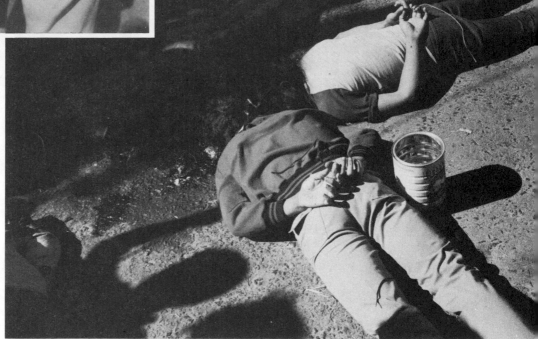

became one of the most powerful symbols of the Salvadoran death squads, was portrayed as a quaint, faintly whimsical custom of the local constabulary. The powerful coffee-growers emerged as a group of benign eccentrics: "Planters love their coffee. They talk it, live it, and drink it. 'Those fellows have interest in nothing but growing coffee,' the secretary of the [coffee] Association said. 'They don't care about politics or anything else. All they want is to be left alone to grow and pamper their beloved coffee in peace.'"

Nor would the reader find any trace in Marden's report of the momentous events of 1932, which had been consigned to the *oubliette* of history. Like sugar in Cuba, coffee in El Salvador had been a prime casualty of the Depres-

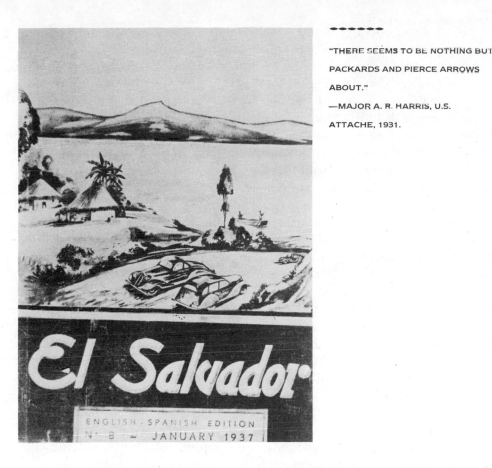

sion, its value slumping so badly that most farmers decided it was uneconomical to harvest the 1930 crop and left the berries to decay on the bushes. Peasant wages fell to eight cents a day, and "the country became permeated with the sick-sweet smell of rotting coffee fruits," wrote Thomas Anderson in his classic *Matanza,* for many years the only published account of what happened.

Major A. R. Harris, U.S. attaché for Central American military affairs, was sent on a tour of inspection a few days after the coup that brought Martínez to power in December 1931. "The first thing one observes when he goes to San Salvador," he wrote, "is the number of expensive automobiles on the streets. . . . There seems to be nothing between these high-priced cars and the ox-cart with its barefooted attendant. There is practically no middle class between the very rich and the poor. Roughly 90 percent of the wealth of the country is held by about one-half of one percent of the population. They live in almost regal splendor with many attendants, send their children to Europe or the United States to be educated, and spend money lavishly on themselves. The population has practically nothing."

Harris's superiors were particularly interested in his assessment of the threat from local Bolsheviks. Washington had been mildly concerned about

El Salvador since 1930, when the Fish committee, looking into the workings of international communism, had concluded that "Salvador has been selected as a center of propaganda." Harris's verdict was that "a socialistic or communistic revolution may be delayed for several years: ten, or even twenty, but when it comes it will be a bloody one." However, he added, "the authorities seem to realize that the situation is dangerous and are quite alert in their fight against communistic influences."

Harris's prediction of revolution was correct, and his assessment of the government's resolve was well founded. But his timetable was overly optimistic. On January 22, 1932, just a month after his report was filed, the first communist-led uprising in the Americas erupted in El Salvador's western coffee-growing district. Within three days, the United States had warships standing by to land the marines if needed. But the Salvadoran authorities, mindful of the marines' five-year stay in Nicaragua, declined the offer and took care of the problem themselves.

Anderson recounts what happened next: "Around Izalco a roundup of suspects began. As most of the rebels, except the leaders, were difficult to identify, arbitrary classifications were set up. All those who were found carrying machetes were guilty. All those of a strongly Indian cast of features, or who dressed in a scruffy, *campesino* costume, were considered guilty. To facilitate the roundup, all those who had *not* taken part in the uprising were invited to present themselves at the *comandancia* to receive clearance papers. When they arrived they were examined and those with the above-mentioned attributes seized. Tied by the thumbs to those before and behind them in the customary Salvadoran manner, groups of fifty were led to the back wall of the church of Asunción in Izalco, and against that massive wall were cut down by firing squads."

••••••

MASS GRAVES, 1932. "OUTSIDE OF THE CANAL ZONE, SAN SALVADOR IS ABOUT THE MOST MODERN AND PROGRESSIVE CITY I HAVE VISITED ON THIS TRIP. . . . THE TASTES OF ALL THE UPPER CLASSES HAVE BEEN CULTIVATED ALONG MUCH THE SAME LINES AS THOSE OF AMERICANS."
—FRANK G. CARPENTER, *LANDS OF THE CARIBBEAN*, 1925.

The net caught all the ringleaders of the failed revolt: Agustín Farabundo Martí, Mario Zapata, Alfonso Luna—all captured by future president Aguirre's police—and "a short, rough little Indian" named Francisco (Chico) Sánchez. When an aide reproached Martínez for the scale of the bloodletting, he answered by quoting an Indian religious text. His retribution had no malice, he said: "I am only the instrument of the fates to fulfill destiny." Anderson estimated that while the rebels killed perhaps a hundred people, government troops killed between eight and ten thousand. It was difficult to be more precise, because the Salvadoran authorities, too, had shrouded the event in their own brand of amnesia, systematically removing from the National Archives any reference, account, or newspaper report. All official papers relating to the slaughter, including photographs, were entrusted to a right-wing journalist from Guatemala, and never saw the light of day in the United States.

FIRST GROUP OF U.S.-TRAINED SOLDIERS, EL SALVADOR, 1948.

FOUR
•••••••
BAD
NEIGHBORS
1947–67

AMERICA REINVENTED ITSELF EACH DAY; WHY COULDN'T
THE WORLD DO LIKEWISE? . . . THAT THERE COULD BE MORE
THAN ONE REALITY IN THE WORLD ALWAYS CAME AS A
SURPRISE TO AMERICANS, AND AN INSULT THAT THE LOCAL
REALITY WAS ALWAYS THE CONTROLLING REALITY.
—WARD JUST,
THE AMERICAN AMBASSADOR

The United States emerged from World War II as the most powerful nation in history. Yet again its mainland territory had been spared from invasion and attack. War was the engine that drove the U.S. economy, even as it was ruining the economies of its European competitors. The United States's new position would rest on a new set of global arrangements: sole possession of the atomic bomb, the United Nations, Western military alliances to contain the Soviet Union, and negotiated "spheres of influence." Within this system, Central America would have a special place as a secure hinterland whose loyalty to the West was beyond question. In May 1945, as the war ended, Secretary of War Stimson told his number-two man, John J. McCloy, that while Soviet influence in Eastern Europe was offensive, U.S. control of its own neighbors was of a different sort. "I think that it's not asking too much," he told McCloy, "to have our little region over here which never has bothered anybody."

In the eyes of the Truman administration, the crucial distinction was that the Soviets, in the name of national security, demanded the right to shape their neighbors' internal policies. All the United States asked was for Central America to follow its lead in international affairs and demonstrate hostility to the Soviet bloc. As long as that was guaranteed, each country's domestic arrangements were its own affair. In practice, this often meant, as it had in the 1930s, accepting dictatorship in the name of noninterference.

The language of the postwar years was superficially the same as that of Woodrow Wilson and Franklin Roosevelt: the Americas formed a natural community of shared values and ideals, which had built a shield of loyalty against Hitler and could now turn it against the menace of Stalin. But the tone was harder and edged with fear. During World War II, Washington had affected a chummy hear-no-evil, see-no-evil stance toward neighboring governments, and spoke about Central America as if it were a kind of extended Rotary Club. After 1945, however, Americans began to perceive a relentless contest for global supremacy. Their anxieties were reminiscent of attitudes in 1898: on one hand, the public saw the United States's new power as the logical reward for virtue; on the other, it was far from comfortable with life as a superpower. The sense of alien threat, always a strong ingredient of American life, now produced an atmosphere of suspicion and rancor at home in which dissent was readily seen as betrayal. In the international arena, the United States demanded a more stringent set of loyalty oaths from its allies, especially those responsible for keeping order in the environs of the Panama Canal.

Central Americans who hoped that loyalty would be rewarded by lavish economic aid along the lines of Europe's postwar Marshall Plan were soon disappointed. The region was trapped in a paradox: politically, it was the first line of American defense; economically, it was one of the lowest priorities in the world, with the exception of Puerto Rico, where Operation Bootstrap was the first attempt by the United States to industrialize an undeveloped country. The Truman administration responded that Central American prosperity would come not from aid but from a dynamic private sector. And to countries lacking any kind of democratic standards, Truman offered the same tacit assumption as his predecessors: if the central freedom, that of enterprise, were guaranteed, the freedoms of speech, assembly, and religion would all follow.

In Central America, however, that is not quite how it worked. Instead, the small elite who controlled exports (four-fifths of which were now headed for the United States) also tended to be the ones who could afford to consume the imports (four-fifths of which also came from the United States). In the process, they Americanized their life-styles to such an extent that Washington came to regard them as the natural repository of American democratic values. In fact, they only clung more jealously to their privileges and wealth. As social inequalities grew, so did instability, which in turn was countered more and more by strong-arm tactics. In the short run, however, the situation appeared friendly, stable, and pro-American, and in the years of Harry S. Truman and Dwight D. Eisenhower, that was the main concern.

The dangerous logic of the Cold War, and the risk that the accompanying rhetoric would paint the United States into one corner after another, was clear enough. The Truman Doctrine, unveiled in March 1947, when the United States intervened in the Greek Civil War, assumed the right to police the globe against communist threats wherever they were detected, even if the target area was a strategically insignificant backwater. Surely then, many commentators argued, the United States was leaving itself hostage to any tottering despot smart enough to blame his problems on communism.

Above all else, containment of the Soviet Union on every front was a matter of credibility. If the United States failed to follow through on its tough talk, it would suffer a serious loss of face, and the wound would be no less humiliating for being self-inflicted. Logically, the closer, smaller, and weaker the country in question, the more traumatic the loss of face would be. Nevertheless, though some members of the Washington establishment were un-

The New Good Neighbor Policy

"IT SEEMS TO BE TAKEN FOR GRANTED, UPON ALL SIDES OF THE HOUSE, THAT WE ARE TO PROCEED WITH THIS PROCESS OF AMERICANIZING CENTRAL AMERICA. . . . I WISH TO KNOW, IN THE FIRST PLACE, BY WHAT RIGHT WE PROPOSE TO RENDER THIS SERVICE TO OUR SOUTHERN NEIGHBORS. HAVE THEY INVITED US TO AMERICANIZE THEIR INSTITUTIONS?"
—REPRESENTATIVE EMORY B. POTTLE OF NEW YORK, 1858.

comfortable with what the Truman Doctrine might lead to, it went down well with the public, in large part because, as Senator Arthur Vandenberg pointed out, Truman had chosen to "scare the hell out of the American people" with apocalyptic visions of freedom under siege.

In July 1947, the National Security Act created the Central Intelligence Agency, a single Defense Department, and the National Security Council. This was followed in September by a conference in Rio de Janeiro, where the Latin American countries agreed to reorganize hemispheric defense to reflect the imperatives of the Cold War. They would adopt standardized U.S. weaponry and equipment and integrate themselves into a single training and command structure headed by the United States—a prospect the cartoonist Herblock of the *Washington Post* depicted as putting lethal weapons in the hands of unruly adolescents. The task of the Latin American military as a whole was to keep the continent's resources out of communist hands; the purpose of each national army was not to fight foreign wars but to guarantee domestic stability.

The first test of U.S. Cold War policy in Central America came in the same year. In Nicaragua, the State Department had been hoping to see a peaceful transition to democracy, and was shocked when Somoza, who was constitutionally barred from reelection, announced that he intended to seek it anyway. Truman's ambassador, Fletcher Warren, cautioned, "We would be foolish to make an enemy of a chief-of-state who has consistently been our friend," but his superiors eventually persuaded the dictator to step down. As his stand-in, he endorsed the aging Liberal Leonardo Argüello. To Somoza's consternation, Argüello was swamped by his opponent at the polls. The National Guard, however, was in charge of counting the ballots, and on May 1, Argüello was duly sworn in as president. Disconcertingly, he proved to have a mind of his own, and set about replacing Somoza cronies with opposition figures. An enraged Somoza put up with just three weeks of this independent behavior before having congress declare Argüello "mentally incompetent." A second puppet president lasted precisely three days before Somoza mounted a bloodless coup and returned to his throne.

Some Latin Americans hoped that the sequence of fraud, ouster, and coup might embarrass the Truman administration into disowning Somoza. But when a few chilly months of withholding recognition failed to push the general into holding fresh elections, Washington's bluff had been called. Somoza was manifestly in control of Nicaragua, his international posture was unswervingly pro-American, and he claimed that his opponents were communists. His government was quietly recognized, and for nine more years he remained in power. It was the first of many occasions in the postwar years when Washington, in the name of stability, passed up the opportunity to encourage the democratic process in Central America.

—— —— ——

Nicaragua and its neighbors seemed to slump into a torpor of neglect. Central American files gathered dust in the State Department; the diplomats posted

FRESHWATER SHARK,
LAKE MANAGUA.
"THERE ARE ALSO A HANDFUL
OF TOP-CLASS RESORTS OFFERING
EXCELLENT SPORT FISHING,
WITH GUIDES AND EQUIPMENT
TO ASSIST EVEN THE RANKEST
AMATEUR."
—JAMES LEMOYNE, TRAVEL
SECTION, *NEW YORK TIMES*,
JANUARY 24, 1988.

to the region were generally mediocre; the area was considered secure. Apart from an occasional stopover in Guatemala to check on the progress of President Arévalo's modest democratic reforms, the press, too, steered clear of the area. Carleton Beals, the liberal journalist who had located Sandino in 1928 and written widely on the region in the 1930s, now complained that his editors at magazines like the *New Republic* and the *Nation* showed no interest in the subject: It was "almost impossible to get anything published on Latin America, not even banalities, let alone any attempted analyses of what is going on."

The region's only identity seemed to be as a safely exotic, if rather comical, tourist playground for Americans after the rigors of wartime. Somoza's fiefdom became the subject of a whimsical 1946 hit song recorded by Kay Kyser and his orchestra:

Managua, Nicaragua, is a beautiful town,
You buy a hacienda for a few dollars down. . . .
Managua, Nicaragua, what a wonderful spot!
There's coffee and bananas and a temp'rature hot,
So take a trip and on a ship go sailing away—
Across the agua to Managua, Nicaragua. Olé! . . .

The Pacific coast of Central America proved a paradise for big-game fisherman, who still found something of the outdoor appeal that Teddy Roosevelt and Richard Harding Davis had discovered a half-century before. Businessmen looking to invest in Nicaragua might expect to be invited for the week-

end to Somoza's seaside estate and entertained with a day's deep-sea fishing
on the dictator's boat, trying for marlin, barracuda, or sailfish. The more adventurous could spend a few days at a tarpon camp on the Río San Juan along
the Costa Rican border, hoping to catch one of Lake Nicaragua's rare freshwater sharks. Even the more obscure destinations experienced a modest tourist boom, as returning travelers convinced their friends that it was possible to
get American-style home cooking in San Salvador or Tegucigalpa.

-- -- --

Cuba, however, continued to rule the roost as a tourist resort. Its first great
boom had come with Prohibition, which Irving Berlin had written about in
"I'll See You in C-U-B-A": "Everybody's going there this year," the song
went:

> *The season opened last July,*
> *Ever since the U.S.A. went dry.*

In the 1950s, Cuba was Ernest Hemingway and Errol Flynn and George
Raft; it was young honeymooners on the fabled Varadero Beach, and corrupt
New Jersey mobsters using their casino profits to build strings of luxury
hotels. Havana appealed to wholesome midwestern families relishing the
affluence of the Eisenhower years, and to another kind of tourist who was
fleeing the stultifying conformity of that era and could find anything in Havana from narcotics and striptease joints to gay bars and child prostitution.
For both sets of visitors, the lure was similar. Cuba was what it had always
been: a forbidden, slightly overripe fruit, an offshore refuge where you could
do anything that was considered illegal or immoral at home.

Gifted musicians like Chico O'Farrill and Frank Raúl Grillo ("Machito")
migrated to New York from such Havana nightspots as El Casino de la Playa.
Jazz-saxophone great Charlie Parker recorded with Machito and his orchestra
in 1949–50, while Xavier Cugat's society band and Stan Kenton's "Peanut
Vendor" popularized Cuban rhythms for a mass audience. The "dance of the
millions" that had accompanied the Cuban sugar boom of the 1920s was again
in full swing. "Exuberant Havana is one of the world's fabled fleshpots,"
reported *Time* in 1952. "The whole world dances to its sexy rumbas and
mambos. Its socialites dine off gold plate, and its sumptuous casinos are
snowed under by the pesos of sugar-rich playboys."

Corruption was nothing new in Cuba. Nor did it all result from the domi-
nant American influence on the island. Shady business and abuse of government power had been ingrained in nineteenth-century Spanish colonial rule.
If anything, it seemed to escalate when the government was nominally democratic. Both the governments of Ramón Grau San Martín (1944–48) and
Carlos Prío Socorrás (1948–52) came to power through the ballot box, but it
was common knowledge that fabulous sums were paid out to buy both elections. After April 1952, however, when Fulgencio Batista, leader of the Ser-

FIFTIETH ANNIVERSARY OF THE AMERICAN CLUB, HAVANA, 1955. "THE HIGHER CLASS OF THE PUBLIC MEN OF OUR COUNTRY HAVE ALWAYS BEEN INTERESTED IN CUBA, AND SHE HAS HAD A CHARM FOR OUR PEOPLE IN PROPORTION TO THE ELEVATION OF THEIR INTELLIGENCE." —MURAT HALSTEAD, 1896.

THE ONE-ARMED BANDIT, 1957.
"FROM THE 1880S ONWARDS CUBA
WAS A SOCIETY OF ADVENTURERS.
POLITICAL INDEPENDENCE
BROUGHT INTERLUDES OF HECTIC
PROSPERITY, NEVER FREEDOM
FROM UNREST. WEALTH WAS MADE
BY SPECULATION. NORTH
AMERICANS BURST INTO THE
COUNTRY IN THE GOOD TIMES, AND
BROKE OUT AGAIN IN THE BAD."
—HUGH THOMAS.

geants' Revolt back in 1933, disposed of the Prío regime in a bloodless predawn coup, graft reached new extremes.

Cuba had been a source of fascination, even obsession, in the United States for more than fifty years. But the Batista coup was the first time it had made the cover of *Time*. After his surprising defeat at the polls in 1944, and his even more surprising decision to stand by the result, Batista had gone to Florida. He lived in exile in Daytona Beach, keeping trim on an exercise machine or in a rowing shell on the Halifax River, and busying himself with his real-estate holdings in Miami. Batista was fifty-one now, "a hairy, muscular man's man," according to *Time*. The newsweekly registered its distaste for the coup but tried to put it in the context of the Latin American character. Democracy was a fragile flower, it ruminated: "Self-discipline in the exercise of personal liberties is also needed to keep democracy stable. Latinos are individualists, insistent upon personal as distinct from political liberty. They are men of passion, men of honor. . . . Sometimes, in the flurry of upholding honor and individual rights, some of the quieter ground rules of social conduct have a tendency to get lost in the shuffle."

The Eisenhower administration was also indulgent, recognizing the Ba-

TV GAME SHOW, 1957. "EVEN OUR BAD TASTE WAS IMPORTED." —PABLO ARMANDO FERNÁNDEZ.

tista regime without delay. With his return to power, Cuba lurched from bad
to worse. "The Cuban political system, such as it was, had already been
tortured to death," wrote Hugh Thomas. "The accumulated follies of fifty
years were bearing their rotten fruit." He called Batista's coup "an event
comparable in the life of an individual to a nervous breakdown after years of
chronic illness."

Cabinet ministers bought their jobs by fixing the lotteries and padding the
bills for public-works projects. U.S. companies doing business in Cuba, especially on government contracts, could routinely expect to pay hefty bribes
to officials. With the return of Batista, top army officers made vast fortunes
from vice rackets and smuggling. *New York Times* correspondent Robert
Alden was taken one Christmas to a casino that was favored by cabinet members and the military. "The women wore chinchilla capes and sported diamonds as big as robins' eggs. Thousands of dollars changed hands at each
throw of the dice." Anger against these symbols of Batista's corruption built
steadily until the triumph of Castro's revolution, New Year's Day 1959, when
crowds would sack the casinos and rip down all the parking meters in the
streets of Havana.

There was a resident American colony of 6,500 in Batista's Havana, most
of them business executives or retirees who owned Cuban real estate. They
gathered for cocktails and gossip at the Country Club, the Miramar, or the
Havana Yacht Club. Wives belonged to the Women's Club, which did chari-
table work, or the Mothers' Club, which organized special tea dances for the
children. In a building owned by the Masons, the Little Theater and the
Choral Society put on regular productions. At the same time, wrote Thomas,
"the Cuban upper middle class was imitative and easily copied U.S. modes
of behavior. All rich Cubans had money in North America, most had been
educated there, many looked on North America as their social guarantor;
some were really more North American than Caribbean."

The activities of the American colony and the short-stay tourists during
the Batista era were chronicled by Constantino Arias, the house photographer
at the U.S.-owned Hotel Nacional, Havana's finest. His photographs of the
gamblers, the Folies Bergères dancers at the Teatro Blanquita, and the amateur dramatics at the Casa de la Comunidad were not so remote from the
image of Cuba purveyed by the tour operators in New York and Miami. The
only difference was Arias's sense of irony, which surely escaped his subjects.

••   ••   ••

As Batista settled into the presidential office in Havana, attentive readers in
the U.S. were noticing an increasing number of stories with a Guatemala City
dateline in their morning newspapers. A great deal of this news "was supplied, edited, and sometimes made by United Fruit's public-relations department in New York," according to Thomas McCann, the company's former PR
director. United Fruit, with its pamphlets on the history of the banana and its
culinary and cultural advice to wartime housewives, had always had an agile
PR operation. Its push to influence news coverage of Guatemala began in

April 1951, when a company consultant, the public-relations wizard Edward Bernays, persuaded *New York Times* publisher Arthur Hays Sulzberger to send a reporter down. Bernays described the results as "masterpieces of objective reporting."

The Bernays-Sulzberger meeting came hard on the heels of the election of a new Guatemalan president, Jacobo Arbenz Guzmán, who promised to extend the reforms of his predecessor, Arévalo. United Fruit was particularly upset about Arbenz's plan to build a new highway and railroad to the Atlantic coast, breaking the company monopoly on Guatemala's export trade. It grew even more alarmed in 1952, when Arbenz announced a modest agrarian-reform program that would give small holdings to a hundred thousand land-less families. Part of the land was to come from company property that was standing idle.

Between 1952 and 1954, Bernays put together a series of press junkets to Guatemala. "Designed with the precision of a space-shot," wrote McCann,

CUBA'S BATISTA
He got past democracy's sentries.

"TOTALITARIANISM WE REFUSE TO
COOPERATE WITH ... WITH
DICTATORSHIPS WE WILL."
—FRANCIS ADAMS TRUSLOW,
COUNCIL ON
FOREIGN RELATIONS, 1949.

they were "a serious attempt to compromise objectivity." Bernays, who was convinced that the Arbenz reforms were the thin edge of a Soviet wedge that would end with the seizure of Central America, wrote with satisfaction that, "as I anticipated, public interest in the Caribbean skyrocketed in this country."

In 1953, *Life* devoted a lavish photo spread to the "Red" land reform. The photographer was Cornell Capa, who twenty years later produced an impressive book of images of poverty in El Salvador and Honduras for the Population Reference Bureau. But the sensitivity of Capa's photographs was crushed beneath the steamroller of *Life*'s prose. The article reported that Guatemala was "openly and diligently toiling to create a Communist state in Central America . . . only two hours' bombing time from the Panama Canal." The Guatemalan Reds, *Life* wrote, had picked on the United Fruit Company because they were "forever in need of something to hate."

The timing of Bernays's press campaign was perfect. The public was gripped by fear of the Soviet menace; a Soviet power-play in America's backyard could be counted on to grab the attention of editors, few of whom were willing to risk dissent in the prevailing Cold War climate; and the Eisenhower administration was delighted to find a winnable confrontation with communism in such a sensitive theater. Visitors to the office of Secretary of State John Foster Dulles reported him "purring like a giant cat" at the impending showdown.

It is hard to pick out the high-water mark of a period as laden with extremes as the Cold War. Some would say late 1949 and early 1950, when the Republican Party launched its witch-hunt to root out those it blamed for "losing" China, and Senator Joe McCarthy brandished his list of 205 known communists in the State Department. Others might say 1951, the year of the Hollywood blacklist. Or 1957, perhaps, when a collective frenzy seemed to seize the land with the news of the Soviet Union's *Sputnik* space probe. David Caute, in *The Great Fear*, his study of the Cold War, feels that mid-1954 was probably "the high summer of the great fear." It was in May of that year that the Emergency Civil Liberties Committee delivered the warning, "The threat to civil liberties in the United States today is the most serious in the history of our country." In the same month, the CIA put into motion Operation Success, to overthrow Arbenz. It was the largest covert operation up to that time, and arguably the symbolic pinnacle of the international Cold War.

Arbenz had legalized the Guatemalan Communist Party in 1951. As one of a dozen new parties formed since the overthrow of Ubico seven years earlier, it had only a limited following and just four members in the fifty-six-member congress. Party officials were influential in the labor unions and land reform. These signs were enough to convince John Peurifoy, the U.S. ambassador, that "if the president is not a communist, he will certainly do until one comes along." Alexander Wiley, chairman of the Senate Foreign Relations Committee, agreed that Guatemala had "become a serious beachhead for international communism in this hemisphere."

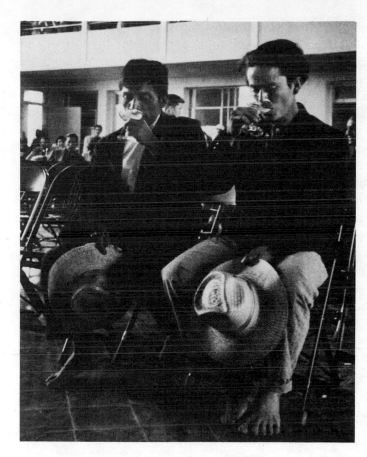

●━━━━━●

"COMMUNIST LEADERS KNOW THEY
HAVE LITTLE TO FEAR IN A LAND
WHERE JOSÉ MANUEL FORTUNY,
GUATEMALA'S NO. 1 RED, CAN
SUMMON A CABINET OFFICER AT
WILL, AND WHERE BAREFOOT
PEASANTS, UNACCUSTOMED AS
THEY MAY BE, ARE LEARNING
TO SIP CHAMPAGNE."
—*LIFE*, OCTOBER 12, 1953.

The CIA, which had overthrown the nationalist government of Mo-
hammed Mossadegh in Iran the previous year, found the pretext it needed
for getting rid of Arbenz on May 15, 1954, when a Swedish freighter, the
Alfhem, unloaded a cargo of Czech-made weapons for the Guatemalan Army.
For the previous six years, Guatemala had been under a U.S. arms embargo,
and it had turned to Soviet-bloc suppliers as a last resort. CIA Director Allen
Dulles determined that the weapons would enable Arbenz to crush his neighbors and move on the Panama Canal—though why he should have the remot-
est desire to do so was a question that no one, in the atmosphere of the day,
stopped to ask.

The U.S. press, liberal as well as conservative, accepted the conspiracy
theory. "If the Arbenz forces are successful," fretted Clay Felker in *Life*, "the
Kremlin will gain a de facto foothold in the Western Hemisphere." Like other
reporters, Felker dismissed news of anti-U.S. protests in the region as part of
a "Red-run" plot. In February 1954, *Newsweek* surveyed Guatemala's neighbors and summed up the situation with a medical metaphor—diseased and
healthy bodies, infection and immunity, spreading cancer that has since
been applied repeatedly to Cuba and Nicaragua: "The other Central American countries seem to be relatively clean for the moment. But Red expansion
will always be a possibility while the focus of the infection remains in Gua-

temala." *Newsweek* also swallowed an almost ludicrously transparent story that the CIA had planted to advance the domino theory. In a May 17 piece in Guatemala, the magazine reported that the Somoza government had sighted an unidentified submarine off the coast of Nicaragua, and shortly afterward discovered a cache of machine guns, rifles, grenades, and ammunition. "They were of European make, he said, were wrapped in water-repellent material, and the rifles were stamped with hammer-and-sickle." Somoza told reporters that this could betoken "a new Korean situation" in Central America.

One of the most remarkable features of Operation Success was its propaganda activities, run by a young CIA agent named E. Howard Hunt, who later achieved renown for his role in Watergate. By means of ominous clandestine radio broadcasts, the agency managed to convince Arbenz that he was facing an invading army supported by the might of the United States, when in reality the rebel force was about two hundred strong, backed up by mercenary pilots who ran a couple of psychologically damaging bombing raids on Guatemala City from bases in Nicaragua. The Arbenz government caved in on June 27. On July 2 Ambassador Peurifoy flew into the capital aboard his private plane, accompanied by an obscure army colonel named Carlos Castillo Armas, whom Washington had chosen to head a new government. Two days later, Peurifoy and his wife invited five hundred conservative Guatemalans to their home to celebrate the Fourth of July. The Guatemalans sang "The Star-Spangled Banner," and Betty Jane Peurifoy dashed off a celebration verse that *Time* published. It ended:

> *. . . pistol-packing Peurifoy looks mighty optimistic*
> *For the land of Guatemala is no longer Communistic!*

The Eisenhower administration milked the episode for all its symbolic value. Guatemala became a blank slate on which to project U.S. fantasies.

••••••

NIXON INSPECTS CAPTURED COMMUNIST
LITERATURE, GUATEMALA.
"AS WE BOARDED THE PLANE TO DEPART FOR
HOME, MY ASSOCIATES AND I WERE COMPLETELY
WORN OUT. OUR NERVES WERE SHOT FROM
TENSION, ANTICIPATING NIXON-LIKE INCIDENTS. SO
WHEN WE WERE WELL IN THE AIR, WE ALL BURST
INTO HEARTY CHEERING, HAD A FEW DRINKS, AND
SAT BACK TO BREATHE."
—MILTON EISENHOWER, LEAVING GUATEMALA,
1958.

The Americas had been cleansed of Soviet contamination. The world had seen that when America talked tough, it meant business. Guatemala was to become "a showcase for democracy." Castillo Armas made a state visit to Washington, received a twenty-one-gun salute, and visited Eisenhower in his hospital room in Denver, where he was recovering from a heart attack. The following February, Vice-President Richard Nixon, who had built his reputation as a Cold War inquisitor at home, made an official tour of eight Central American and Caribbean countries, beginning in Cuba and ending in Guatemala. He examined piles of captured "Red" literature and inspected a display of the Czech weapons from the *Alfhem*, most of which were obsolete and useless. He declared, "This is the first instance in history where a Communist government has been replaced by a free one"—a claim that was to be repeated, almost word for word, after U.S. forces invaded Grenada in October 1983.

On January 5, 1956, the *New York Times* reported, "There are indications of the return of confidence of native businessmen in the economic possibilities of Guatemala, now that political stability has been achieved and labor-management strife has been eliminated." The new stability meant thirty years of military rule and perhaps a hundred thousand violent civilian deaths. But as far as Americans were concerned, Guatemala was allowed to slide back into obscurity. Only in 1982, twenty-eight years after the event, did two books finally piece together the story of Operation Success. In *Bitter Fruit*, Stephen Schlesinger and Stephen Kinzer dwelt heavily on United Fruit's role, but Richard Immerman, in *The CIA in Guatemala*, may have come closer to the heart of the matter, suggesting that corporate arrogance was less the issue than Washington's need for a demonstration victory in the Cold War. As John Foster Dulles had said of the Arbenz government, "If they gave a gold piece for every banana, the problem would still be Communist infiltration."

-- -- --

The silence that shrouded Central America in the late 1950s was broken only twice: once in July 1957, when Castillo Armas was assassinated, and once the previous September, when Anastasio Somoza García was shot four times by a poet named Rigoberto López Pérez. Somoza had just finished dancing the cha-cha at a reception; the twentieth anniversary of his rule was only three months away. When Ambassador Thomas E. Whelan, a frequent companion at the poker table, expressed concern, Somoza replied, "I'm a goner."

Both events served to confirm two things: the United States counted on steadfast neighbors who stood by its side in the fight against alien enemies; and political life "down there" was marked by irrational, intractable violence. Eisenhower mourned the death of Castillo Armas, who was killed instantly, as "a great loss to Guatemala and the world." Somoza lingered on for a week, and Ike rushed a team of top military doctors from Washington's Walter Reed Hospital (named for the man who had conquered yellow fever in Cuba) to join a second team at the Canal Zone's Gorgas Hospital (named for the man

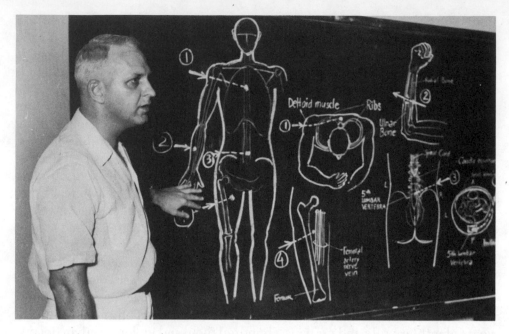

••••••

DR. BERNART WILLET, CHEST
SPECIALIST AT THE U.S.
GOVERNMENT'S GORGAS HOSPITAL
AT ANCÓN, ONE OF FOUR SURGEONS
WHO OPERATED ON PRESIDENT
ANASTASIO SOMOZA OF
NICARAGUA, AFTER HE WAS SHOT
BY AN ASSASSIN, EXPLAINS HOW
THE BULLETS ENTERED
SOMOZA'S BODY, 1956.

who had beaten tropical disease in Panama). Colonel Charles O. Bruce, medical director of the Canal Zone, and chest specialist Dr. Bernart Willet kept
the press briefed on the extent of Somoza's wounds.

After seven days in a coma, the dictator succumbed. "Cheek-by-cheek
cooperation with the United States has been his guiding principle," said
Newsweek's deathwatch story. Ike sent a personal honor guard to accompany
the coffin, and Secretary of State Dulles promised that Somoza's "constantly
demonstrated friendship for the U.S. will never be forgotten." By the time
news of his death was broken, his eldest son, Luis, had taken over as president, and his younger son, Anastasio Somoza Debayle, or "Tachito," was
installed as chief of the National Guard. The dictatorship had become a dynasty.

•• •• ••

One of the few journalists who disagreed with the accepted wisdom about
Guatemala was an experienced *Times* reporter named Herbert Matthews. He
had been with the paper since 1932, covering the Spanish Civil War and
doing stints as bureau chief in Paris, Rome, London, and New Delhi. Since
1949, he had been an editorial writer specializing in Latin America. To be
sure, his dissent over Arbenz was more one of nuance than of substance. After
a fact-finding trip in 1952, his verdict was that Arbenz was "young, inexperienced, and enthusiastic." He and his colleagues were "naïve enough to think
that communism must take its part in any truly liberal regime, and they never
could be made to realize the dangers of communism to their country and to
themselves." Even as late as 1971, when he wrote his memoirs, Matthews
made it clear that he had no qualms about the overthrow of Arbenz; he simply

thought it could have been achieved less messily by helping the army and police to stage a coup.

Matthews had followed events in Cuba closely for years. An increasingly despotic Batista had faced the threat of armed revolution since 1953, when a band of rebels led by Fidel Castro had attacked the Moncada barracks. After a brief spell in jail and then self-imposed exile, Castro had returned in 1956 aboard the yacht *Granma* to begin a guerrilla war in the mountains of the Sierra Maestra. His little army was soon encircled and cut off from the outside world. The United Press reported that he had been killed, and Batista's PR adviser, former CBS executive Edmund Chester, even gave the dictator the date of Fidel's death and burial—December 9, 1956.

Out of the blue, however, in February 1957, Herbert Matthews received word from the *Times*'s Havana stringer, Ruby Hart Philips, that Castro was alive and eager to give an interview. Matthews prepared his trip to the Sierra amidst the strictest secrecy. "The last place to get the slightest inkling of what was happening had to be the American embassy," he wrote.

Relations between the Eisenhower administration and Batista had never been cosier. Until the late 1940s, diplomats in the region were often well-informed scholars who took an active role in formulating policy. Dana Munro, U.S. chargé d'affaires in Managua during the war against Sandino and author of a classic study of the five Central American republics, was a good example. But the U.S. ambassador in Havana, Arthur Gardner, was typical of a new breed of know-nothing political appointees who had come into the service after the Cold War purge of many career diplomats and were objects of con-

"YOU CAN BE SURE WE HAVE NO ANIMOSITY TOWARD THE UNITED STATES AND THE AMERICAN PEOPLE."
—FIDEL CASTRO TO HERBERT MATTHEWS, 1957.

tempt among their European counterparts. Gardner was ostentatiously close
to Batista, and had even tried to persuade him that the FBI or CIA should
dispatch a hit man into the Sierra to kill Castro. "Except for Cuban government circles and the American and Cuban business community," Matthews
wrote, "Gardner was hated by the Cubans."

Traveling south from Havana by car, Matthews took his wife along on the
assignment for "camouflage" to get through military checkpoints, reasoning
that in Cuba "nothing could have looked more innocent than a middle-aged
couple of American tourists." He interviewed Castro on February 17, 1957,
and the first of his three-part series hit the front page of the *Times* a week
later. It caused a firestorm, and for years to come key phrases would be
scrutinized to provide ammunition for those who blamed Matthews for "losing" Cuba. Castro emerged as a Jeffersonian figure, with ideas that were
"radical, democratic, and therefore anti-Communist." He stressed that "we
have no animosity toward the United States and the American people." The
Cuban government was enraged most of all by Matthews's assessment (accurate, as it turned out) that "General Batista cannot possibly hope to suppress
the Castro revolt." The regime accused Matthews of fabricating the entire
story, to which the *Times* responded four days later by printing a photograph
of Matthews conducting the interview while Castro lit one of his trademark
cigars.

It was, as Matthews himself said, "the biggest scoop of our times." But
much more than that, it was one of those rare moments when a single news
story managed to cut through the haze of official untruth—whether the rigid
censorship of Batista's police state or the drowsy complacency that had settled over America in Eisenhower's second term. It also opened a wound that
has never healed, and could probably have been caused by no other country
than this loose piece of Florida that had inexplicably come adrift ninety miles
offshore.

Paying attention to the realities of Cuba for the first time in years, U.S.
opinion created an instant drama of heroes and villains. With its decision to
impose an arms embargo in March 1958, the State Department served notice
that Batista's days were numbered. Castro in turn became a folk hero, larger
than life, Robin Hood to Batista's grotesque Sheriff of Nottingham. Hard on
the heels of Matthews's reports came a CBS documentary titled *Cuba's Jungle
Fighters*. Fidel, giving his second interview, stared into the camera lens and
assured American viewers he was not a communist. In April 1959, three
months after his triumphal entry into Havana, Castro came to the United
States as the guest of the American Society of Newspaper Editors. The press
lionized him. The CIA briefed him for two hours on the Red menace.

The visit provoked one of Matthews's sharpest insights. "In reality," he
wrote, "Americans were welcoming a figure who did not exist, expecting
what could not and what would not happen, and then blaming Fidel Castro
for their own blindness and ignorance." Castro soon made it apparent that
while posing for photographs at the Lincoln Memorial was all very well, there
were limits to how far he was willing to follow an American script. His

militant brand of Cuban nationalism and the United States began to move, as
in a law of physics, in opposing directions. This left Americans with two choices:
accept the consequences of U.S.-Cuban history and assume responsibility
for the past; or deny history, preserve innocence, and demand vengeance.

•• •• ••

As U.S.-Cuban relations careened from one crisis to another between 1959
and 1961, culminating in Castro's defiant embrace of the Soviet Union, the
cry of betrayal filled the air. It searched for alien influences and fifth-colum-
nists, and found scapegoats in State Department officials like Roy Rubottom
("He favored Castro, there is no question about it," former ambassador Gardner raged) and William Wieland of the Caribbean desk, who had lived in
Cuba in the 1920s and 1930s. But the main target was Matthews, who became
a lightning rod for the failure of the intelligence community to detect Castro's
sympathies. (Even as late as 1959, after Castro had taken power, Allen Dulles
assured the Senate that the Cuban leader did not have "any communist lean-
ings.") The liberal Matthews found himself stigmatized as a fellow-traveler,
a useful fool, and a traitor—insults that stuck to him until the end of his
career. A cartoon in the arch-conservative *National Review* in May 1960,
brilliantly parodying the *Times*'s own advertising slogan, summed up the
mood of rancor.

•• •• ••

By the time the cartoon appeared, the atmosphere was irretrievably poisoned.
Conservatives like Spruille Braden, ambassador to Havana in the 1940s,
thought Cuba was "the gravest threat there has ever been to the security of

"IN MY THIRTY YEARS ON THE *NEW
YORK TIMES*, I HAVE NEVER SEEN
A BIG STORY SO MISUNDERSTOOD,
SO BADLY HANDLED,
AND SO MISINTERPRETED
AS THE CUBAN REVOLUTION."
—HERBERT MATTHEWS, 1961.

"I got my job through the New York Times."

our country and the hemisphere." By March 1960, Eisenhower had decided that Washington could no longer coexist with Castro, and he authorized a program of covert actions to get rid of the Cuban leader. Over the next several years, the CIA would attempt to assassinate Castro with exploding cigars and poisoned milkshakes, and humiliate him with depilatory powders that would make his beard fall out.

Americans heard a lot about Castro's iniquities, but nothing about the moves to topple him. At best, they read hopeful features that promised a return to traditional U.S.-Cuban friendship—one day. The March 1961 *National Geographic* carried a colorful report about life on the Guantánamo naval base, which one enthusiastic pilot thought was "kind of like Hawaii with Cubans." The reporter found guests at the Officers' Club sprawled in lawn chairs at one of eight open-air movie theaters, watching Vincente Minelli's new hit musical, *Bells Are Ringing.* The magazine catalogued the other attractions of "Gitmo": its neat cinder-block houses, seventeen softball fields, six baseball diamonds, four hobby shops, a darkroom, a roller-skating rink, and a twenty-seven-hole golf course. Some of the base wives, though, were less keen: "In fifteen minutes you can drive from one end of it to the other. . . . It's the same old thing day after day."

The only real problem was the "anti-U.S. headlines of Cuban papers hawked at the gates." But to compensate for these, there were "repeated demonstrations—on a person-to-person level—of Cuban-American friendship." The best example was the annual Fourth of July baseball game between the base and a Cuban all-stars team. The navy had won the 1960 game 4–3 in extra innings.

Otherwise the press was silent. In November 1960, the *Nation* reported that anti-Castro Cubans were being trained on a secret base in Guatemala, but the story died. The Miami papers knew from the talk on the streets that something big was in the air, but agreed with the CIA not to print the news. The *New Republic* and the *New York Times* killed or severely cut stories that detailed plans for an invasion of Cuba. In its January 13 issue, *Time* was still sneering at "Castro's continued tawdry little melodrama of invasion." So virulent was the dislike of Castro that no paper was willing to tip him off about the largest CIA operation in history, with as many as seven hundred agents holed up in an abandoned navy air base in the Miami suburb of Opa-Locka. The word from the White House—now occupied by John F. Kennedy, who had inherited Eisenhower's plans for Cuba—was that national security was at stake, and, as the *Times*'s Theodore Bernstein explained, "Editors cannot have the information or specialized knowledge that would allow them to dispute an official determination that the country's safety might be jeopardized."

On April 17, fourteen hundred men hit the Cuban beaches at the Bay of Pigs. Facing an army of thirty-five thousand, they were overwhelmed. It was, as Theodore Draper put it, "one of those rare politico-military events: a perfect failure." Many called it the most humiliating defeat in American history.

The humiliation was represented on so many stinging levels—from the image of undertrained, outnumbered troops stumbling ashore over coral reefs and swamps, to the bitter symbolism of defeat at the hands of a foreign leader cast as a virtual Antichrist. The fact that Cuba held a special place in U.S. history —San Juan Hill, the *Maine*, the Good Neighbor, the winter playground— rubbed salt in the wounds. Just three months into his presidency, Kennedy was humiliated in all that he prized most: virile action, boldness in the defense of freedom.

Those who accused Kennedy of betraying Brigade 2506 said the entire affair could have ended differently if he had ordered protective air strikes. The postmortems in Washington, too, tended to emphasize the technical aspects of the fiasco: rusty outboard motors, insufficient ammunition, bureaucratic snafus. Press comment also found the Bay of Pigs an embarrassment rather than an impropriety, and few papers condemned the principle of the invasion. No one saw that the seeds of the disaster could be found in its origins. "If the [CIA] had not had Guatemala, it probably would not have had Cuba," reflected E. Howard Hunt, who served in both operations. The Bay of Pigs and the overthrow of Arbenz employed the same team; the architect of both was CIA Deputy Director Richard Bissell. Agents assigned to the Cuba invasion initially called it Operation Guatemala. They used the same headquarters, the Opa-Locka base. The pilots flew from the same Nicaraguan airstrips.

The men who engineered the downfall of Arbenz in 1954 were so intoxicated by their success that they thought it could be repeated—as if making foreign policy were like executing dance steps, following footprints painted

CASTRO IN MOSCOW WITH

NIKITA KHRUSHCHEV, 1963.

"HAS CUBA GAINED,

AND, ABOVE ALL, HAVE WE IN THE

UNITED STATES GAINED BY THE

BATISTA-CASTRO EXCHANGE?"

—COLUMNIST JOSEPH ALSOP.

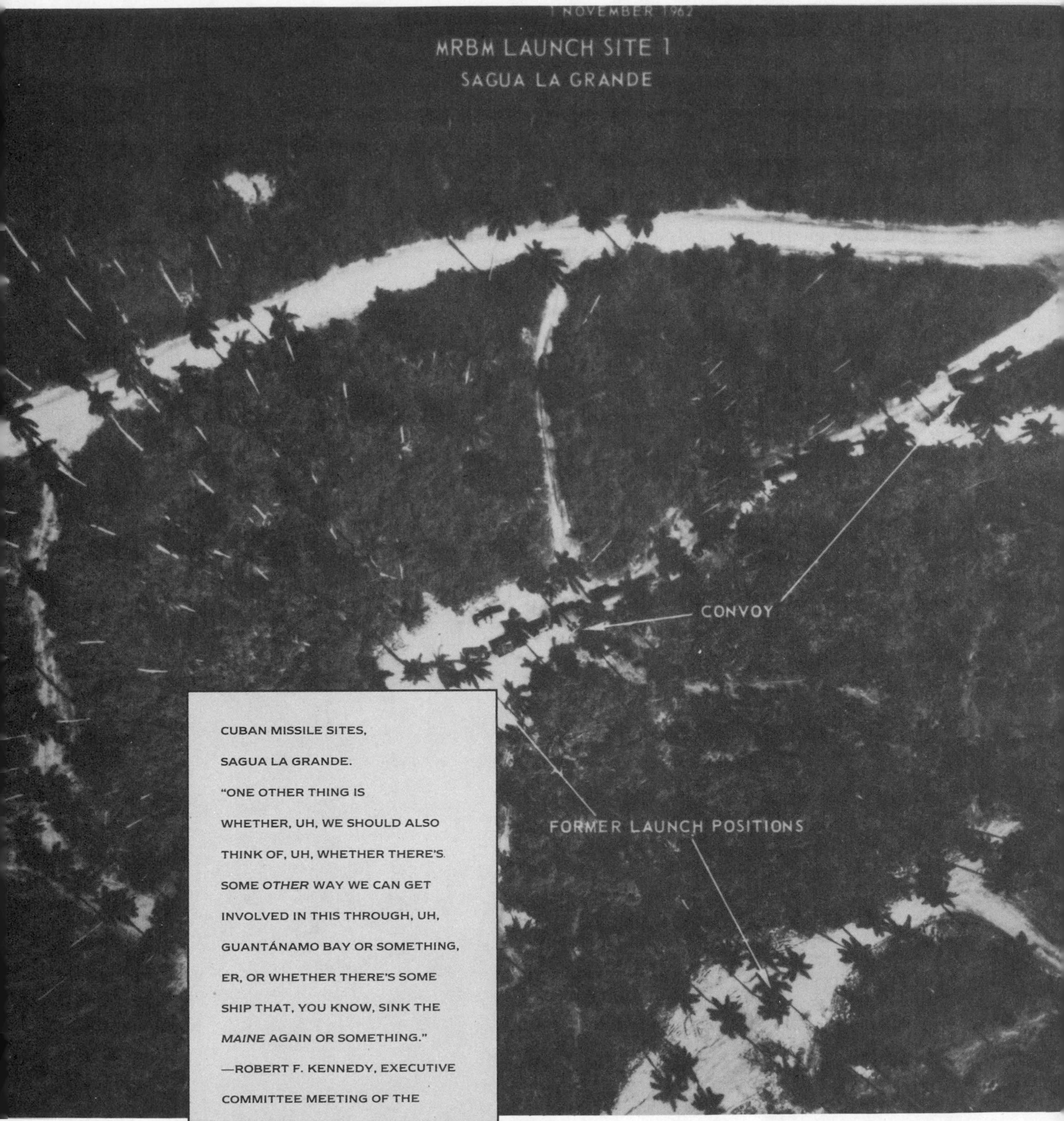

1 NOVEMBER 1962

MRBM LAUNCH SITE 1
SAGUA LA GRANDE

CONVOY

FORMER LAUNCH POSITIONS

CUBAN MISSILE SITES,
SAGUA LA GRANDE.
"ONE OTHER THING IS
WHETHER, UH, WE SHOULD ALSO
THINK OF, UH, WHETHER THERE'S
SOME *OTHER* WAY WE CAN GET
INVOLVED IN THIS THROUGH, UH,
GUANTÁNAMO BAY OR SOMETHING,
ER, OR WHETHER THERE'S SOME
SHIP THAT, YOU KNOW, SINK THE
MAINE AGAIN OR SOMETHING."
—ROBERT F. KENNEDY, EXECUTIVE
COMMITTEE MEETING OF THE
NATIONAL SECURITY COUNCIL,
OCTOBER 16, 1962.

on the floor. Bissell thought Castro would lose his nerve as Arbenz had, and failed to see any difference between the two men—in part, perhaps, because he came to believe the agency rhetoric that had depicted the moderate Arbenz as a flaming Red. The CIA saw history only as a useful guide to operational tactics, and never appreciated that the Cubans, too, might have studied the Guatemala episode and drawn entirely different lessons. As it happened, Castro's top lieutenant, Ernesto (Che) Guevara, had arrived in Guatemala in 1953 and had witnessed the entire affair. The first article he ever wrote was titled, "I Saw the Fall of Jacobo Arbenz." The Cubans had observed Arbenz's failure to secure his regime militarily and did not intend to repeat his mistake. The army was loyal to Castro, and the mass uprising on which the CIA had staked its hopes never took place.

The Bay of Pigs sealed Castro's alignment with the Soviet Union and directly paved the way for the missile crisis the following year. While Castro was looking for a cast-iron guarantee against future invasions, Nikita Khrushchev had observed Kennedy's refusal to send in U.S. troops to back up the invading brigade, and decided to test his opponent's strength. On October 14, 1962, a U-2 spy plane flying over Cuba photographed a number of nuclear-weapons launching sites at San Cristóbal. Kennedy ordered a naval blockade of Cuba, to prevent Soviet vessels that might be carrying missiles from reaching the island. For almost two weeks the world appeared to stand on the brink of a nuclear exchange. In the end, Soviet ships turned back. "We're eyeball to eyeball" was the memorable comment of Secretary of State Dean Rusk, "and I think the other fellow just blinked." The crisis ended with an understanding that the Soviets would not station offensive weapons in Cuba; in return, the United States pledged not to invade the island. (In fact, as Dean Rusk revealed in 1987, Kennedy had been prepared to go the extra mile by linking the Cuba settlement to the removal of antiquated U.S. Jupiter missiles from Turkey.)

Only after the missile crisis did the United States finally secure the release of the prisoners taken at the Bay of Pigs. The very idea of negotiating with Castro had aroused a storm of protest. "If the United States wants these men back," ran a typical May 1961 editorial in the *Indianapolis Star*, "let us

••••••

PRESIDENT KENNEDY: "YOU DIDN'T
GET ANY HELP FROM US."
EDDIE FERRER (CUBAN CIA PILOT):
"NO, MR. PRESIDENT, BUT I EXPECT
IT THE NEXT TIME."
KENNEDY: "YOU BETTER BELIEVE
THAT THERE'S GOING TO BE
A NEXT TIME."

simply go and take them." Eventually, the prisoners came back to Miami the week after Christmas 1962. Presidential aides advised Kennedy that a meeting with them would be a needlessly belligerent gesture. But his brother Robert, the attorney general, who felt the United States had no higher priority in the world than overthrowing Castro, told him to go ahead. In a much-photographed welcome rally in Miami's Orange Bowl, accompanied by his wife, Jackie (who made a speech in Spanish), Kennedy committed the immense symbolic weight of the presidency to the Bay of Pigs veterans, telling them they represented America's highest values. The survivors of Brigade 2506 presented Kennedy with their banner, and he vowed, "This flag will be returned to this brigade in free Havana."

The Bay of Pigs and the missile crisis introduced a new and virulent theme to American politics, that of betrayal. Just as Washington had lambasted Castro for betraying the revolution, now the anti-Castro exiles accused Kennedy of betraying them. The Bay of Pigs was the first time that the United States was accused of leaving its allies to twist in the wind because it was unwilling to put American lives on the line—a charge which returned to haunt Washington in Southeast Asia and can still be heard in debates over Central America. Cuban-Americans, seeking a replay of the Bay of Pigs that they could win, began to make themselves felt in the mainstream of American politics, as well as the lunatic fringe. They were recruited as the Watergate burglars of Howard Hunt—of Guatemala fame—who told them they would find evidence of Castro's support for George McGovern's 1972 presidential campaign. Veterans of the Bay of Pigs became key covert operatives and bureaucrats in the Southeast Asian war of the 1960s and 1970s, and in the contra war against Nicaragua a decade later.

•• •• ••

The trauma of the Bay of Pigs all but eclipsed a new program Kennedy had announced the previous month. The Alliance for Progress, which Kennedy called the most important foreign-policy initiative of his presidency, was a massive aid program, to be administered by the newly created Agency for International Development. The alliance was the second half of Kennedy's answer to the Cuban revolution, and its goal was to prove that the United States could offer a model of development and social welfare that would beat Castro on his own terms. The symbol of the enterprise was a handshake, wrapped in the Stars and Stripes.

Also announced in March 1961 was the Peace Corps, perhaps the quintessential idea of the Kennedy era. It was to operate worldwide, but its roots, as the recruiting posters made clear, also lay in Cuba. At the Peace Corps Training Center in Puerto Rico, the closest available simulation of Third World conditions, new recruits were put through a three-month course in American institutions and values, the culture and language of the country to which they were assigned, and survival training. "If you impress the peoples of these countries with your commitment to freedom, to your pride in your country

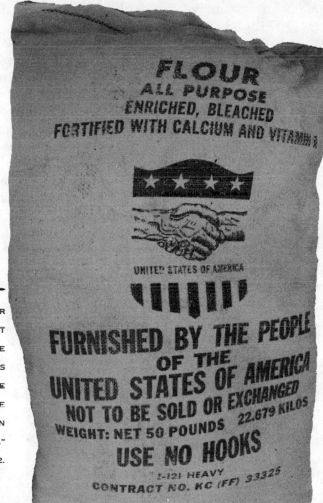

"THE BELIEF IN AN EVEN BETTER
TOMORROW, THE CONVICTION THAT
OBSTACLES EXIST TO BE OVERCOME
AND THAT THE UNITED STATES HAS
A STRONG AND BENEFICIAL ROLE
TO PLAY IN THE WORLD—THESE
CONSTITUTE THE AMERICAN
SECULAR RELIGION."
—*TIME* EDITORIAL, 1982.

SALVADORAN PCN SYMBOL
ON 1982 ELECTION BALLOT.

and its best traditions and what it stands for, the influence may be far-reaching," JFK told the first trainees at a White House luncheon. By June 1964, there were more than ten thousand volunteers in the field. Two out of every five were in Latin America. The image of the ugly American was pervasive during this period; so what better antidote than the image of heroic young idealists in jeans and sneakers living in mud huts at great personal sacrifice?

Children, too, were exposed in the early and mid-1960s to a wave of revised images of Central America through a booming market for school texts of the life-in-other-lands variety. Their flavor was the Good Neighborliness of the 1940s with a new spin: the crusading zeal of Kennedy's youthful Camelot. But the surface sheen of the Alliance for Progress did not have to be scratched very hard for more familiar and enduring attitudes to emerge.

On Guatemala: "It is difficult to develop stable and democratic government because so many of the nation's Indians are illiterate and superstitious" (*Let's Visit Central America,* 1964). And this: "The Indians pose one of the major problems of Central America. They are an ideal group for Communist agents to work on" (*Central America: Lands Seeking Unity,* 1966).

On Nicaragua, from the same book: "Excitable and changeable, Nicaraguans often pour their energies into fighting. If they struggled as willingly

••••••

"FROM THE FRONT PORCHES OF THE UNITED STATES, THE VIEW OF THE PEACE CORPS IS JUST BEAUTIFUL."
—*TIME,* 1963.

against rugged mountains, rain forests, and swamps, they might advance more rapidly." And most typical of all, on the United States: "As you watch your new friends strive to create a better life, you can be proud that our country is helping them toward their goal" (*Getting to Know Costa Rica, El Salvador, and Nicaragua*, 1964).

The bare bones of the alliance had been worked out under Eisenhower, and at least part of the dilemma had been apparent even then to officials like Milton Eisenhower, who acted as his brother's special envoy to Latin America. "We must convince Latin Americans that our concern for their welfare is deep, abiding, and genuine," he said, "that it is not merely a gambit in the Cold War." He knew it would not be easy, for "the long and fearsome shadow of our past behavior precedes us." Yet in the apparent readiness to acknowledge past errors, there was still the same naïveté about the legacy of history that had bedeviled Wilson, Hoover, and Franklin Roosevelt—all of whom had said very similar things about Central America and the Caribbean. These men believed the problem was to demonstrate U.S. goodwill and turn over a new leaf. What none of them saw was that past U.S. conduct had left not only psychological scars but political systems with their own logic and momentum. One could not simply shake hands and start over.

Kennedy knew that change in Central America was inevitable, but thought that stability, in such a volatile region, had to come first. Just as instability in the 1920s had opened the door to "Mexican Bolshevism," instability in the 1960s invited the worst nightmare of all, a "second Cuba." So Kennedy armed the defenders of the status quo, whose monopoly of power was the root of the problem. The United States opened the School of the Americas to teach local armies how to maintain internal security, and created a regional military alliance, CONDECA, that was informally headed by the Somozas in Nicaragua.

With the help of funds from the Alliance for Progress, the Central American economies grew rapidly in the 1960s and early 1970s. A new generation of fly-by-night U.S. investors, encouraged by federal investment guarantees, arrived from the Sunbelt states, hoping to turn quick profits from tourism and exotic fruits and vegetables. Larger corporations like Maidenform and Texas Instruments, lured by the promise of tax breaks and cheap labor, converged on the new free zone in El Salvador. But almost none of the new wealth trickled down. The elites got richer, the middle class—JFK's hope for the future—grew disillusioned, and Cuban-influenced guerrillas sprang up. Nicaragua's Sandinistas, taking their name from the man who had defied the marines in the 1920s, were born four months into the Alliance for Progress and three months after the Bay of Pigs. The two halves of the alliance slipped giddily out of balance, the demand for military security drowning out the call for civilian reform, and the whole arrangement bred instability on a massive scale. Central America, which had been intended as a showcase for the alliance, became the symbol of its collapse.

-- -- --

Fixated on Cuba, both Eisenhower and Kennedy allowed El Salvador and Guatemala to become lands of squandered opportunity. In October 1960, a new reform-minded junta in El Salvador promised free elections, but the Eisenhower administration, fearing that some of its members might harbor leftist sympathies, withheld recognition. The junta lasted three months before it was overthrown by right-wing officers heralding a regime of National Transformation that would turn El Salvador into a Central American Taiwan. It was January 25, 1961, and John F. Kennedy had been president for five days. He welcomed the coup with the opinion that "governments of the civil-military type of El Salvador are the most effective in containing communist penetration in Latin America." In 1962, the Salvadoran military formed a new official party, which adopted the Alliance for Progress's handshake symbol as its logo and ruled the country until 1979.

In Guatemala, meanwhile a group of young nationalist officers were so incensed by the training of Cuban exiles for the Bay of Pigs on Guatemalan soil that they attempted a coup in November 1960. The Eisenhower administration stationed warships and two thousand marines offshore while General Miguel Ydígoras Fuentes crushed the revolt; nothing was to disrupt preparations for the invasion. The nationalist officers retreated to the hills to organize a guerrilla movement that is still fighting today.

In 1963 Guatemala prepared for elections. Favored to win was Juan José Arévalo, the reformer who had held office from 1945 to 1951. But the United States had invested too much in Operation Success in 1954 to allow the return of a man who was now characterized in the U.S. press as an "extreme leftist." On the day after his return to Guatemala, ultraconservative officers toppled the government and canceled the elections. According to some reports, Kennedy gave the green light to the coup in a secret meeting in Washington. "Free elections are stopped without protest from us, if not with our connivance, where we fear the results," the independent journalist I. F. Stone commented acerbically. "The test is not whether Guatemalans trust Arévalo, but whether we do."

••   ••   ••

The Alliance for Progress, already grievously wounded, was all but killed off by Kennedy's assassination. Lyndon B. Johnson had little time for Latins: the Organization of American States, he remarked, "couldn't pour piss out of a boot if the instructions were written on the heel." His disdain was symptomatic of broader public attitudes, which cartoonists soon began to reflect. In 1961 and 1962, in the first flush of the Alliance for Progress, they had tended to savage military dictators and question whether Cuba was really the root of the problem. By 1963, however, the voices of Teddy Roosevelt, Woodrow Wilson, and Calvin Coolidge echoed again. Old attitudes about the slothfulness and incompetence of Latin American politicians were resurrected. Official Washington was irritated that the region had failed to keep its end of the alliance bargain by making a "determined effort" at self-help. The public's

●—●—●—●—●—●

"THE CLASS WILL PLEASE COME TO

ORDER—SOMEBODY?"

—*NEW YORK TIMES*, 1963

"THE CENTRAL-AMERICAN CITIZEN

IS NO MORE FIT FOR A REPUBLICAN

FORM OF GOVERNMENT THAN HE IS

FOR AN ARCTIC EXPEDITION."

—RICHARD HARDING DAVIS, 1896.

patience ran out quickly. Why couldn't Latin Americans learn the ways of democracy? After all, they had had more than two years.

Crawford's cartoon, which could easily have appeared in 1915 or 1926, ran as part of a special *New York Times* feature in December 1963. Flanking it were two other cartoons: in one, Latin America appeared as a mad bull charging the matador; in the other, as a passive figure in a sombrero hunched over a bar as the stern-faced new barman, LBJ, mixed a cocktail. That week, Johnson had symbolized a shift in policy by appointing Thomas Mann, a conservative Texan who had served Eisenhower in the same post, to head his Latin American programs. Mann is perhaps best remembered for his comment, "I know my Latins. They understand only two things—a buck in the pocket and a kick in the ass." Congress by this time had decided that it had put too many bucks in Latin pockets. Concluding that the alliance was a boondoggle, it cut appropriations by a quarter. Johnson's priority was the chaos in South Vietnam that grew after the assassination on November 2 of Premier Ngo Dinh Diem, three weeks before the assassination of Kennedy, who had approved it.

Meanwhile, the *Times* feature reported, the Cuban revolution was nearing its fifth anniversary, "bearing all the aspects of a willful, moody, undisciplined, but relatively robust child." Public hostility had ebbed since the missile crisis, but fighting Cuban subversion was "urgent business," said

Johnson, who chose to spurn a series of peace feelers from Castro. New
Cuban outrages dotted that day's news pages in the *Times:* aid to terrorist
groups in Venezuela and, perhaps, Bolivia. Closer to home, the paper noted
the emergence of "Castroite" guerrillas in the Dominican Republic, ignoring
the fact that they were fighting to reinstate the elected social-democratic
government of Juan Bosch, who had been overthrown by the military in
September.

•• •• ••

In Johnson's first eighteen months as president, he plunged into two crises
in Central America and the Caribbean. He saw both as Castro-inspired power
plays, though their roots went back several decades. The first came in Panama
in January 1964, over the issue of whose flag should fly over the Canal Zone.
Anti-U.S. sentiment among Panamanians went back a long way, to the early
days of the canal. In the early 1920s, one visitor reported, it was easy to see
"their resentment at our hardly concealed contempt for them." A Panamanian
employed in the zone as a clerk or mechanic was treated "with frank contempt for his undersize, his lack of education, and for his large proportion of
negro blood. He responds by calling North Americans 'gringos' and hating
[us] with a deep, malevolent rancor that needs only a fit occasion to blaze
forth in riot and massacre."

It blazed forth at intervals over the next forty years. There were riots in
1947, when the United States tried to negotiate an extension of wartime
basing rights, and in 1958, when students raised fifty Panamanian flags over
the Canal Zone in what they called Operation Sovereignty. Canal police tore
them down, but the incident disturbed the Eisenhower administration
enough to grant Panama the right to fly its flag "in selected locations, at least
on ceremonial occasions." The Pentagon refused to accept the arrangement,
and more riots followed in 1959, when demonstrators attacked U.S.-owned
property.

In 1963, when a joint U.S.-Panamanian commission recommended raising
the flags of both countries over some canal buildings, militant "Zonians"
smelled a sellout by Washington. Much like the sailors at Cuba's Guantánamo
base, they had little interest in abstractions like sovereignty. "Few Americans
abroad lead a more comfortable life or are more self-consciously American,"
wrote *Time*. Average salaries were three times higher than on the mainland;
only one Zonian in five spoke Spanish. "There are some people here," said
one, "who haven't been to Panama for ten or twenty years. And they're proud
of it." Seeing an insult to their country, American students at Balboa High
School took the law into their own hands and ran up the Stars and Stripes.
When Panamanian students arrived to protest the absence of their flag, violence erupted. Over the next four days of street fighting, twenty-four Panamanian civilians and four U.S. soldiers died.

Johnson sent Mann down to deal with the crisis. Though some of the more
fastidious types in Washington might have found the Zonian rednecks a bit
crude, there was little disagreement on the basic issues. Secretary of State

"PANAMA RIOTING STARTED WITH
THIS: AMERICAN STUDENTS AT
BALBOA HIGH SCHOOL IN THE
CANAL ZONE WAVE AMERICAN
FLAGS BENEATH THE FLAGPOLE UP
WHICH THEY RAN ANOTHER U.S.
FLAG THURSDAY NIGHT TO TOUCH
OFF THE RIOTING THAT HAS TAKEN
TWENTY-THREE LIVES."
—ASSOCIATED PRESS.

Rusk declared that Cuban-trained communist agents were behind the protests. "These people need the application of a little muscle and common
sense," Mann decided. Conservatives like Representative Daniel Flood of
Pennsylvania thought Panamanian demands for control of the canal were
"part of the audacious, cunning, and far-reaching strategy of the Soviets."

For the public, looking at TV news images and wire-service photographs,
the issue must have seemed simple. They saw Old Glory raised by clean-cut
high-school kids, and then desecrated and burned by foreigners. The eruption of Panamanian anger, the slogan *"Yanqui* go home!" daubed on the
walls, was as hard for Americans to comprehend as the demonstrations that
had greeted Richard Nixon's Latin American tour in 1958, when nationalists
had hurled rocks and spat on the vice president's car. The question to be
asked, in tones of aggrieved innocence, was, "Why do they hate us?"

For many in Congress, such expressions of dissent or independence by
small countries could only be read as a national humiliation, calling into

question the nation's credibility as a superpower. "We are in the amazing position," said Senate Minority Leader Everett Dirksen of Illinois, "of having a country with one-third the population of Chicago kick us around. If we crumble in Panama, the reverberations of our actions will be felt around the world." It was widely agreed that the riots were a fitting epitaph for the Alliance for Progress. A *Wall Street Journal* editorial suggested that "This disgraceful business ought to be a sharp reminder to all the sentimentalists who believe we can uplift Latin America, and be loved for it, simply by handing out billions of dollars."

•• •• ••

Any last flickering signs of life in the Alliance for Progress were extinguished in the Dominican Republic in 1965. In May 1961, the megalomaniacal dictator Trujillo, who had run the country for thirty years, was assassinated. In the most eloquent and precise summary of the logic behind the alliance, Kennedy told Arthur Schlesinger, Jr., "There are three possibilities in descending order of preference: a decent democratic regime, a continuation of the Trujillo regime, or a Castro regime. We ought to aim at the first, but we really cannot renounce the second until we are sure we can avoid the third."

U.S. TROOPS IN SANTO DOMINGO, APRIL 1965.

"WHY NOT GET

THE BREEDING GROUND?"

CHICAGO TRIBUNE.

In crude terms, what happened was this: Washington failed to throw its weight behind the "decent democratic regime" that emerged from free elections; in the chaos that followed its overthrow, defenders of the constitutional order were joined by a handful of communists, raising the specter of a "Castro regime"; and after U.S. troops had intervened to restore order, Dominicans ended up with "a continuation of the Trujillo regime."

In December 1962, the hugely popular social democrat Juan Bosch swept to power with a two-to-one victory margin at the polls. His new party was fragile and inexperienced, as one would expect in a country where for thirty years all political activity had been stifled. Within weeks, the CIA began to report leftist infiltration. In September 1963, after just nine months, the government was ousted by the military. Although Kennedy never actively relished the prospect of a military regime anywhere, he often found it the only option. In the Dominican Republic he insisted on a civilian figurehead, and the armed forces obliged. In return, Kennedy pumped in $100 million worth of aid to demonstrate the degree of U.S. commitment to the new regime. But it proved corrupt and repressive, and on April 24, 1965, officers loyal to Bosch tried to reinstate his elected government. After three days of fighting, they were on the verge of winning.

Again, Johnson's troubleshooter was Thomas Mann. On April 25, he cabled the U.S. embassy to say he feared "Castroite extremists" would seize control. So why had the embassy not told him if U.S. lives were in danger? This seemed remiss. Taking the broad hint, the embassy replied that yes, American lives were indeed threatened. Johnson went on television and told viewers, "The American nation cannot, must not, and will not permit the establishment of another communist government in the Western Hemisphere." The 82nd Airborne Division went in on April 28, and before long there were 23,000 U.S. troops in the country.

It was the first use of U.S. combat forces in the region since 1933, but at home it seemed like another splendid little war, as the press provided familiar, reassuring images of humane American order imposing itself on Caribbean chaos. *Time* commented, "If ever a firm hand was needed to keep order, last week was the time and the Dominican Republic was the place," and led off its cover story with a photograph of marines in the streets of Santo Domingo, over the caption: "The only hope of safety in a city gone berserk."

The fighting was quick and cathartic, setting up a straw man of Cuban involvement and then bloodying Castro's nose with little cost. Only twenty-six Americans died, though 2,850 Dominicans were killed. A Gallup poll found more than three-quarters of Americans approved of the invasion, which, like many U.S. actions in the region, was less about itself than about the larger signals it sent. It demonstrated, to the point of paranoid delusion, that the United States would not accept a "second Cuba." And it sent a tough message to North Vietnam. Public support for the invasion led Johnson to believe that he would get similar backing for an escalated war in Southeast Asia, and in July he increased combat strength there from eighteen battalions to sixty-two.

•• •• ••

Luke Thompson, a master sergeant in the Special Forces, served in a covert team of Green Berets in the Dominican Republic in 1965, on a mission to monitor the activities of U.S. citizens and ensure their safety. But Thompson's unit soon discovered that many of them, especially the Peace Corps volunteers, actively sympathized with the pro-Bosch resistance. The Green Berets' mission shifted from protecting their compatriots to spying on them.

Many Peace Corps volunteers returning from the Dominican Republic joined the swelling antiwar movement. Between Johnson's 1965 troop buildup and the Tet offensive of 1968, the fabric of American innocence was ripped apart, and this battered innocence turned to bitter disillusionment. It was a time when radicals began to call the country Amerika, when the writer Susan Sontag visited North Vietnam and pronounced the United States "a cancerous society," explaining, "It is self-evident the *Reader's Digest* and Lawrence Welk and Hilton Hotels are organically connected with the Special Forces napalming villages." The mass-produced icon of the antiwar movement, and even of less politicized segments of American youth, was Alberto Korda's heroic photograph of Argentine-Cuban revolutionary Che Guevara.

Luke Thompson never returned to Latin America himself, but in 1982 he revealed to the *New York Times* details of the Green Berets' next assignment in the region, after the Dominican Republic. This was to Bolivia, in the late summer of 1967, where they were sent to help local Rangers track down Guevara and kill him. Guevara, a doctor, had accompanied Fidel Castro to

Cuba on the yacht *Granma* in 1956. After the revolution, he became a Cuban citizen and was appointed president of the National Bank, then minister of industry. In the spring of 1965, he abruptly disappeared. Some said he had been eliminated by Castro; others reported sighting him beside rebel troops in the Dominican Republic, or in Vietnam, Laos, Venezuela, the Congo. There was no firm news until April 1967, when a message reached Havana. In it, Guevara wrote, "How close and brilliant the future would seem if two, three, many Vietnams flourished throughout the world." He was in Bolivia.

While a team of ten or twelve Green Berets from the Eighth Special Forces in Panama taught the Rangers jungle warfare, the CIA pinpointed Guevara in a ravine in the eastern spur of the Andes. "He was caught and executed on the spot," said a former Green Beret who was there. "The Boliv-

••••••

"THE COMMUNIST ATTITUDE
TOWARD LIFE IS TO SHOW BY
EXAMPLE THE ROAD TO FOLLOW.
—CHE"
—HAVANA UNIVERSITY, 1971.

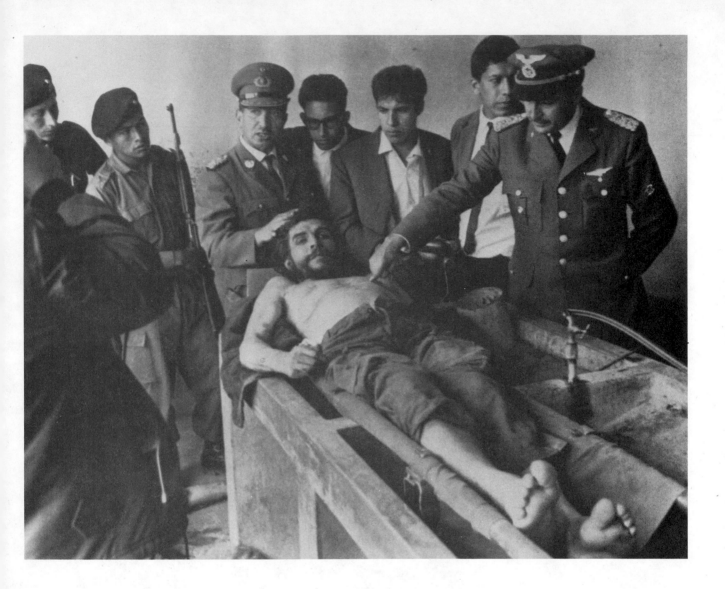

ians pulled the trigger. They needed to get the credit." Guevara's body was brought back to the camp, where it was identified by two U.S. intelligence agents who had flown in from Panama. One of them was a Cuban Bay of Pigs veteran named Félix Rodríguez, who took to wearing Guevara's wristwatch as a souvenir. The body was then taken to a shack in the town of Villagrande for display to the press. The photograph sent out over the UPI wire was compared by the British critic John Berger to Rembrandt's painting *The Anatomy Lesson of Professor Tulp*. Both were formal and didactic displays of a corpse, designed to make an example of the dead, "one for the advancement of medicine, the other as a political warning."

"If Ernesto Che Guevara was really killed in Bolivia, as now seems probable," the *New York Times* commented, "a myth as well as a man has been laid to rest." Nobody missed the symbolic force of the image, though its interpretation was in the eye of the beholder. Sontag hoped it would be "useful to young people . . . in advancing the development of a revolutionary consciousness." For more mainstream commentators, it was "Fidel's Bay of Pigs," the metaphorical death of the Cuban threat. *Time* was pleased that Guevara's "departure from the scene takes away much of the mystery and romanticism that has been associated with that [Cuban] subversion." *Newsweek* hoped he would be remembered as "a zealot, humorless, arrogant, ruthless, and sometimes brutal in his dedication to his own simplistic version of history."

An image so idealized, or laden with such mythic weight, easily becomes an abstraction. And it is easy to remove abstractions to a safe distance or even, in the end, reduce them to parody. Within a year, Omar Sharif was starring in the movie *Che!* which was filmed in Puerto Rico. In it, Guevara tells a Bolivian peasant that he has come to free him. The peasant replies, "To free me from what? Ever since you came to these mountains with your guns and your fighting, my goats give no milk." At the end of the movie, the audience is reassured, falsely, that "the CIA was not involved [in Guevara's death] in any way."

By 1971, when Woody Allen made his film *Bananas*, bearded revolutionaries were strictly slapstick. As soon as the Castro-clone Esposito comes to power, he decrees that Swedish will be the official language and orders all citizens to change their underwear every half hour. Officialdom had declared Castro and Guevara politically dead; the popular culture had turned them into objects of derision. No longer even banana republics, Central America and the Caribbean were now just places where people went bananas.

VOTING LINES
IN EL SALVADOR, 1982.
"IT WAS A PUBLIC RELATIONS
TRIUMPH. IT GOT THE
REPORTERS AND THE
EUROPEANS OFF ALL THIS OTHER
SHIT ABOUT HUMAN RIGHTS."
—STATE DEPARTMENT
PRESS OFFICER.

FIVE
THE DEMOCRACY GAME
1967–82

Two events in the late 1960s had briefly rescued Central America from oblivion, only to be dismissed as routine spasms of characteristic violence, of no more lasting news significance than a two-headed calf. The first was a bloodbath in Nicaragua, where the Somozas were engineering a family dynasty—quietly where possible, but messily where necessary. Luis Somoza had taken over smoothly after his father's death in 1956. He had ruled until February 1963, when a family crony, René Schick Gutiérrez, took office. Then in August 1966, Tachito Somoza, the National Guard commander who had always played bad cop to his brother's good cop, accepted the presidential nomination. As the vote drew near, the Guard saw action in the mountains against a group of Sandinista guerrillas. But Tachito shrugged them off as a minor nuisance, and volunteered a contingent of his best troops to serve in Vietnam—an offer the

United States, perhaps fearing embarrassment, quietly refused. By the beginning of 1967, it was apparent to the opposition that another election fraud was likely, and on January 22, tens of thousands of demonstrators marched to a rally for the Conservative opposition candidate, Fernando Agüero. The Guard opened fire on the crowd, killing sixty. Agüero supporters took refuge in the Gran Hotel, on the Avenida Roosevelt, with a group of hostages that included twenty Americans. Yet even then, the State Department announced, "We do not have any intention of becoming involved in the internal affairs of Nicaragua." On February 5, the election went ahead. The official count gave Tachito three-quarters of the vote.

Election fraud and violence also blighted what might have been a democratic transition in El Salvador five years later. Always considered the runt of the litter in Central America, El Salvador had made news only once in recent years, in 1969, when it fought a bitter four-day war with its neighbor Honduras. The fighting was a warning signal of the growing despair in the Salvadoran countryside. Thousands of landless peasants had spilled over the border into Honduras, only to be expelled in a frenzy of anti-Salvadoran feeling. The flash point, however, came when the intensity of the two World Cup soccer qualifying games provoked rowdyism and minor outbreaks of violence between rival fans. The U.S. press was now on safer ground. The conflict needed no deep analysis; it was just another case of volatile Central Americans getting out of hand, to be written off with a good-natured sneer as the "Soccer War."

On February 21, 1972, all other foreign stories were swept off the front pages by Richard Nixon's landmark trip to China. Though El Salvador had voted in a crucial election the day before, Central America's main place in the day's news was as the exotic backdrop for a celebrity-watching story: Howard Hughes, the reclusive billionaire, had been sighted in Managua. Late editions carried reports that the Salvadoran voting had ended amidst confusion and charges of fraud, with the army suspending the count after early returns showed a likely victory by the center-left opposition. But the story was relegated to a few lines on the inside pages, next to news of a bloodless coup in Ecuador—two further examples of the irrational merry-go-round of Latin American politics. (In contrast, the 1982 election, an event touted as the showcase of the Reagan administration's Central American policy, was a media circus that drew seven hundred journalists. "Where were all you guys ten years ago?" demanded José Napoleón Duarte.)

The reports from San Salvador relied almost entirely on AP and UPI , and they, in turn, appeared to rely on press handouts from the armed forces. They even had trouble getting the opposition candidate's name right. José Napoleón Duarte, the former mayor of San Salvador and a centrist Christian Democrat, appeared in several reports as Eduardo Duarte. Nor did the press have much notion of the Salvadoran political spectrum. Americans make a fetish of elections, but they also expect them to conform to their two-party model of Democrats and Republicans. Most reports described the official army candidate, Colonel Arturo Armando Molina, as a "centrist," and his military opponent as a "conservative." That left Duarte as a "leftist." In a damaging canard that began as an army press release, the *New York Times* characterized Duarte's UNO as "a left-wing coalition . . . styled after Chile's governing Popular Unity movement." The *Miami Herald* reported that Duarte's candidacy "has raised fears that if he were elected he might proceed to 'Chileanize' El Salvador"—particularly ironic, since Duarte's sister party in Chile eagerly backed the 1973 military coup that killed President Salvador Allende Gossens.

The fraud stood. A month after the election, officers loyal to Duarte revolted. Confronting a similar situation seven years earlier, rightist officers in the Dominican Republic had appealed to Washington for help. Their Salvadoran counterparts, however, made do with aerial support from Nicaragua and Guatemala. Two hundred people were killed. Duarte was seized, beaten up, and packed off into exile in Venezuela.

The fraud and the violence convinced many Salvadoran politicians that there was no hope of bringing about change through elections. Some parted ways with the Christian Democrats and joined the guerrillas; others stayed with the party and, remembering what had happened to Duarte, opted for a lower profile next time around. In both Guatemala in 1974 and El Salvador in 1977, the Christian Democrats nominated retired military officers; both men lost as the result of fraud. But that alone did not justify the airfare for many U.S. media. What had brought the reporters and cameramen down to Nicaragua in 1967 and El Salvador in 1972 was less the voting than the violence. As far as most American readers in the 1970s were concerned, El Salvador and Guatemala went to the polls in decent obscurity.

The 1972 election would not be Duarte's only bitter experience of Washington's selective moral vision. He hoped the election of Jimmy Carter might herald brighter days, and as the 1977 vote approached, he flew to Washington to lobby the new administration. "My welcome to the United States has fluctuated over the years in direct ratio to my political fortunes," Duarte recalls in his memoirs. "During the exile years, each time I came through the U.S. customs the FBI would question me for hours." In 1977, the only sympathetic hearing he found was from Senators Tom Harkin of Iowa and Edward Kennedy of Massachusetts, both active human-rights advocates, and the Washington Office on Latin America (WOLA), a liberal public-policy group. In the corridors of the Capitol, Vice-President Walter Mondale grabbed Duarte's hand for a quick photo opportunity before ducking into an elevator. "That," Duarte remembers with some bitterness, "was the extent of my contact with the Carter government until 1979. . . . It was not until after the Sandinista guerrillas marched victoriously into Managua in July 1979 that any U.S. government official tried to reach me to discuss the problems in El Salvador."

•• •• ••

Central America, whose spine lies along a tremendous geological fault, has always been highly prone to natural disasters. And of all catastrophes, it is

MANAGUA EARTHQUAKE, 1972.
"PAT AND I WISH YOU AND YOUR
FAMILY A HAPPY CHRISTMAS, IF YOU
CAN HAVE A HAPPY CHRISTMAS
UNDER THOSE CIRCUMSTANCES."
—RICHARD NIXON TO ANASTASIO
SOMOZA DEBAYLE.

earthquakes that most lend themselves to photography. Even more than floods, fires, or mudslides, they generate images of intense pathos, of humanity at its most passive and powerless. When a huge quake flattened the center of Managua, at twenty-three minutes past midnight on December 23, 1972, those images—of ruined buildings, raging fires, and grieving relatives—flashed around the world.

The U.S. Agency for International Development issued a portfolio of photographs to dramatize the humanitarian response of the Nixon administration, which totaled almost $30 million. The survival, on a ruined wall, of a tattered poster showing Santa Claus drinking Coca Cola was AID's poignant reminder that the disaster had struck just before Christmas. Other photographs showed the arrival of six hundred members of the U.S. Army Corps of Engineers from Panama, proof that the United States was again moving vigorously to halt the spread of disease and bring order to Central America's chaos.

Disaster stories, however, tend to become monotonous after a few days. There are the last trapped survivors to bring out; the body count rises; new estimates come in on the cost of the destruction, which in Managua's case ran to more than $1 billion. But such a story cries out for a human-interest dimension that will resonate with readers and viewers back home. Managua provided several. First came the saga of Howard Hughes. Surprised by the earthquake in his germ-free suite at the Intercontinental Hotel, Hughes was carried by aides to the hotel parking lot, where he spent the remainder of the night in his Mercedes Benz limousine before leaving the country with not a flicker of interest in the welfare of the inhabitants. Next came the departure for Managua of Rolling Stones singer Mick Jagger and his glamorous Nicaraguan wife, Bianca.

But for Americans, the most dramatic piece of related news ended up eclipsing the story of the earthquake itself. Late on New Year's Eve, Puerto Rican baseball hero Roberto Clemente died when his plane, loaded with relief supplies for Managua, plunged into the sea seconds after taking off from the San Juan airport. Clemente was the most famous Hispanic sporting figure in history. A four-time National League batting champion with a lifetime .317 average, he was one of only eleven players to reach three thousand hits. In the 1971 World Series, at the age of thirty-seven, he had been the keystone of the underdog Pittsburgh Pirates' improbable come-from-behind victory over the Baltimore Orioles. As soon as he heard of the earthquake in Managua, which he had visited two months earlier as manager of the Puerto Rican team for the Amateur World Series, Clemente set up a relief fund that raised $160,000 within a week. Ignoring the advice of friends, he insisted on boarding the ancient, overloaded DC-7 because he was afraid of corruption and profiteering by the Managua authorities and wanted to make sure that the aid reached those who most needed it.

Clemente's premonitions were right on target. Somoza's National Guard moved through the rubble of Managua looting whatever it could lay hands on, and loading relief supplies straight onto military trucks at the airport for later resale. Guard demolition crews commanded by the dictator's son made off with toilet fittings, furniture, street lights, and electrical wiring. From improvised storefronts, one observer reported, Guardsmen sold "anything from a small electric generator to a water purifier, electric torches, pickaxes and spades, complete factory-sealed blood transfusion equipment."

••••••

UMPIRE DOUG HARVEY

PRESENTS ROBERTO CLEMENTE

WITH THE BALL

AFTER HIS THREE-THOUSANDTH

AND LAST BASE HIT, 1972.

Companies owned by the Somoza family cornered the market in demolition contracts, construction materials, and real estate. Instead of rebuilding downtown Managua, the regime encouraged a sprawl of new shopping malls, middle-class housing, and fast-food outlets on the new highways ringing southern Managua. On the road to Masaya, a McDonald's franchise opened; a local postcard company chose the Golden Arches as the symbol of Managua's "rise from the ashes." American visitors found the city more of a suburban U.S. look-alike than ever. Quick fortunes were the order of the day.

MANAGUA RISES FROM ITS ASHES.
"[AN AMERICAN] WOULD HEAR
MANY OLD, FAMILIAR U.S. SONGS ON
THE RADIO—IN ENGLISH. A TRIP TO
MANAGUA . . . WILL DISCLOSE THE
UBIQUITOUS MC DONALD'S,
BILLBOARDS EXTOLLING THE NEW
VISA BANK CARDS AND THE DINER'S
CLUB, AS WELL AS
BANKAMERICARDS AND AMERICAN
MOVIES. . . . HE CAN FILL HIS TANK
AT A TEXACO, CHEVRON, OR ESSO
STATION FOR $1 A GALLON."
—OTTO J. SCOTT, 1978.

Managua surge de sus cenizas!

But it was not the majority of businesses, nor even the U.S. investors attracted by the post-earthquake boom, who made them. It was the Somoza family. Until 1972, under a kind of gentlemen's agreement, local businessmen had surrendered political power to the Somozas in exchange for guaranteed rights over defined areas of the economy. But Tachito took advantage of the earthquake to break the rules of the game. After 1972, the phrase on every businessman's lips was *competencia desleal*, unfair competition. Like Duarte in El Salvador, however, it was several years before they found anyone in Washington who was interested in their plight.

What riveted public attention in the late 1970s was not the fate of defrauded democrats in El Salvador or offended businessmen in Nicaragua but that most elemental of U.S. concerns, the Panama Canal. U.S.-Panamanian talks on its future had been proceeding quietly since the riots of 1964. But it was only

ten years later, when Secretary of State Henry Kissinger announced that the
United States was willing in principle to restore Panamanian sovereignty
over the Canal Zone, that the matter flared up as a public controversy.

In 1977 the Carter administration opened a drive to give Panama full
control by the end of the century. The fight over the canal treaties was bitter
and intense, seeming to touch every raw nerve about the United States's role
in the world. For the administration, it was the boldest possible statement
that the United States was a mature power, self-confident enough to acknowledge that the outside world had changed and that international relations
could no longer be conducted on the basis of a power play made by Teddy
Roosevelt in 1903. For conservatives, the canal treaties were a surrender of
emotional treasure and a symbol of appeasement. After the traumas of the
1970s—Vietnam, Watergate, and OPEC price hikes—keeping control of the
canal was a reaffirmation of the national will, and a purging of the national
psyche, a specific antidote to the national "malaise" of which Carter spoke.

Along with abortion, Panama was the first rallying point for the new right,
and Ronald Reagan, the movement's main spokesman and figurehead, felt the
feelings aroused by the canal debate made "all the other issues possible."
The new conservatives were rather different from traditional mainsteam Republicans. They looked out on a world teeming with hostility, and showed

••••••

"IT'S OURS.

WE STOLE IT FAIR AND SQUARE."

—RONALD REAGAN.

no interest in compromise. Instead they intended, in the opinion of Democratic senator Thomas J. McIntyre, "to annihilate those they see as enemies." The determination to avoid "losing" Central America lay at the very heart of their world view.

Panama was the centerpiece of Reagan's effort to win the 1976 Republican nomination for president, recognizing that the canal was a litmus test, both for party conservatives disenchanted with Gerald Ford and for the broader public. "People sense in this issue," commented one Reagan campaign strategist, "some way, after Vietnam, and Watergate, and Angola, of reasserting the glory of the country. People once more see a chance for Americans to stand up as Americans."

Rarely has a foreign-policy debate stirred fiercer passions among the public at large. Opinion polls showed public sentiment running as much as four-to-one against the treaties proposed by the Carter administration, though few Americans evaluated the issue on the basis of fact. As one zone official said, "Unfortunately half of these Americans are not sure where the Panama Canal is located." Instead, their feelings tended to be a matter of reflex, crystallizing around the images they had memorized from grade-school textbooks. Democratic senator Gale McGee thought many opponents of the treaties were "still riding up the hill with Teddy Roosevelt." For them, the issue was clear-cut: the canal was the highest example of Yankee enterprise, and the keystone of U.S. national security—even if the Pentagon acknowledged that it could not be defended against the modern threats of nuclear attack or guerrilla warfare.

Reagan, for one, displayed little interest in the factual side of U.S.-Panamanian history, appearing to take literally Coolidge's famous slip of the tongue that Panama was "an outlying possession of the United States." He told cheering audiences in Texas, quite falsely, that the Canal Zone was "sovereign United States territory just the same as Alaska is and as the part of Texas that came out of the Gadsden Purchase and the states that were carved out of the Louisiana Purchase." The zone, he said, "is ours, and we intend to keep it." Reagan went on television to debate the treaties with conservative commentator William F. Buckley, Jr., and declared that it was essential to stand firm in Panama after what he described as "our bug-out in Vietnam."

Through 1977 and into the early months of 1978, the Carter administration battled hard for Senate ratification of the new treaties. Reagan told TV audiences that the rest of the world would interpret ratification as a sign that, "once again, Uncle Sam put his tail between his legs and crept away rather than face trouble." Grass-roots conservatives organized a "Truth Squad" to turn around Senate votes. Hundreds of demonstrators kept up a picket of the Capitol, carrying signs that read, "Today the Panama Canal, tomorrow Taiwan." Their crude caricatures of Panama's nationalist leader, General Omar Torrijos, were labeled, "No deals with Marxist dictators." The conservatives' campaign ultimately failed, and the Senate ratified the treaties. But within months, a new, unstable element was introduced into the political chemistry of Central America. Hoping to favor his friend Carter in the 1980 U.S. elec-

●●●●●●

EDÉN PASTORA,

LEAVING MANAGUA AIRPORT

AFTER THE SUCCESSFUL SEIZURE

OF THE NATIONAL PALACE,

AUGUST 1978.

tion, Torrijos allowed the terminally sick Shah of Iran to take up residence. The Panamanian island of Contadora was the Shah's Elba.

A small number of conservatives, with Reagan prominent among them, tried to link canal treaty votes with U.S. policy toward the Somoza regime in Nicaragua. Since 1975, reports of atrocities had been filtering out of rural Nicaragua, and the Carter administration had made the country one of the focal points of its human-rights policy. In response, Somoza, no novice to the ways of Washington, launched a well-funded public-relations drive on Capitol Hill. This included hiring two Georgia lawyers, at $1,000 a day each plus expenses, to carry out an "independent" human-rights investigation. The lawyers' report duly gave Somoza a clean bill of health, even though one of them, Bobby Lee Cook, could not even spell the name of the country he had supposedly investigated.

Reagan was among the first to speak out in defense of Nicaragua's strongman—although, during his later campaigns for aid to the Nicaraguan contras, he was careful to distance himself from "the hated dictator Somoza." In one of his regular broadcasts over San Francisco's news radio KGO in January 1978, he blamed the fuss over human rights on an "intensive campaign . . . dedicated to 'destabilizing' the government of Nicaragua," which "has never

HAVANA, JANUARY 1, 1959;
MANAGUA, JULY 19, 1979.
"THE TROOPS ARE SIMILARLY DRESSED.
THEY WEAR THE SAME OLIVE DRAB WITH
THE SAME INCREDIBLE VARIETY OF
HEADGEAR. THERE ARE BERETS HERE,
GARRISON CAPS, CAMPAIGN HATS, EVEN
A PITH HELMET. THEY ALMOST ALL WALK
AND TALK THE SAME WAY, WITH THE
SAME WARM FEELING TOWARD
EVERYONE."
—BERNARD DIEDERICH, THE ONLY
JOURNALIST PRESENT ON BOTH
OCCASIONS.

been known as a major violator of human rights." On the contrary, "Nicaragua has been a staunch supporter of the United States in world forums, and is strongly anti-Communist." Reagan blamed a cabal of leftists for "attempted manipulation and intimidation of government officials." Those responsible, he said, were WOLA (the group which had tried to open doors for Duarte in 1977); NACLA (North American Congress on Latin America, the New York–based publisher of the journal *Report on the Americas*); Democratic congressman (and later mayor of New York) Ed Koch; columnist Jack Anderson; and free-lance journalist Penny Lernoux.

•• — ••

The crumbling of the Somoza regime became dramatically apparent in August 1978, when a group of Sandinista guerrillas seized the National Palace, took the entire congress hostage to win the release of fifty-nine political prisoners, and flew out of the country for Panama. At the top of the airplane steps, the group's leader, Edén Pastora, alias "Commander Zero," turned and posed for photographers. It was one of the decade's most famous news pictures, and it made Pastora a folk hero. Within a year, the Sandinistas were back in Managua, this time as leaders of a successful nationwide insurrection. Like Fidel Castro's *barbudos* twenty years before, they rode into the city crammed on top of commandeered tanks, trucks, and buses, waving fists, machine guns, and ancient rifles in the air in the euphoria of victory. Again, the picture circled the world on the cover of every news magazine.

Just as the CIA-backed coups in Iran and Guatemala had embodied the power of the United States in the 1950s, the fall of the Shah and Somoza within five months of each other in 1979 symbolized, for U.S. conservatives, the collapse of American prestige and national will. Iran and Nicaragua were the twin, interwoven neuroses that demonstrated the limits of U.S. power in the modern world, and in the end came close to ruining the Reagan administration. Conservatives seized on the pictures from Managua to prove their worst nightmares. Pastora's beret, the grenades strapped to his chest, seemed to summon up the ghost of Che Guevara; the adolescent holding a machine gun aloft, whether Latin American or Palestinian, became one of the political icons of the 1980s, the decade in which "international terrorism" entered the everyday vocabulary.

The photographs were in fact profoundly ambiguous, their hidden codes locked in the imagination of the viewer. In one sense, triumphant guerrillas entering Havana or Managua were simply the present-day version of a stock routine: armies as liberators. U.S. troops entering Manila or Berlin in World War II had been photographed in identical poses, surrounded by the same cheering crowds. But it was a long time since the image had been generated by "our side." After 1979, it tended to take its place next to pictures of crowds in Teheran carrying portraits of the Ayatollah Khomeini and chanting, "Death to America!"

Liberals, still believing they had risen above what Carter had called the United States's "inordinate fear of communism," searched hard for evidence of "moderate," pro-U.S. sentiment. Pastora proved a rich vein for students of ambiguity. What was the meaning of the figure at the top of the airline steps? A cartoon by Tony Auth in the *Philadelphia Inquirer* showed a confused Nicaraguan wondering what lay in store, in the bubble of his imagination the Pastora figure, with the caption, "Liberation, Marxism, or Worse."

The most likely to ham for the cameras and reinforce every cliché of the gun-toting revolutionary, Pastora was in fact the only conservative in the upper echelons of the Sandinista front. Within two years, he would be out of office; within three, a leader of one of the contra factions. Now, as later, Pastora played the press like a violin. When he told reporters he was a Catholic conservative, many concluded that this went for a substantial part of the movement, since he was its most charismatic personality. The inordinate fear of communism had given way to self-delusion, each in its own way the consequence of a kind of innocence. When the Sandinistas turned out, after all, to be radical, unsentimental nationalists, this left little option but to accuse them of betrayal.

Those who made this charges might have reflected on what Herbert Matthews had said of reporters who lionized Castro twenty years earlier and then turned on him: they had initially welcomed a figure who did not exist, and had little to blame for their disillusionment but their own ignorance.

-- -- --

Reagan's advisers were aware that Carter had used Central America as a setting for the grand gesture, and they were determined to respond in kind. Carter was guilty of "losing Nicaragua" and transferring the Panama Canal, in Jeane Kirkpatrick's words, "to a swaggering Latin dictator of Castroite bent." Reagan, in the sharpest possible contrast, would "draw the line" against communism in El Salvador and roll it back in Nicaragua. Each president in his own way fell into the trap of believing that U.S. power and technical skill could mold Central America like putty, even at a time when its social systems were breaking apart. Carter badly underestimated the consequences of choosing Somoza as a test case of his human-rights policy; Reagan had no inkling of how hard it would be to turn back the clock.

Carter himself had signaled the retreat from his own more liberal policies with the "discovery" in August 1979 of a Soviet combat brigade in Cuba, a month after the Sandinista victory. (The soldiers had been there for years.) The episode killed off the SALT II treaty and froze over any possible thaw in U.S.-Cuban relations. Then, in April 1980, the indelible image of more than 125,000 refugees streaming out of the Cuban port of Mariel aboard a flotilla of small boats reinforced most Americans' vision of Castro's Cuba as a hell on earth.

Reagan's thesis was simple, not to say simplistic: to a public worn out by the moral complexities and alarming setbacks of the 1970s, he explained, "The Soviet Union underlies all the unrest that is going on. If they weren't engaged in this game of dominoes, there wouldn't be any hot-spots in the world." The new secretary of state, Alexander Haig, added that Soviet-backed

MARIELITOS, APRIL 1980.

terrorism would henceforth replace human rights as the central concern of U.S. foreign policy. The administration selected El Salvador as the latest in the series of "splendid little wars"—Cuba in 1898, Guatemala in 1954, the Dominican Republic in 1965—that Central America and the Caribbean had obligingly provided. As so often before, the target country was less a living place than a dramatic cipher. "El Salvador itself doesn't really matter," one Reagan aide acknowledged. The real point was, "We have to establish credibility."

With a mastery of the visual and symbolic aspects of the modern presidency, the Reagan administration orchestrated a remarkable campaign to shape public perceptions of Central America. Part of this was technical: a grasp of Washington's ability to control access to information and set news priorities, an expert use of props and photo opportunities. Part of it was an understanding of the kind of image that would touch nerves in the American psyche. The fight to "save" Central America drew on old memories and fanned old fears: the secure backyard; the permanent affront of Cuba; the enemy at the gate; the sea-lanes and choke points of the Caribbean; Mexico as the last domino. Television was used to great effect, showing animated maps with pulsing concentric circles emanating from Cuba, and curving arrows sweeping up to the Texas border. Maps also suggested that the fire this time was right next door. As the State Department said in 1981 (and Lieutenant Colonel Oliver North repeated in 1987 in his testimony before Congress), "Vietnam was nearly halfway round the globe from the continental United States; El Salvador is less than two hours by air."

Since the administration's aim was to tap the nation's collective memory, there was little in the images themselves that was new. The portrait of Central Americans remained heavily traditional. If they accepted their poverty quietly, like the Hondurans, they could be disregarded, or at best pitied, as passive victims. If they rebelled against it, like the Nicaraguans, they would be categorized as communists. In the time-honored formula, Honduras was stable, Nicaragua was unstable. This left the countries of the region with two options: to choose "freedom," which after 1983 effectively meant support for the Nicaraguan contras, or to be considered a Soviet beachhead in the Western Hemisphere.

There was a major flaw in Reagan's approach: it was impossible to eradicate the "Vietnam syndrome" without taking into account the deep wounds the war had left with the U.S. public, and the limits they imposed on policy. Victory in Central America was designed to erase the trauma of defeat in Vietnam, but it had to be achieved with two important provisos. U.S. forces must never again soil the nation's sense of moral virtue by taking Zippo lighters to peasant huts on television; and American boys must not come home in body bags unless there was a clear and demonstrable threat to national security. The dilemma was not a new one: even the most avid imperialists at the turn of the century had struggled to reconcile the crusading zeal with their reluctance to spill American blood. "The whole nation is not worth the life of one American soldier," the caption had read under one official military photograph of Filipino prisoners of war in 1898.

Conservatives complained that the Vietnam syndrome forced them to fight with one hand tied behind their backs. It certainly meant that the United States would have to rely on its local allies to do the dirty work, and that any U.S. casualties would be doubly traumatic. When the allies' dirty work and the U.S. casualties were combined, public opinion recoiled.

On June 20, 1979, Americans turned on the nightly news and saw their worst fears realized. As ABC News correspondent Bill Stewart approached a National Guard checkpoint in Managua, holding out his press credentials and a white flag, a soldier ordered him to lie face down on the ground. Unaware that Stewart's camera crew, back in its van, was filming the whole thing, the Guardsman walked up to Stewart, kicked him in the side, walked away, thought for a few moments, walked back to him, and shot him in the head. The shocking videotape was the lead item on all three networks.

Much of the public was already queasy about the long U.S. alliance with Somoza. Stewart's execution, bringing the war into Americans' living rooms and triggering all the old anxieties that Vietnam had provoked, turned their doubts to outright revulsion, and robbed the situation in Nicaragua of any familiar moral touchstones. "Our side" was no longer a guarantor of stability and order but the very image of chaos. As far as the press was concerned, the episode stripped Somoza of any right to "objective" reporting. Many reporters left Managua, either in protest or out of fear. Cartoonists declared open season on the dictator. One depicted him as a monster with blood dripping from his hands; another, Conrad in the *Los Angeles Times,* brought the issue of moral responsibility closer to home in a way that would have been unthinkable until the 1970s. It simply showed a bullet stamped, "Made in U.S.A."

A wave of violence against churchpeople in Central America came to a

climax in 1980: Salvadoran archbishop Oscar Romero was shot dead during mass in March, more than a dozen priests killed by death squads in Guatemala, and, most shockingly, four U.S. churchwomen raped and murdered by Salvadoran National Guardsmen in December. The disinterment of their bodies from a shallow grave dominated TV and the print media. At an emotional level, the picture conveyed the horror and chaos of what was going on "down there." At a political level, it became a crucial test of whether Salvadoran authorities were willing or able to prosecute members of the security forces for human-rights violations.

It is a standing joke among the more cynical members of the press corps that human life is valued on a sliding scale: a hundred peasants equal one priest; ten priests, one American. The response of administration officials to the churchwomen's murder suggested that there was a sliding scale for Americans, too. "The nuns were not just nuns," UN ambassador Jeane Kirkpatrick told a reporter. "They were political activists on behalf of the *Frente*." Secretary of State Haig suggested to the House Foreign Affairs Committee that "perhaps the vehicle that the nuns were riding in may have tried to run a roadblock," and later in his testimony wisecracked about "pistol-packing nuns."

The administration took a very different tone regarding other U.S. casualties. The killing of four marines at a sidewalk café in San Salvador in June 1985 triggered one of the most visceral images of the Reagan years: the row of flag-draped coffins, the president delivering a funeral oration that invested each individual victim of terrorism with the symbolism of the entire nation. Reagan vowed, "We and the Salvadoran leaders will move any mountain and ford any river to find the jackals and bring them and their colleagues in terror to justice." Sixteen months later, when a planeload of mercenaries was shot down over Nicaragua while ferrying arms to the contras, Assistant Secretary of State Elliott Abrams hailed the dead crewmen as heroes.

Public and congressional disgust with the conduct of U.S. allies produced a violent reaction among Central American rightists. They in turn denounced the United States as an unreliable partner, and their accusations of betrayal gave an ugly and venomous edge to a polemic that was already unusually bitter. Betrayal, in fact, became a leitmotiv of the entire debate. Conservatives and liberals alike condemned the Sandinistas for betraying their revolution; traditional U.S. allies asked why Washington was pulling the plug on its old friends and betraying their anticommunist cause. In an April 1979 speech, Carter's outgoing ambassador to Managua, the Cuban-born Mauricio Solaun, described the sense of betrayal in Somoza's circle.

"Nicaragua was a faithful client of the United States," Solaun said. "The Somozas were our friends. To this date it is rare that top Nicaraguan officials do not proclaim their allegiance to the U.S.—'*somos americanistas*,' 'we love your country,' are expressions often heard, delivered with the sincere and strong emotivity so common to many Nicaraguans. . . . 'When you needed us —Guatemala, 1954; Cuba, 1961; the Dominican Republic, 1965—we gave you our support. Why do you betray us now, withholding your support from

UNEARTHING OF THREE
ASSASSINATED AMERICAN NUNS
AND LAY WORKER FROM
UNMARKED GRAVES,
SANTIAGO NONUALCO,
EL SALVADOR,
DECEMBER, 1980.

us?' 'You are leaving us alone to face the hatred of our common enemies,' were statements often repeated by Somoza himself to me." In exile in Paraguay in 1980, after his overthrow, Somoza dictated an autobiography called *Nicaragua Betrayed.* (Fulgencio Batista's, written twenty years earlier, had been called *Cuba Betrayed.*)

-- -- --

The themes of betrayal and endemic violence and the dilemmas of the American conscience became the raw material for a spate of popular movies in the mid-1980s, many of them based on real events. The days of Carmen Miranda and José Carioca were long gone, yet the subject matter was not unfamiliar. With the exception of *El Norte* (1983), Gregory Nava and Anna Thomas's moving portrayal of a Guatemalan brother and sister fleeing an army massacre in their village to seek a new life in the United States, all these films were less about Central America itself than about the question of American innocence: was it real or phony? intact or irreparably damaged? misunderstood? irrelevant?

One genre centered on the external threat to a Norman Rockwell America. In *Red Dawn*, a gung-ho fantasy made in 1984, Cuban and Soviet troops occupy Colorado, while Nicaraguan forces sweep up through Texas. Chuck Norris's *Invasion U. S. A.* (1985) played on fears of terrorist infiltration through the porous borders of Florida. And Jack Cox, ghostwriter of Somoza's autobiography, produced an apologia for the Somoza regime called *Last Plane Out* (1983). In the climactic scene, Somoza (played by Lloyd Battista) tells Cox (Jan-Michael Vincent), "I wouldn't be running now if Washington hadn't turned its back on me. . . . Is it possible that the president of the United States is a communist?"

A second type of movie stressed the well-worn image of Central America as a region of political chaos and ungovernable passions, with shoot-'em-up plot lines that showed the same fondness for violence as the network news. *Under Fire* (1983) wove its story around the death of Bill Stewart, and was distinguished both for some fine acting by Gene Hackman and for a wildly fanciful depiction of the Sandinistas as followers of a messianic (and dead) Che Guevara–like leader named Carlos. *The Mosquito Coast* (1986), based on the novel by Paul Theroux, was set in old Richard Harding Davis and O. Henry territory, the Caribbean coast of Honduras. The subject was a familiar one—Yankee inventiveness and the taming of wild jungle frontiers— but with a couple of new twists: Theroux's hero, Allie Fox (Harrison Ford), rejects the debased culture of the modern United States, but the result of his quest is delusion and madness. Oliver Stone's *Salvador,* released in 1986, is also fearful of the entropy of Central America and just as skeptical about the kind of order the United States offers as a solution. It is a portrait of Americans caught in a delirious landscape of violence and obscenity, but its anti heroes, played by James Woods and Jim Belushi, are hardly more appealing than their Salvadoran tormentors.

"THEY FOUGHT FOR THEY KNEW NOT WHAT, AND, TRUE TO THE TRADITION OF THE TROPICS, NEITHER GAVE NOR ASKED FOR QUARTER."

—SAMUEL CROWTHER, *THE ROMANCE AND RISE OF THE AMERICAN TROPICS*, 1929.

Salvador has at least one foot in a third category—movies of conscience, usually by liberal filmmakers, about the moral choices made by Americans. *Choices of the Heart* (1983) was a made-for-TV life of Jean Donovan, one of the missioners killed in El Salvador. *Latino*, directed in 1985 by Haskell Wexler, looked at the ethical dilemmas of the Chicano Green Beret adviser to the Nicaraguan contras in Honduras. And a 1987 release, Alex Cox's *Walker*, depicted the life and death of the nineteenth-century Tennessee filibuster, with a subtext about contemporary U.S. interference in Nicaragua.

None of the movies escaped the charge of propaganda. By 1983, when the first of them appeared, the Central America issue was a political minefield. As the war in El Salvador, far from being a quick, easy victory, bogged down into a frustrating stalemate, the administration's language grew harsher, in an effort to break down the resistance of liberal legislators who found the human-rights situation in that country hard to stomach. In a televised address to an extraordinary joint session of Congress in April 1983, President Reagan declared, "The national security of all the Americas is at stake in Central America." By then the news was out that the United States had embarked on a supposedly covert war against Nicaragua.

The conflict's dirty little secrets—its reliance on advisers from Argentina's military regime, the mining of Nicaragua's harbors, well-reported contra atrocities, the "assassination manual" distributed by the CIA to contras in Honduras—prompted anguished reflections on American morality abroad. At the same time, the administration's insistence on Cuban and Soviet influence in Nicaragua cowed most Democrats, who were unwilling to appear "soft on communism," into their own pattern of invective against the Sandinistas.

Opinion polls showed the public passive, poorly informed, and mildly fearful on the subject of Central America. This may have been partly because, when it tuned in to Congress and the editorial pages, the polemic sounded like so much white noise. Most lawmakers' opinions were quickly set in stone. Hardly any changed their minds, and after 1983, few new arguments of substance were advanced. Floor debates became ritual exercises in hyperbole. For Republicans, Nicaragua was a "cancer" to be "excised" (or treated by "chemotherapy"). For most Democrats, the favored word was still "betrayal." The social realities of Central America seemed to exist in some disembodied parallel universe. What was really at stake was an unresolved struggle for the soul of America, with not even a glimmer of consensus on the extent and use of U.S. power in the contemporary world. Most legislators could agree with the formula offered by Republican senator Richard Lugar— "No more Cubas, no more Vietnams"—but on closer inspection that was less the blueprint for a bipartisan policy than a Hobson's choice.

The public was likely to be further confused by television news, with its tendency to compress complex information into a fifteen-second package. As ABC executive Av Westin asks in his book *Newswatch*, why should a story on Nicaragua begin, "The Cubans are there, and the Russians are coming"? Because "there has to be something that will relate the story to the basic concerns of the television viewer. . . . The simplest way is to tie it to American interests. . . . Central America is just south of our borders; Cuban interests and other dangerous forces are at work there. An understanding of that locale in terms of American national security interests makes it all the more important for the distracted viewer to pay attention." Westin assumes that the average viewer has "zero knowledge and zero interest in the subject we intend to cover."

In this overheated environment, it was hard for any picture from Central America to remain value-free. Whatever the photographer might intend, any image could be made into an icon, or a piece of political ammunition. Like the news reports they accompanied, the timing and content of photographs were keyed less to events on the ground than to the rhythm of debates in Congress. The conventions of modern photojournalism only made matters worse. The age of the photo essay, in magazines like *Life* or *Look*, was long gone. Today, photographers for the big French and U.S. agencies are at the mercy of the newsweeklies, which demand single, powerful images—roadmaps that will guide the cursory reader to the essence of the story. The reader's convenience is the photographer's straitjacket: even the most imaginative and conscientious know what an editor needs before they shoot, and once the roll of film is shipped to New York they have no control over how it will be used or captioned.

Central America offered proof positive that the camera could lie, or, more

•••••••

PASSERBY?...

accurately, that the user of an image—whether editor, intelligence analyst, or government official—could lie about its original intent. During an outbreak of street fighting in San Salvador in 1980, the worst year of right-wing death-squad violence, photographer Étienne Montes caught members of the National Police using an ice-cream vendor as a human shield. Montes was one of a pack of reporters at the scene. Another, former UPI photographer Jean-Louis Clariond, published a shot of the incident in his book, *Quo Vadis Centroamérica*, which was dedicated to Ronald Reagan and given out to the media by the Salvadoran armed-forces press office. It accompanied a text about the urban terrorism of the left, and was captioned, "Arrest of a suspect after street fighting, 1980."

Right-wing ideologues have no monopoly on the misleading use of captions. Days after the Sandinista victory in Nicaragua, the award-winning photographer Susan Meiselas took a photograph that she identified as "Distributing free meat and milk, Matagalpa, July 1979." *Business Week* ran the image in its January 24, 1983, issue, over the caption, "Nicaraguan citizens form lines outside government supermarkets awaiting food rations." The text reduced a government social-welfare program to one of the grimmest clichés of life in a Soviet-bloc society.

In another instance, the August 2, 1982, edition of *Time* ran an article reviewing the state of the Nicaraguan revolution on its third anniversary, wrapped around a photograph of the Sandinista leadership. The caption

•••••••

FREE FOOD OR RATION LINES?

•••••••

MOSCOW OR MASAYA?

matched the tone of the article: "Sandinista leaders . . . celebrate in Moscow. Strident Marxism, disregard for human rights, and dependence on the Cubans." In fact, the celebration was not in Moscow but in the small provincial town of Masaya, eighteen miles outside Managua.

Misuse of photographs by news magazines was bad enough; it was even worse when government officials got the idea. In February 1982, after a meeting with union leaders in Florida, Secretary of State Haig cited a color photograph of burning bodies that had been published in the weekly magazine of the French conservative newspaper *Le Figaro*. The caption read, "The massacre of fiercely anti Castro Miskito Indians." Haig said the picture "showed the most atrocious genocidal actions that are being taken by the Nicaraguan government against their Indian populations." Later, in a speech to the Conservative Political Action Conference, he used the picture to demonstrate bias in the U.S. news media: "I want to ask the question why the

ATLANTIC COAST OR ESTELÍ?

very, very impressive photographs which appeared in *Figaro,* which graphi-
cally and horribly depicted the genocide occurring on the East Coast of Nicaragua, have not received the same attention as the alleged right-wing
atrocities in El Salvador are receiving." In fact, *Newsweek* had already run
the same shot, back in its October 2, 1978, edition, but correctly identified. It
showed Red Cross workers burning, as a hygienic measure, the corpses of
civilians killed by Somoza's troops in the town of Estelí.

During its first three years in power, the Sandinista government did commit some serious abuses of human rights on the Atlantic coast. In December
1981, troops killed between fourteen and seventeen detainees in the village
of Leimus on the Honduran border, apparently in reprisal for contra attacks.
At the same time, they forcibly evacuated several thousand Miskitos from the
war zone. The following year, seven young Miskitos were killed by Sandinista soldiers, who were later punished by their superiors. But these incidents fell well short of the State Department's charge of genocide. In May
1984, President Reagan was still insisting, "There has been an attempt to
wipe out an entire culture, the Miskito Indians, thousands of whom have
been slaughtered or herded into detention camps."

The charges of Sandinista genocide against the Miskitos were part of a
concerted public-relations campaign whose central theme was as old as the
Monroe Doctrine: disorder in Nicaragua was the result of interference by
hostile foreign powers from beyond the Western Hemisphere. Often using
sophisticated visual props, the administration threw all its energies into con-
vincing the American public that the nightmare of Cuba was being repeated.
On March 9, 1982, in a dramatic instance of this technique, Washington reporters were invited to a briefing-cum-slideshow on Nicaragua's military
buildup. In a piece of symbolism that nobody missed, the presenter was John
R. Hughes of the Defense Intelligence Agency, the premier photo interpreter
of the U.S. intelligence community and the man who had revealed the aerial
photographs of Soviet missiles in Cuba in 1962.

Hughes's grainy slides showed "Soviet-style obstacle courses . . . East
German-built trucks . . . a vehicle-storage and maintenance area . . . characteristic of Cuban design." It was hardly another missile crisis, and the news
media—though by this point almost uniformly hostile to the Sandinistas—
were not impressed. *Newsweek,* for example, presented the images with a
degree of ironic detachment that would have been unthinkable twenty years
earlier. The subject was less the aerial photos themselves than Hughes, with
his pointer, giving what the magazine called a "carefully orchestrated show-
and-tell session."

The Hughes briefing was widely ridiculed. In Garry Trudeau's *Doonesbury* cartoon, Romanian-backed Nicaraguans in North Korean–made sneakers performed Cuban-style push-ups before retiring to the Bulgarian-built
mess tent to eat Soviet-style pizza. Even so, the administration maintained its
fondness for photographs, which it used at various times to show Soviet
freighters off-loading weapons at Nicaraguan ports, dugout canoes allegedly

carrying arms to Salvadoran guerrillas, and Cuban construction workers building an airport on the island of Grenada. The Reagan administration's use of these photos suggested an infatuation both with high technology and with clandestinity. The most compelling facts were always those gathered by secret means (CIA operatives boasted they could hear a toilet flush in Managua); and a skeptical public could be won over if it was allowed to peep through the lens of the government's hidden camera. So when the United States needed to understand the character of its neighbors, it should turn not to the economist, the historian, or the anthropologist but to the high-resolution surveillance cameras aboard a U-2 spy plane flying at ninety thousand feet.

The technique was particularly favored by Lieutenant Colonel Oliver North, who gave his slideshow presentation to dozens of groups and reporters. One North briefing, for NBC News anchor Tom Brokaw, suggested how poorly "intelligence" substituted for a knowledge of Nicaraguan history. Again echoing the Cuban missile crisis, where aerial photos had revealed the layout of soccer fields (not a Cuban sport, and therefore evidence of the Soviet

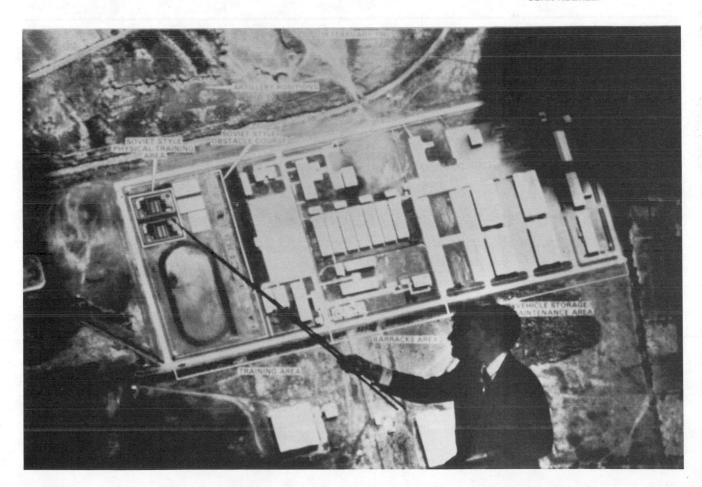

presence), North showed a slide with the familiar outline of a baseball dia-
mond. "Nicaraguans don't play baseball," he told Brokaw, "Cubans play
baseball." Had North been in Managua in 1979, he would have noticed that
the exploits of Nicaraguan pitcher Denis Martínez of the Baltimore Orioles
was almost the only story that could compete with news of the revolution.
The following year he might have been impressed by the national euphoria
over a goodwill tour by the Orioles. Nicaraguans had been *fanáticos* for
baseball ever since 1902, when the sport was introduced to the Atlantic coast
by the occupation force of the U.S. Marines.

-- -- --

Evoking the external threat in the Caribbean and Central America had always
been only half the story. Just as important was the drive, in moments of crisis,
to have the region's disorderly societies embrace American values as their
own. After 1981, the formal trappings of democracy in the region, so often

LEVEY AND KIDD, U.S. MARINES IN
MANAGUA, 1928.
"THE BALL PARK ON SUNDAY IS THE
MAIN MEETING PLACE IN MANAGUA.
. . . SOMETIMES OUR AMERICAN
MARINES PLAY IN THE GAME AND
MORE FREQUENTLY UMPIRE IT. YOU
SEE THE NATIVE PLAYERS GROW
EXCITED AND SOMETIMES STAB OR
KILL ONE OF THE NINE."
—G. L. MORRILL, 1916.

ignored and abused, became the object of a virtual crusade. This raised special difficulties. In the absence of a democratic history, and with much of the
region's political center killed off by right wing violence in the 1970s, elections were at best like building a house on sand, at worst like building the
house's roof before the walls. With the substance so shaky in the spate of
elections that were held in Honduras (1981 and 1985), El Salvador (1982,
1984, and 1985), Guatemala (1984 and 1985), and Haiti (1986 and 1987),
perception was everything.

After 1983, when Congress dropped its main objections to military aid, El
Salvador became a sideshow. But in 1982, it was the main event. Some seven
hundred journalists descended on San Salvador for the Constituent Assembly
elections that March. For the entire week of the vote, U.S. television network
news gave El Salvador an average of five minutes a night. ABC reporter
Richard Threlkeld summed up, perhaps unwittingly, the real significance of
the event when he described it as "a kind of final examination to see whether
this place is democratic enough to deserve our help." The comment was
reminiscent of nothing so much as the Nicaraguan elections of 1928: though
the actors were Central Americans, their play was being staged for the benefit
of a U.S. audience.

To Americans fearful of "another Vietnam," the Reagan administration's
intentions had to appear to be benevolent, its support for democracy sincere.
The Salvadorans had to give evidence that they wanted to emulate U.S. democratic ways, and the country's new leaders had to be, in the words of the
Foreign Policy Association's Raymond Leslie Buell back in 1930, men "at
least tolerably acceptable to articulate opinion." Christian Democrat José
Napoleón Duarte, defender of the center against the violent extremes, with
his rumpled suits and his broken English learned at Notre Dame, was ideal,
even if Washington had done little to uphold his cause in the past.

The event was tailor-made for television, a medium which demands two
sides as clear-cut as those in a football game. In the midst of a raging civil
war, the elections represented order against turmoil; a vision of what might
be against the nightmare of what was. The culture was violent; the people
wanted peace. All these messages were embraced in the images of long voting lines that dominated the front pages and the newscasts. Voters stood in
the blazing sun for hours, or "dodged guerrilla bullets" to reach the polling
places. If the guerrillas of the FMLN-FDR chose to boycott the election, this
was because they had an innate preference for bullets rather than ballots, not
because the entire leadership of the leftist alliance had been abducted and
killed in November 1980, or because their successors had been included on
a "traitors list" published by the armed forces in March 1981.

If a guerrilla perspective on the elections was lacking, the biases of the
press corps were not entirely to blame, for the Salvadoran military did their
part to ensure that journalists would steer clear of such controversial topics.
Ten days before the vote, reporters were summoned to the San Salvador
morgue. Laid out in stark wooden coffins under the harsh glare of the camera-

men's klieg lights were the bodies of a four-man Dutch television crew, shot dead as they traveled to keep an appointment in a rebel-held area. The military announced that they had been "killed in crossfire," but the corpses had been mutilated, the pants pulled down to expose their bloodied genitals. Like the presentation of Che Guevara's body to the cameras in 1967, this was a formal display of the dead for demonstration purposes, and there was little room for ambiguity about the message. The same day, an anonymous death list was circulated with the names of thirty-five foreign journalists. In the months leading up to the March election, major newspapers, including the *New York Times* and the *Washington Post,* had run reports from behind rebel lines, which the U.S. embassy accused of romanticizing the guerrillas. These now abruptly ceased.

Instead, there was euphoria about the pageant. The image of the voting lines embodied the grandest of all abstract ideas—Democracy—and *we* were its sponsors. Best of all, it could be measured in the statistics and percentages that Americans love. Dan Rather led off his election-night broadcast on CBS News with an exclamation of delight: "It was a triumph! A million people at

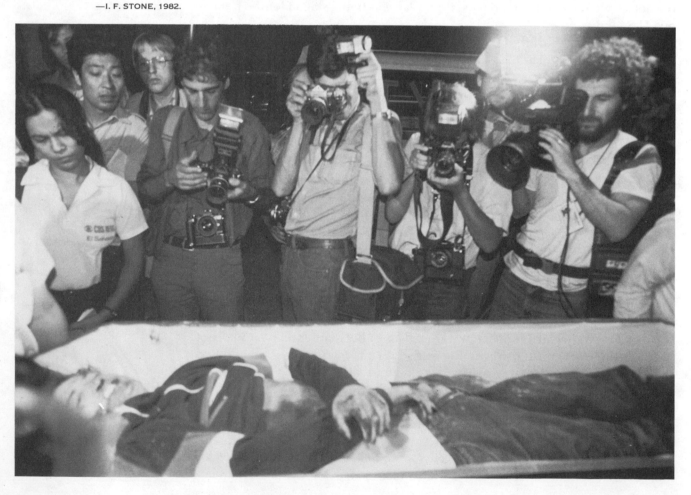

the polls." With 70 percent of eligible voters having cast their ballots, the turnout was in fact fractionally lower than the 72 percent cast in the fraudulent elections of 1972 and 1977. But that history played little part in reports of the 1982 vote, and the embassy had little patience with journalists who insisted on raising it. "Why keep dredging up the past?" one U.S. official asked a reporter. "Don't you understand this is Day One in El Salvador?" His attitude went to the very heart of the matter. since the turn of the century, the United States had seen Central America's past not as an inescapable burden on the present but as something to be transcended and reinvented through American ingenuity.

MEDICAL STUDENTS FROM ST.
GEORGE'S UNIVERSITY RETURN
TO CHARLESTON AIR FORCE BASE.
"APOCALYPSO NOW!"
—*TIME* HEADLINE ON GRENADA.

SIX

UN-AMERICAN
ACTIVITIES

1983—88

SO FOUL A SKY CLEARS NOT WITHOUT A STORM.
—SHAKESPEARE, QUOTED BY JOSEPH CONRAD
AS THE EPIGRAPH TO *NOSTROMO*

As the first theater in its fight for democracy, the Reagan administration had selected a country the size of Massachusetts. For the second, it chose Grenada, an eastern Caribbean island of 133 square miles, more than half of whose nationals live in Brooklyn. Between October 12 and 19, 1983, Grenada's four-year-old revolutionary regime disintegrated; a clique of zealots from the central committee of the ruling New Jewel Movement took power; Prime Minister Maurice Bishop was murdered; and the island was placed under a shoot-to-kill curfew. On October 25, nineteen hundred U.S. troops stormed ashore "to protect American citizens and to help restore democratic institutions."

At the most obvious level, this was a strikingly unequal contest—Goliath overwhelming David. But for the administration and most of the press, it was a richly symbolic encounter, and the real adversary was not Grenada, or even its new rulers. "U.S. Invades Grenada in Warning to Russia and Cuba About Expansion in the Caribbean," read a typical headline from the *Wall Street Journal*. The island itself had only a marginal existence in news reports, serving primarily as an arena for the conflict of larger forces. The Grenadian population had a walk-on part, praising the U.S. forces effusively for rescuing them. Secretary of State George Shultz thought the place was "a lovely piece of real estate."

For the previous two years, the administration had fanned a fierce debate, again supported by spy-plane and satellite photos, about a new ten-thousand-foot runway under construction on Grenada's southern tip. The island had no capacity to handle large jets, and tourists had to stop over in Barbados. British companies had the main construction contracts, but Cuban technical volunteers were doing most of the work. The great airport debate showed how far U.S. policies had come to be dictated by the almost metaphysical contingency plans of the Pentagon. What mattered about Grenada's airport was not that it would, in all likelihood, be a magnet for European and North American tourists but that it might one day serve as a takeoff point for Soviet Backfire bombers if the United States could not guarantee the reliability of the Grenadian government.

For the U.S. public, the Grenada invasion, coming on the heels of a terrorist bombing that killed 241 marines in Beirut, was the archetypal "splendid little war." Only eighteen U.S. soldiers died. Richard Hofstadter's comment on morality and expediency in the Spanish-American War could have been written about Grenada: "The quick victories won by American arms strengthened the psychological position of the imperialists. The feeling that one may be guilty of wrongdoing can be heightened when the questionable act is followed by adversity. Conversely, it may be minimized by the successful execution of a venture. Misfortune is construed as Providential punishment; but success, as in the Calvinist scheme, is taken as an outward sign of an inward state of grace."

As a calculated morality play of U.S. virtue and power, Grenada went much further. It was the first combat between U.S. and Cuban forces, a long-awaited act of revenge for the Bay of Pigs. It also provided the opportunity to strike back at the press for its failure to "get on the team" in Vietnam. The Pentagon excluded journalists from the island for the first two days. Photographers were reduced instead to recording a set of theatrical sideshows, such as the ground-kissing ceremony by American students from the St. George's University Medical School returning to Charleston Air Force Base. This was doubly galling for journalists, since they knew it played straight into the hands of the president who had barred them from covering the main event.

At the broadest level of symbolism, the events in Grenada were an irresistible opportunity to discredit the idea of revolution in the Third World. When reporters were finally allowed on the island, troops of the 82nd Airborne Division gave them conducted tours of stockpiled Soviet-bloc weapons. Later, the administration released selections of captured documents, many of them in Cyrillic script, and transcripts of the final sessions of the Grenadian central committee, which were examples of Leninspeak at its worst. The influential columnist Charles Krauthammer offered a typical comment in the *New Republic*: "Revolution is a large idea, and Grenada a small

••••••

CUBAN PRISONERS ON GRENADA,
1983. "THEY ARE COUNTRIES WHICH
MIGHT HAVE BECOME THE PREY OF
IMPERIALISTIC NATIONS OVERSEAS
HAD THE POWER OF THE UNITED
STATES NOT BEEN AVAILABLE TO
PROTECT THEM."
—PROFESSOR WILLIAM R.
SHEPHERD, COLUMBIA UNIVERSITY,
JANUARY 1928.

PRISONERS AT THE BAY OF PIGS,
1961. "BRING ME A COUPLE OF
HAIRS FROM CASTRO'S BEARD."
—LUIS SOMOZA TO FLYERS LEAVING
A SECRET AIR BASE IN NICARAGUA.

island. Of such incongruities comedy is made." It "becomes more empty of meaning, more powerful a tool, and thus more attractive to the next gang of thugs, posturers, and dreamers." The message was that American liberals and neoliberals should never again be fooled into sympathizing with revolutionaries, as they had been in Vietnam or, closer to home, Nicaragua. In such circumstances, the use of force was morally justifiable. National sovereignty and international law were meaningless abstractions when compared to the demands of order. This echoed the belief of Henry Stimson, back in 1927, that the United States had every right to intervene in the Caribbean area, "if those independent governments do not adequately fulfill the responsibility of independence."

The message of Grenada was taken most seriously by the Sandinistas, who were aware not only of the threat of U.S. armed attack but also of the failure of the Grenadian leaders to hold themselves accountable to the population through elections. Back in July 1979, a week before it took power, the Sandinistas' provisional junta had written a letter to the Organization of American States (OAS) that promised, among other things, "to call Nicaraguans to our country's first free elections in this century." In 1981, a speech by Defense Minister Humberto Ortega Saavedra suggested that a Western-style multiparty election was not necessarily what they had in mind. "Never forget," he said, "that our elections will be to perfect revolutionary power, not to hold a raffle among those who seek to hold power." Ortega also set a date: 1985.

Grenada brought that timetable forward. At the same time, declining support from Western European countries persuaded the Sandinistas that a genuine multiparty contest was in order. As a senior foreign ministry official explained to a delegation of observers from the Latin American Studies Association (LASA), the vote was "a key element in our national defense strategy. Our internal legitimacy is not in question. What *is* in question is our international legitimacy." The elections were set for November 4, two days before the U.S. presidential vote, so that Nicaragua could present Washington with a fait accompli.

Three parties to the right of the Sandinistas took part, and three to their left. Within Nicaragua, then, it appeared to be a seven-party contest with a wide variety of choices. As far as U.S. observers were concerned, however, there was only one litmus test to judge whether the vote was legitimate. This was whether an opposition grouping called the Coordinadora Democrática decided to run. It was headed by Arturo Cruz, a banker who had lived in Washington since 1970, spending only a brief period in 1979–80 inside Nicaragua. Cruz was highly regarded in the U.S. Congress, but there was no solid evidence that his Coordinadora enjoyed widespread domestic support.

Cruz pulled out with the election just a month away, and on October 21, a story by *New York Times* reporter Philip Taubman helped explain why. According to a senior U.S. official quoted in the article, "The Administration never contemplated letting Cruz stay in the race, because then the Sandinistas could justifiably claim that the elections were legitimate, making it much

harder for the United States to oppose the Nicaraguan government." It was
the business federation COSEP, "which was in frequent contact with the
CIA about the elections," that brought the crucial pressure to bear on Cruz.

Despite Taubman's story, the great majority of U.S. news reports ceased
to take the elections seriously once Cruz had pulled out. Though the voting
lines were just as long, and the sun just as hot, as in El Salvador, they did not
appeal as much to U.S. photo editors. Many papers did not even report the
results, which gave the Sandinistas 67 percent of the valid vote, with 29
percent going to conservative and center-left parties. Most reporters did not
even stay in Managua for the election-night count, which showed a 75 percent
turnout, a little higher than in El Salvador. Instead, the LASA delegation
reported, the results "were literally buried under an avalanche of alarmist
news reports, based on secret intelligence information deliberately leaked to
the U.S. television networks by Reagan administration officials, which portrayed a massive, Soviet-supplied arms buildup in Nicaragua, allegedly
aimed at giving the Sandinistas the capacity to invade neighboring countries." The highlight was the docking of the Soviet freighter *Bakuriani* at the
Pacific port of Corinto, supposedly carrying MIG-21 fighter aircraft. The story
was pure fabrication, but it worked. What lodged in the memory of U.S.
readers from November 1984 was not the Nicaraguan election but the "MIG
crisis." And in the official Washington version of history, the Sandinistas went
down as Marxist-Leninists who had broken their promises to the OAS.

During a speech in February 1985, Vice-President George Bush displayed
a Nicaraguan postage stamp bearing the bearded face of Karl Marx, as proof
of the essential nature of the Sandinista regime. It was not the first time the
image from a stamp had been used for political reasons. Recall Frenchman

SOVIET FREIGHTER *BAKURIANI* IN PORT AT
CORINTO, NICARAGUA.
"THE CARIBBEAN IS AN UNFENCED
NEIGHBORHOOD THAT WE SHARE WITH 27
ISLAND AND COASTAL NATIONS. . . . IF THE
REGION SHOULD BECOME PREY TO SOCIAL
AND ECONOMIC UPHEAVAL, AND
DOMINATED BY REGIMES HOSTILE TO US,
THE CONSEQUENCES FOR OUR SECURITY
WOULD BE IMMEDIATE AND FAR-REACHING."
—SECRETARY OF STATE GEORGE SHULTZ.

NICARAGUA SALUTES THE

ANNIVERSARIES OF TWO

OF ITS HEROES.

Philippe Bunau-Varilla, lobbying for Panama in the debate over an inter-oceanic canal: "Look at the Nicaraguan postage stamps," he wrote in one pamphlet in 1901. "Young nations like to put on their coats of arms what best symbolizes their moral domain or characterizes their native soil. What have the Nicaraguans chosen to characterize their country on their coat of arms, on their postage stamps? Volcanoes!"

In one sense Bush and Bunau-Varilla were both correct about the importance of a young nation's postage stamps. The problem was that the set marking the centenary of Marx's death was only one of many commemorative issues. Bush might even have boosted his case by pointing to a set honoring Lenin's 115th birthday, or a stamp featuring Bulgarian Comintern leader Giorgi Dimitrov. But casting the net wider would also have revealed a set dedicated to Pope John Paul II, not to mention a lavish series of seven stamps to mark the 250th birthday of George Washington, which depicted the great American hero signing the Constitution, crossing the Delaware, and shivering at Valley Forge. Indeed, Bush's claims prompted a letter to the *New York Times* from a reader in Cleveland, who reported receiving "an envelope from Nicaragua on which were affixed two brightly colored stamps dedicated to Babe Ruth, complete with a baseball, the Stars and Stripes, and the Babe in the characteristic process of swatting a ball into the bleachers."

The diverse range of personalities celebrated on the Sandinistas' stamps reflected a long-established current in Nicaraguan history. Augusto César Sandino, the guerrilla leader of the 1920s, had espoused a jumble of philosophies, including some crude socialist ideals from his days as an oilfield worker in Mexico and a strong dose of mysticism. To his followers, there was no contradiction between his anti-*yanqui* passion and respect for such figures as Washington, Jefferson, and Lincoln, whom they considered the representatives of a similar nationalist outlook.

Since his murder in 1934, many groups had laid claim to Sandino's inheritance—almost everyone, in fact, but the local communists, who recalled that Agustín Farabundo Martí, leader of the communist revolt of 1932 in El Salvador, had parted company with the Nicaraguan on the ground that he was not ideologically pure. The Sandinistas adopted Sandino's name in 1961, at a time when it was risky to speak it aloud in Nicaragua, and have always pointed to his heterodox ideas as evidence of the breadth of their own nationalist-Marxist philosophy. Since 1979, opposition groups have claimed that the Sandinistas, as "Marxist-Leninists," have falsely appropriated the hero's name. Some, like the Sandino Revolutionary Front, the contra faction led by Edén Pastora, adopted it for themselves. Even the U.S. administration accused the Sandinistas of having "demeaned the name of their patron, César Augusto [*sic*] Sandino"—whose life was devoted to driving the United States out of his country.

A similar polemic has surrounded the figure of José Martí, the hero of Cuba's war of independence from Spain. Fidel Castro venerates Martí as a nationalist; anti-Castro exiles in Miami claim him as their own because he was not a Marxist. The Reagan administration took this dispute to new lengths when it set up a radio station to broadcast to Cuba, and called it Radio Martí. It was a calculated provocation, which the Cuban government found insuffer-

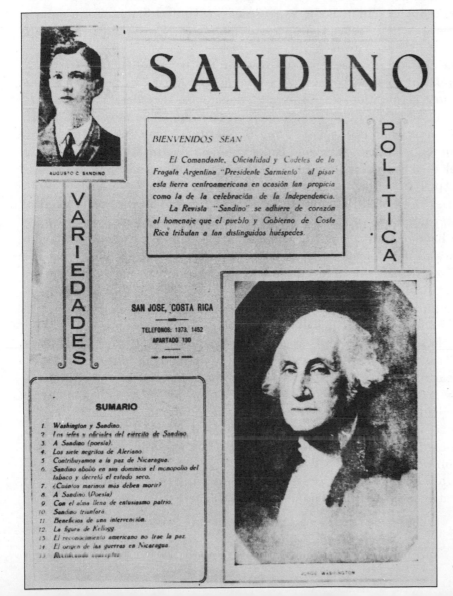

'THE MAN WHOM [THE SANDINISTAS] HONOR, SANDINO, HE SAID HE WAS A COMMUNIST."
—RONALD REAGAN, IN *TIME*, MARCH 1986.

"THE COMMANDANTES EVEN BETRAYED THE MEMORY OF THE NICARAGUAN REBEL LEADER SANDINO, WHOSE LEGACY THEY FALSELY CLAIM. FOR THE REAL SANDINO, BECAUSE HE WAS A GENUINE NATIONALIST, WAS OPPOSED TO COMMUNISM."
—RONALD REAGAN, JUNE 24, 1986.

able, for the central plank in Martí's philosophy was that the greatest danger facing his country was "our formidable neighbor who scorns and does not understand us."

This kind of verbal warfare over political symbols touches on the United States's most deeply held convictions about the New World and the ideologies that can be allowed to take root here. Alone among the Western nations, the United States has no real domestic experience of socialism, whether of the social democratic or Marxist variety. Since it assumes a natural community of interests with its neighbors, any appearance of socialist ideas in the backyard can only be evidence of an alien organism at work. By this reasoning, a political movement in Central America may be nationalist, or it may be Marxist, but it cannot be both.

To Europeans, the notion of a movement in Nicaragua using Marxist ideas to advance nationalist goals, where other tools have failed, does not present any particular intellectual problem. To Americans, it appears to defy the laws of nature, and any movement that acts this way can only be using the language of nationalism to camouflage its "real" agenda—advancing the strategic interests of the Soviet Union at the expense of the United States. For a culture whose Puritan roots remain strong, accusations of heresy and betrayal are then only a short step away.

Those accusations reached a crescendo in the spring of 1985, as Congress voted on a further round of aid to the contras. On April 23, at the end of one of the most acrimonious foreign-policy debates in memory, the House rejected a request for $14 million in "nonmilitary aid." The next day, a series of amendments failed, the last losing by just two votes. Nicaragua, meanwhile, announced that President Daniel Ortega Saavedra would leave within the week on a twelve-nation European trip that included a stop in Moscow.

On April 29, Ortega met with Soviet leader Mikhail Gorbachev. With Western sources of aid largely cut off, Nicaragua was in desperate need of petroleum supplies. And though Ortega's timing may have seemed atrocious, he must have reasoned that Nicaragua's image problems in Washington were secondary to the demands of survival. Although Gorbachev, following the logic of *perestroika*, was reluctant to have Nicaragua become another money pit like Cuba, he was willing to make the relatively modest investment necessary to guarantee the Sandinistas' survival, fend off the contras, and gain prestige in the eyes of Latin nationalists at the United States's expense.

The photos of the Ortega-Gorbachev meeting released by the Soviet press agency Tass were decidedly restrained, and in marked contrast to the extravagant bear hugs and raised fists of the famous Castro-Khrushchev photos of the early 1960s. Yet coming after a furious debate in which many Democrats felt they had taken a political risk by opposing a popular president over the issue of communism, the reaction in Washington was, if anything, more extreme. Senators brandished the Tass picture as they approved a bipartisan resolution deploring the visit. Carrying on an age-old tradition that viewed Washington as the first constituency of Central American politicians, liberal Democrats were particularly prone to phrases like "stab in the back" or "slap

••••••

ORTEGA VISITS MOSCOW,
APRIL 1985.
"SUPPOSE YOU SEE A BIRD
WALKING AROUND IN A FARMYARD.
THE BIRD WEARS NO LABEL THAT
SAYS 'DUCK.' BUT THE BIRD
CERTAINLY LOOKS LIKE A DUCK.
ALSO HE GOES TO THE POND AND
YOU NOTICE HE SWIMS LIKE A DUCK.
THEN HE OPENS HIS BEAK AND
QUACKS LIKE A DUCK. WELL, BY
THIS TIME YOU HAVE PROBABLY
REACHED THE CONCLUSION THAT
THE BIRD IS A DUCK, WHETHER HE'S
WEARING A LABEL OR NOT."
—U.S. AMBASSADOR TO
GUATEMALA RICHARD C.
PATTERSON, JR., 1949.

in the face." Representative Charles E. Schumer, Democrat of New York, summed up the mood when he said, "There's huge anger at Ortega. People regard his trip as a personal rebuke to Congress."

On April 30, 1985, as President Reagan left for his controversial visit to German war graves at Bitburg, he declared an economic embargo against Nicaragua. According to the text of the announcement, "The policies and actions of the Government of Nicaragua constitute an unusual and extraordinary threat to the national security and foreign policy of the United States." The hyperbole was just a hint of what was in store as the administration grew ever more frustrated at Congress's reluctance to fund the overthrow of the Sandinistas.

Nicaragua was in many ways a greater affront to U.S. conservatives than Cuba had been. It was unthinkable that a traditional client state, a shade smaller than Arkansas or Alabama, with only three million people, should refuse to submit to Washington's will—or, in Reagan's phrase, to "say uncle." But when adversaries are turned into demons, the meaning of language can easily break down. And as obsession takes hold, even a realistic sense of physical scale can begin to dissolve. Herblock picked up on this in one of his *Washington Post* cartoons, which showed Reagan gesturing to a globe to prove that, "as you can see from this diagram, . . . Nicaragua covers the earth."

The figure of Daniel Ortega, so determinedly uncharismatic, was also elevated to something of an obsession. His reluctance to act out the role of a new Castro, Khomeini, or Qaddafi—the United States's three great modern demons—only seemed to add to the administration's frustration and anger. With the help of a New York public-relations firm, Nicaragua slowly developed some publicity skills of its own, and Ortega, in his own stoic way, became a semi-public figure, jogging with Secret Service agents in Central Park, eating at Chinese restaurants in New York, appearing on the Phil Donahue show, posing for photographs with his seven children wearing New York Mets caps. The worst personal weakness that could be pinned on him was a visit to a New York optician to buy $3,000 worth of eyeglasses. As the vices of dictators go, it was fairly trivial, but it accounted for hundreds of column inches, and gave the cartoonists something to work with at last. Officials took to mentioning Ortega's glasses in speeches. Reagan called him "the little dictator in green fatigues." Although the press was often wary of this exaggeration, it tended increasingly to speak of Nicaragua in the terms normally reserved for major world powers: it was no longer "the Nicaraguan government," but "the Ortega regime," or something called "Managua"—on a par with "London" or "Moscow."

"There seems to be no crime to which the Sandinistas will not stoop," Reagan said in a March 1986 nationally televised speech, as yet another contra-aid vote drew near. "This is an outlaw regime." More accurately, it

••••••

THE DICTATOR IN DESIGNER

GLASSES.

seemed that there were no limits to how far the administration would go in its drive for contra aid. This time the president accused the Sandinistas of fomenting subversion in Brazil—a charge the Brazilian government rejected the next day. He also made great play of the Sandinistas' anti-Semitism—which numerous Jewish leaders promptly denied.

But most damningly, Reagan tried to tie the Sandinistas to the international cocaine trade. "I know," he said, "that every American parent concerned about the drug problem will be outraged to learn that top Nicaraguan government officials are deeply involved in drug trafficking." Visual props and photographic images were again a major part of Reagan's repertoire. To prove the charge of subversion, a map of Latin America with a spreading red stain; to substantiate the drug-trafficking allegations, a blurry black-and-white photograph taken with a camera hidden by the CIA aboard the aircraft of a big-time drug-smuggler-turned-informant named Barry Seal. According to Reagan, the photograph showed Federico Vaughan, allegedly a top aide to interior minister Tomás Borge, loading cocaine onto a plane at an airfield outside Managua.

As the president's own Drug Enforcement Administration admitted the day after the speech, there was no evidence to back up this charge. Indeed, as a number of reporters established, the weight of the evidence pointed in just the opposite direction, to an extensive contra role in the cocaine trade,

━━━━━━

Q.: "DO YOU THINK IT IS MORE IMPORTANT FOR THE UNITED STATES TO PUT A STOP TO [ANTI-COMMUNIST CENTRAL AMERICAN LEADERS'] DRUG DEALINGS, OR MORE IMPORTANT FOR THE UNITED STATES TO SUPPORT THEM AGAINST COMMUNISM?"

A.: STOP DRUG DEALINGS: 63% SUPPORT ANTI-COMMUNISM: 21%

—*NEW YORK TIMES*/CBS NEWS POLL, APRIL 1988.

with relationships of convenience between the Nicaraguan rebels (not to mention Panamanian, Honduran, and Haitian military officers) and the Colombian Medellín drug cartel. But the attack on the Sandinistas was not a reasoned, factual debate. It was an effort to trigger atavistic fears about the United States's physical and moral security in a hostile world, and to generate public pressure on foot-dragging members of Congress.

The claim of a communist menace was a familiar one; cocaine was a potent new addition to the demonic chaos that loomed on America's doorstep. Nineteen eighty-six was the year of the Reagan administration's "Just say no" antidrug campaign. Its terms of reference were traditional, speaking of American innocence fighting to resist contamination from abroad. From a point of origin in Colombia, Peru, or Bolivia, drugs seeped in through the United States's porous Caribbean frontier—an idea that was central to the quintessential 1980s television show, *Miami Vice*. The city of Miami bred its own fascination, the greatest since the 1930s, when it was the jumping-off point for Havana and the novel adventure of Pan-American Airways. In 1987 alone, Miami was celebrated in three books, by Joan Didion, T. D. Allman, and David Rieff. All of them found the city both romantic and repellent, with its pink flamingos and sunshine, its drug wars and art-deco architecture. Miami was the gateway to Latin America, home to the anti-Castro Cubans—who had become a serious force in domestic politics—and of course the nerve center of contra operations. None of the writers were even able to decide whether Miami was really an American city. It seemed a kind of boundary between U.S. civilization and the outside world, recalling one of those sixteenth-century maps in which the borders of the known world end, and a formless, uncharted mass begins, with the legend, "Here be savages."

Like JFK greeting the Bay of Pigs veterans at the Orange Bowl, Reagan aggressively worked to wrap the contra leadership in the personal authority of the presidency and the mantle of the United States's most cherished national values. There were fighting speeches at the White House podium, as well as more casual, populist moments, as when Reagan donned a T-shirt that read, "I'm a Contra Too," or a button that said, "If you liked Cuba, you'll love Nicaragua." The effort to turn back the Sandinista revolution was, in short, the most crucial personal issue of Reagan's two-term presidency. The contras, too, used the Washington platform to sell their cause, recognizing that congressionally approved dollars rather than support inside Nicaragua were their main sustenance, and agreeing, like José María Moncada sixty years before, "to designate the State Department as the arbiter of our fights and differences."

The president's problem was that his appeals failed to work, or worked only with the expenditure of enormous political capital. Congress was split down the middle: for one side, the contras were the only thing that would stave off an invasion by U.S. forces; for the other, they were the first blundering steps into a new quagmire. The administration geared itself up to an emotional pitch every few months, all to secure a few swing votes that just barely kept the contras in the field until the next time. Public opinion remained firmly opposed to contra aid. At most, only two-fifths of those questioned were sympathetic to supporting them.

The dissent over Central America did have clear limits. There was little or no debate, even among liberal Democrats, about the nature of the Nicaraguan regime: the question was whether to destroy it or to contain it, and by what means. Indeed, as a real place, Nicaragua seemed hardly to exist. It functioned as a colony of the imagination, a tabula rasa on which the United States examined its own moral record. Many concluded that American conduct in Central America no longer gave the country the right to see itself as the shining city on the hill of John Winthrop's dream. But the issue was still aberrational U.S. behavior. Few critics—or at least few in positions of influence—were willing to look at the validity of competing ideologies in the region. For the most part, the dissenters' goal was not to rethink basic assumptions about coexistence in an intractably plural world but to restore U.S. behavior to what was imagined to be its true course.

Even within those limits, however, it was a different and more stubborn kind of dissent than any administration had previously had to face over Central America. There had been a vocal minority of anti-imperialists during the Spanish-American War; rather more against the marine occupation of Nicaragua in the late 1920s; and virtually no dispute over Guatemala in 1954, or over Cuba and the Dominican Republic in the 1960s. Perceptive, dissenting voices from within the establishment, or on its fringes, have been a recurring thread in these pages—Clarence K. Streit and Frank L. Kluckhohn of the *New York Times*, Walter Lippmann, *Time* magazine's William Krehm. By the 1980s, voices like these had a new scale and momentum. Despite the Reagan administration's nostalgia for a black-and-white moral universe, the president found that all the things he disliked most about the 1970s—the Vietnam syndrome, Watergate-inspired distrust of the executive branch, fears about abusive covert actions, a commitment to human rights—could not be simply wished away. In fact, the contra policy did more than anything else to breathe new life into those concerns.

•• •• ••

As always, the nation's leading cartoonists were a good barometer of dissent. Many of them, like Tony Auth in a 1983 cartoon, saw Central America as a swamp or quagmire—an obvious reminder of Vietnam. In one sense, liberals and conservatives agreed on this definition: in Sylvester Stallone's *Rambo*, one of the right's key iconic statements of the mid-1980s, the Third World is an unknowable hell of mud, creepers, and leeches. Auth's commentary, however, was also on the reluctance of Congress to oppose a popular president. Conservatives saw these legislators as a timorous bunch without firm moral convictions, who would nickel-and-dime another American enterprise into failure as they had in Vietnam. Faced with an off-again, on-again flow of contra aid, the response of extreme conservatives in the administration was

LOS ANGELES TIMES, 1985.

to bypass Congress altogether. They agreed with Oliver North that honorable fighting men were willing to "die face-down in the mud," and proposed to plunge ahead without informing the squeamish.

By 1985 the administration had lost a lot of credibility and goodwill by its transparent attempt to manage public perceptions of Central America. All the aerial photographs and postage stamps and murky pictures of cocaine-handlers had taken their cumulative toll. Conrad's cartoon from the *Los Angeles Times,* with its clever play on one of the president's frequent mild outbreaks of skin cancer, was one of many suggesting that trust in the truth-fulness of the presidency had not fully recovered from Watergate. In particu-lar, a gulf had opened between Reagan's obsession with Nicaragua and a largely indifferent public that declined to see the country as a national-security threat.

The steady flow of news and presidential warnings did little to shake the public's deep-seated parochialism or its isolationist instincts. Most Americans still did not know where Nicaragua was because they had decided it did not matter to them where it was. In essence, not much had changed since the early part of the century, when Faustin Wirkus's shipmates fancied that Haiti was "somewhere south of Suez." In the *New York Times*–CBS News poll conducted after Oliver North's appearance before the 1987 congressional Iran-*contra* hearings, only 32 percent of respondents could locate Nicaragua as part of Central or Latin America; 21 percent thought it was in South Amer-ica; and another third admitted they did not know. The remaining 15 percent placed Nicaragua on the map not by any cultural or geographical logic but because of its national-security associations. Several located it in the vicinity of Iran or Iraq, many in the Middle East, some in Africa, and a few in Asia or near Vietnam. One person thought it was "just below, I think, Texas." An-other, thinking perhaps of the president's vision of foot-people streaming across the border at Harlingen, Texas, guessed that it was "south of the U.S. —and not very south."

A small minority of cartoonists risked showing the U.S.–Central American relationship from a more radical perspective that questioned the very funda-ments of the United States's rights as a world power. H. Clay Bennett of the *St. Petersburg Times,* for example, in a brilliant, iconoclastic reversal of old myths, depicted an old-fashioned policeman of the Wilsonian era helping a contra burglar to break into Nicaragua's house. For once, we are forced to remember that the United States is in Central America's backyard, as much as the other way round. Cuba may be ninety miles from the U.S. coast, but by the same token the United States is ninety miles from the Cuban coast.

-- -- --

A major part of the aid controversy was a battle over vocabulary: Was the very term "contra" abusive, an invention of the Sandinistas? To partisans, they were "freedom fighters" or, a shade more neutrally, "the democratic resis-tance." To Sandinista supporters, they were "mercenaries." The *New York*

Times, striving for objectivity, settled on "rebels." Perhaps no single state-ment damaged Reagan's standing more than his assertion that the contras were "the moral equal to our Founding Fathers"—a proposition that many cartoonists, like *Newsday*'s M. G. Lord, found irresistible.

Two basic questions were asked about the contras: Were they adequate standard-bearers of American values? Were they effective instruments of American policy? On both counts, the answer seemed to be no. From one day to the next, they were not even politically coherent. Each photograph of the president with the contras seemed to feature a fresh cast of characters. The first rebel directorate, assembled by the CIA in a Fort Lauderdale hotel room, quickly disintegrated. A revised three-man team was hastily put together in time for the April 1985 aid debate, armed with something called the "San José Declaration," which Oliver North said was akin to "our own Declaration of Independence and our own Constitution." The document was drafted, this time in a Miami hotel room, by North and contra leaders Arturo Cruz and Adolfo Calero. As North himself acknowledged in an April 1985 memo to National Security Adviser Robert McFarlane, "The objective was . . . to con-vince the U.S. Congress that the opposition was led by reasonable men."

But over the long haul, the image battle was a losing one. This was partly because the CIA, in its insistence on controlling the fractious movement, sidestepped the people with the most claim to support inside Nicaragua—

••••••

NEWSDAY, 1985.

CONTRAS CROSSING THE RIO COCO

NICARAGUAN REBELS ARE 'THE MORAL EQUIVALENT OF OUR FOUNDING FATHERS' - R. W. REAGAN

"LEAVING THE CONTRAS! WHAT KIND OF
AMERICAN ARE YOU, ANYHOW?"

©1987 HERBLOCK

WASHINGTON POST, 1987.

the more moderate elements of the Miskito Indians, the charismatic but un-
predictable Edén Pastora—in favor of the militarily skilled former officers of
the National Guard and long-term agency assets such as the right-wing former
Coca-Cola bottler Calero. Men like Cruz were drafted because they were
credible with Congress, but it was embarrassingly obvious that they had no
influence over either Calero, the military commanders in Honduras, or the
troops in the field. Cruz himself, with the honesty of the good democrat, was
the first to admit as much.

In the end, in March 1987, Cruz quit. Herblock, having observed the
foibles of U.S. foreign policy for forty years, captured the dilemma of Cruz
(and the administration) sharply. The more the contra leadership was designed to win points on Capitol Hill, as both a military and a moral force, the
more unstable the coalition of Nicaraguans with sharply competing ambitions
was likely to become. Furthermore, every time the administration tried to

calm internal disputes by reshuffling the leadership, its hidden hand became more visible. At the same time, the administration was obliged to downplay the importance of its own former creatures, putting its precarious credibility at even greater risk. Cruz had been held up as proof of the contras' democratic vocation; now, he was depicted as a Hamlet figure, indecisive, and in any case lacking popular support inside Nicaragua. There seemed to be an endless parade of Nicaraguans willing to follow in the footsteps originally laid down in the 1910s and 1920s by Adolfo Díaz and José María Moncada. But by the time the hapless Cruz was replaced, the administration was in considerable disarray.

Even the more hard-line contras proved to be less-docile allies and more perversely nationalistic in their way than the United States had calculated. The *Somocista* leaders in Miami and Honduras, who could never shake their reputation for atrocities, made little secret of their irritation at being made to jump through hoops and clean up their human-rights record in order to qualify for aid. Many of them were also clearly interested in the money for strictly nonpolitical reasons. Large amounts of laboriously defined "humanitarian aid" went to support a lavish life-style in Miami which was mercilessly satirized in two long sequences of *Doonesbury* cartoons.

One senior U.S. official commented angrily that, "like other Latins, they love to screw the gringos"—a remark which, crass though it was, suggested how ambivalent the U.S.–Central American relationship had always been. In order to gain U.S. support, the contra leaders would plead a slavish adherence to American ideals. Indeed, their highest ambition was probably to enjoy unmolested in Managua the accoutrements of a middle-class American existence: a California ranch house with a two-car garage and a modest pool. But at bottom was a current of bitterness at being permanently excluded from the country they envied, never sure from one moment to the next whether the United States was going to act like an eager elder brother or a scolding parent. Anastasio Somoza Debayle had always borne a grudge against the cadets at La Salle Military Academy on Long Island, who had called him a spic. He dealt with it superficially by affecting an English as fluent and idiomatic as that of any American. More deeply, he determined never to entirely trust his sponsors, and, in the end, accused them of betrayal when he had outlived his usefulness and was dumped. The contras, in this respect as in so many others, were truly Somoza's inheritors.

-- -- --

When an antiquated C-130 aircraft was shot down over southern Nicaragua in October 1986, and a sad-faced mercenary from Wisconsin named Eugene Hasenfus was led away from the wreck with his hands tied, the Reagan administration's war against Nicaragua began to unravel. The image spoke of humiliation, of David downing Goliath. It also opened Pandora's box. In the months that followed, the full extent of the contras' dependence on outside aid became apparent. Also, the scope of a covert operation that had aided them behind the backs of Congress would be revealed, at least in part, in-

●●●●●●

CAPTURED EUGENE HASENFUS,
OCTOBER 1986.
"NO MAN IS ABOVE THE LAW AND
NO MAN IS BELOW IT,
NOR DO WE ASK ANY MAN'S
PERMISSION WHEN WE REQUIRE HIM
TO OBEY IT."
—THEODORE ROOSEVELT,
MESSAGE TO CONGRESS, 1904.

cluding what Oliver North called the "neat idea" of selling arms to Iran and diverting the profits to the contras.

It seemed like the end of one of those old movies, in which the faces of those who have acted earlier in the story flit briefly across the screen like ghosts. The former owner of Hasenfus's aircraft was Barry Seal; the plane was the same Fairchild C-130, nicknamed the *Fat Lady*, that the CIA had used to photograph "Nicaraguan officials" loading cocaine. In 1984, the aircraft had also been hired out to NBC for a film starring Morgan Fairchild called *The Time Bomb*, one of that season's crop of witless terrorist scare movies, this one about a gang planning to hijack a load of nuclear-weapons-grade plutonium in Texas. When Hasenfus was asked to name his coworkers at the supply airfield of Ilopango in El Salvador, he identified two Cuban veterans of the Bay of Pigs. One was Félix Rodríguez, the man who still wore Che Guevara's watch as a souvenir; the other, Luis Posada Carriles, had escaped from a Venezuelan jail where he had been held for his role in bombing a Cuban airliner in 1976, killing seventy-three people.

The Hasenfus episode was the start of what was variously called Irangate, Contragate, or simply the Iran-contra affair. Its key player was Oliver North, an obscure, driven marine officer who had run the covert support operation from the National Security Council offices in the White House. North had actually been known to the press for almost two years before the scandal broke. However, although more than fifty news reports had mentioned him, the press seemed to have collectively acceded to the White House's explicit

NOW YOU SEE HIM

WEEKLY EDITION   AUGUST 26, 1

Oliver North, second from right, with President Reagan and contra leaders

White House

request to journalists not to probe too hard. In official terms, North did not exist. He disappeared from White House photographs of Reagan and contra leaders. Just as Cuban newspaper editor Carlos Franqui vanished from a famous photograph with Fidel Castro, so North was neatly excised from the "official" record. Only an accidentally released print betrayed his presence behind Reagan. Journalists acquiesced in the charade, as if still obeying John F. Kennedy's famous stricture after the Bay of Pigs, "Every newspaper now asks itself with respect to every story: 'Is it news?' All I suggest is that you add the question: 'Is it in the interest of national security?' "

The Iran-contra affair made it apparent that acute stress lines had developed in the CIA, the National Security Council, and all the other institutions the United States had set up to manage its global power after World War II. It also demonstrated the full extent of a still-unresolved power struggle between the executive and legislative branches. After Vietnam, there was a widespread feeling on Capitol Hill that the debacle had its roots in Con-

NOW YOU DON'T

WK24-Oct 16)SPECIAL FOR NEW YORK POST-- President Reagan meets, from left, Alfonso Robelo, Arturo Cruz, and Adolfo Calero, three leaders of the Nicaraguan democratic resistance on April 4, 1985.(rca41640 Official White House Photo by Pete Souza)1985   Exclusive to NY Post

●●●●●●

ABOVE, THE TWO OFFICIAL
VERSIONS, MASKED AND CROPPED.
—*NEW YORK POST*, 1985
BELOW, THE MASKED MAN
UNINTENTIONALLY REVEALED, AT
FAR RIGHT.
"BETWEEN THE TWO MEN THERE IS
NOW A STRANGE VOID, A BLANK SPACE
THAT IS REALLY THE BLACK HOLE OF
THE TOTALITARIAN TIME: THE ETERNAL
WRITING AND REWRITING OF THE
CLOTH OF HISTORY."
—G. CABRERA INFANTE.

gress's deference to the wishes of the president. The attempt to strike a counterbalance included the War Powers Act and the establishment of committees to oversee the intelligence community. The Reagan administration resorted to a clandestine bureaucracy to evade obstacles such as these, and the outcome was an acrimonious contest over the direction of Central America policy, a deadlock between the presidency's nostalgia for unfettered power and the Congress's continuing demand for a restraining hand.

Above all, the bureaucratic debacle was a personal humiliation for the most popular president of the postwar era. When Secretary of State Shultz told reporters that Hasenfus "had no connection with the U.S. government at all," some, like Conrad of the *Los Angeles Times*, wondered whether the same comment might not apply to Reagan. Conrad's cartoon was one of the most brutal portrayals of an American president, as scornful as anything leveled at Jimmy Carter during the worst days of the Iran hostage crisis.

Faced with the choice of seeing Reagan as a driven ideologue, perhaps guilty of impeachable offenses ("high crimes and misdemeanors"), or as a disengaged incompetent, Congress opted for the latter, even if Reagan's passionate attachment to the contras made its verdict seem purely an exercise in damage control. As Congress eventually concluded, the arms sales to Iran were motivated as much by the desire to keep the contras alive as by the wish

••••••

LOS ANGELES TIMES, 1986.

" I'M NOT ONE OF OURS ! "

to free American hostages in Beirut. Because they were outraged at being unable to control events in Central America, Reagan and the men who served him were willing to risk the presidency. The measure of their desperation was to stake the *contra* resupply operation on a decrepit airplane that could be shot out of the sky by an eighteen-year-old Sandinista.

The remaining cast of characters, those who played bit parts in the contra supply operation, showed both how little had changed since the United States's first forays into the region in the nineteenth century, and how far things had come. If there was a single common ancestor for their high-flown rhetoric about God, democracy, and freedom, and their unshaven, macho cult of frontier adventure, it was probably William Walker, though the lineage certainly passed, too, through Richard Harding Davis and Lee Christmas, Faustin Wirkus and Brigade 2506. The *Soldier of Fortune* crowd and the U.S. military advisers in El Salvador, with their murky world populated by "Hondus" and "Salvos"; the free-lance outfits, predominantly from the old slave states, like the Alabama-based Civilian Military Assistance, with their Confederate flags and Vietnam T-shirts with helicopter stencils—taken together,

they were an uncanny throwback to Walker's Phalanx of Immortals. "We like to think of ourselves as missionary-mercenaries," said one Vietnam vet, in Central America to refight old battles.

•• — •• — ••

Secretary of State Dean Acheson once looked out at a world in change and reflected, "When you step on a banana peel, you have to keep from falling on your tail. You don't want to be lurching all over the place all the time. Short-term stability is all right, isn't it? Under the circumstances." For almost a century, this philosophy appeared to work in Central America and the Caribbean. Through the efforts of marines and businessmen, covert operatives and vacationers, an illusion was preserved. But short-term measures, by definition, cannot work forever: they suppress and postpone, but they do not provide solutions.

Once upon a time, the rationale for intervention had been business. But when U.S. investments in the region were factored out of the equation, the ideological dimension of the U.S.–Central American relationship took on a life of its own. Many of the old frontier enterprises, the gold mines and railroads and logging concessions, had yielded to the suffocating jungle growth they had once beaten back. Their successors were the ranching operations of avid contra supporters, men like John Hull and Bruce Jones, drawn by the cheap, fertile land on the Costa Rican–Nicaraguan border. Sugar had lost its proud role in international markets, giving way to cheaper substitutes, though in the flatlands of western Nicaragua it was still possible to glimpse an occasional boxcar emblazoned, in English, with the words, "Nicaragua Sugar Estates." The neat, orderly company towns that the United Fruit Company had built still dominated the torrid plains of northern Honduras, but as the banana giants had withdrawn from old controversies, these seemed to the visitor more of an archaic museum than a vital economic force. Teddy Roosevelt's great transoceanic canal still went efficiently about its business, but its transfer to the Panamanians, at midnight on December 31, 1999, was drawing closer.

By the 1980s, the archaic social order of the region had begun to come apart, and the breakdown challenged all the images of Cuba, Nicaragua, Panama, and their neighbors that the United States had generated since 1898. It was in Central America and the Caribbean that the United States first tasted power, and the sense of mission at its most absolute. It is there that the limits of U.S. power and the torments of America's self-image in the modern world —perhaps the end of the "American century" announced by Henry Luce after World War II—have been most devastatingly exposed.

In the wake of Iran-contra, as the Reagan administration entered its final year, a succession of events and images in Central America and the Caribbean seemed to mock the power that had once been so absolute. In Haiti, which had languished in obscurity for so long, known only as a destination for cruise ships and Club Med tourists, the regime of "Baby Doc" Duvalier finally collapsed. Washington saw immediate elections as the solution, but the November 1987 vote disintegrated in a bloodbath that the administration appeared helpless to avert. (The broader culture continued to trivialize events in that wretched country: one major-league manager wondered, in *Sports Illustrated*, whether the turmoil in Haiti, where all U.S. baseballs are manufactured, might not explain the mysterious increase in the number of home runs hit during the 1987 season.) Panama, meanwhile, witnessed a hapless U.S. effort to ditch the dictator Manuel Noriega, a longtime CIA asset indicted by a Miami grand jury for his role in cocaine smuggling. In El Salvador, the diagnosis in June 1988 of President Duarte's terminal cancer seemed symptomatic of the unraveling of U.S. policy in that country. And Honduras was the scene of an airlift of 3,200 U.S. troops in a final, impotent gesture of support for the contras on the eve of their peace talks with the Nicaraguan government; within days, a mob of Honduran students was burning the Stars and Stripes and torching U.S. embassy buildings.

The crisis had its roots in all the pride, complacency, and anger that were wrapped up in the *Maine* and at San Juan Hill; in the banana empire, the winter playground, and the engineering marvels of the Panama Canal; in all the indulgences shown to Batista and Somoza and Trujillo, to Ubico and Martínez and Carías; in Operation Success, the Bay of Pigs, and the missile crisis. It grew, too, out of the refusal to accept the outcome of democratic elections and movements for reform throughout the 1960s and 1970s; out of the fear of "audacious, cunning, and far-reaching" Soviet strategies where none existed; and out of the belief that living with other countries' nationalism meant that Uncle Sam had "put his tail between his legs and crept away."

The force of that nationalism was perhaps Washington's most basic miscalculation. The independent Central American peace process that got under way in 1987 with the peace plan of Costa Rican president Oscar Arias Sánchez suggested that, in the end, the Marxist-oriented, anti-*yanqui* anger of the Sandinistas and the softer requests from countries like Guatemala and Costa Rica for a measure of autonomy had more in common with each other than with Washington's demand for order on its southern flank. In the desire to settle their own conflicts, the Central Americans proved that they had minds of their own. And that was something no U.S. government, from Monroe to Reagan, had ever taken into account.

NOTES

INTRODUCTION

Page xi: The remark by Senator Hannegan is taken from R. W. Van Alstyne's brilliant book *The Rising American Empire* (New York: Quadrangle, 1960), p. 149. His chapter "The Thrust into the Caribbean, 1848–1917" is particularly valuable. On nineteenth-century American attitudes toward Latin America, the most useful starting point is Frederick Merk's *Manifest Destiny and Mission in American History* (New York: Vintage, 1966).

Page xii: There is much valuable discussion of Latin American stereotypes in John J. Johnson's *Latin America in Caricature* (Austin: Texas University Press, 1980). Several of the cartoons in this book, especially for the period from 1900 to 1914, also appear in Johnson's collection.

ONE: INNOCENTS ABROAD: 1898–1918

Page 1: On the conduct of the press in the Spanish-American War, Charles H. Brown's *The Correspondents' War* (New York: Scribner's, 1967) is the best single source. A good popular summary is in Claude Julien, *American Empire* (New York: Pantheon, 1970), pp. 57–71.

Page 4: David McCullough's remarks about San Juan Hill are taken from a Public Broadcasting System documentary by Bill Moyers, "T.R.," made in 1983.

Page 5: The standard work on the Monroe Doctrine is Dexter Perkins, *Hands Off: A History of the Monroe Doctrine* (Boston: Little, Brown, 1941). "At Home this volcano would be a fortune . . ." is from John Lloyd Stephens, *Incidents of Travel in*

Central America, Chiapas and Yucatan (New Brunswick, N.J.: Rutgers University Press, 1949), vol. 2, p. 8.

Page 6: see William Walker's own 1860 account, *The War in Nicaragua* (Mobile: S. H. Goetzel, 1860; facsimile reprint, Tucson: University of Arizona Press, 1985). Albert Z. Carr's *The World and William Walker* (New York: Harper, 1963) is the best-known narrative of the Tennessee filibuster, and provided the factual basis for the 1987 Alex Cox movie, *Walker*. It has its faults, however, especially in its generous explanation of Walker's turn to slavery as an expedient when his fortunes were waning. A fictional account of Walker's life is Robert Houston's *The Nation Thief* (New York: Pantheon, 1984). On the slave states and the Caribbean, see Robert May, *The Southern Dream of a Caribbean Empire* (Baton Rouge: Louisiana State University Press, 1973).

Page 8: Muybridge's photographs are collected in E. Bradford Burns, ed., *Eadweard Muybridge: A Photographer in Guatemala* (Berkeley: University of California Press, 1986).

Page 9: The description of Coralio is from "Caught," in *The Pocket Book of O. Henry Stories* (New York: Washington Square, 1948), p. 114.

Page 11: The Reverend Morse's comments on the Spanish character are taken from Frances FitzGerald, *America Revised* (New York: Vintage, 1980), pp. 49–50.

Page 12: Walter LaFeber's *The New Empire: An Interpretation of American Expansion 1860–1898* (Ithaca: Cornell University Press, 1963) provides a detailed account of the origins of the Spanish-American War. The same author's *Inevitable Revolutions: The United States in Central America* (New York: Norton, 1983) is the best general history of U.S. policy in the region.

Page 14: The Mayer-Bryan exchange on Haiti is cited in Lester Langley, *The Banana Wars* (Lexington: University of Kentucky Press, 1983).

Pages 16–17: Robert L. Beisner, in *Twelve Against Empire: The Anti-Imperialists, 1898–1900* (University of Chicago Press, 1985), gives a fascinating picture of the range of opposition to the Spanish-American War. The quotations from E. L. Godkin and Carl Schurz are both taken from Beisner, pp. 71–72 and 23–24 respectively.

Page 19: Teddy Roosevelt's exploits in Panama are recounted in David McCullough's very readable *The Path Between the Seas: The Creation of the Panama Canal, 1870–1914* (New York: Simon and Schuster, 1977); and in Walter LaFeber's *The Panama Canal: The Crisis in Historical Perspective* (New York: Oxford University Press, 1978). Some of the contemporary accounts of the building of the canal are well worth tracking down, especially W. J. Abbott's *Panama and the Canal* (New York: Syndicate Publishing, 1913).

Page 27: Richard Hofstadter's comment on Wilson is from his chapter "Woodrow Wilson: The Conservative as Liberal" in *The American Political Tradition* (New York: Vintage, 1948), p. 240. It is also worth looking at Mark T. Gilderhus, *Pan American Visions: Woodrow Wilson in the Western Hemisphere, 1913–1921* (Tucson: University of Arizona Press, 1986).

TWO: BANANA REPUBLICS: 1918–33

Pages 31–36: Accounts of the early expansion of the banana giants are Thomas L. Karnes, *Tropical Enterprise: The Standard Fruit and Steamship Company* (Baton Rouge: Louisiana State University Press, 1978), and Thomas P. McCann, *An American Company: The Tragedy of United Fruit* (New York: Crown, 1976). LeFeber tells the story succinctly in *Inevitable Revolutions*, pp. 42–46. The Rolston letter is quoted in Richard Lapper and James Painter, *Honduras: State for Sale* (London: Latin America Bureau, 1985).

Pages 38–41: Wirkus's memoirs were published as *The White King of La Gonave* (Garden City, N.Y.: Garden City Publishing, 1930).

Page 42: The story of the Nicaraguan war is told in Neill Macaulay, *The Sandino Affair* (Chicago: Quadrangle, 1960). It is also the subject of an excellent chapter in Karl Bermann's *Under the Big Stick: Nicaragua and the United States Since 1848* (Boston: South End, 1986), pp. 183–217. The comments by Lippmann are from Ronald Steel, *Walter Lippmann and the American Century* (New York: Vintage, 1980), pp. 237–38.

Page 43: "The curious short-sightedness . . ." is from Arthur B. Ruhl, *The Central Americans: Adventures and Impressions Between Mexico and Panama* (New York: Scribner's, 1928).

Page 46: Carleton Beals's dispatches from Nicaragua appeared in various issues of *The Nation*, February and March, 1928.

Page 51: Beals's anecdote about Lindbergh is in his autobiographical volume, *Glass Houses: Ten Years of Freelancing* (Philadelphia: Lippincott, 1938), p. 333.

Pages 54–56: The story of John Barr Baker and the censorship of copy from the U.S.S. *Maryland* is told in Tebbel and Watts, *The Press and the Presidency* (New York: Oxford University Press, 1985), p. 421. The remainder of this account is drawn from Harry Wilbur Hill, ed., *President Elect Hoover's Good Will Cruise to Central and South America* (San Francisco: Book Press, 1929).

Page 57: For the early history of the Nicaraguan National Guard, the standard work is Richard Millett, *Guardians of the Dynasty* (Maryknoll, N.Y.: Orbis, 1977).

THREE: GOOD NEIGHBORS: 1933–47

Page 60: The basic text on the period is Bryce Wood, *The Making of the Good Neighbor Policy* (New York: Columbia University Press, 1961). On World War II, see also David Greene, *The Containment of Latin America: A History of the Myths and Realities of the Good Neighbor Policy* (Chicago: Quadrangle, 1971). The popular biography by Nathan Miller, *FDR: An Intimate History* (New York: New American Library, 1983), is good on Roosevelt's spell as Assistant Secretary of the Navy. See pp. 100–172. Richard Hofstadter's characterization of FDR is from the chapter "Franklin D. Roosevelt: The Patrician as Opportunist" in *The American Political Tradition* (New York: Vintage, 1948), p. 350.

Page 61: The December 1940 poll is cited in Johnson, *Latin America in Caricature*, p. 317. There are some memorable vignettes of the Central American dictators of the 1940s in William Krehm's *Democracies and Tyrannies of the Caribbean* (Westport, Conn.: Lawrence Hill, 1984).

Page 62: On Somoza García's rise to power, see especially Millett's *Guardians of the Dynasty* and Bernard Diederich, *Somoza and the Legacy of U.S. Involvement in Central America* (London: Junction, 1982).

Pages 62–64: "The motor car, radio and newspaper syndicate . . ." and "A Saturday night dance . . ." are from Ruhl, *The Central Americans*, p. 24.

Page 65: "Within striking distance to the south . . ." is from the introduction to Roger Stephens, *Down That Pan American Highway* (New York: Roger Stephens, 1948).

Page 66: The story of the exploratory drive is told in *The International Pacific Highway, Mexico City to San Salvador Section. Report, Second Pathfinding Expedition of the Automobile Club of Southern California* (Los Angeles, 1931).

Pages 67–68: Descriptions of the rules of Trujillo in the Dominican Republic include Bernard Diederich, *Trujillo: The Death of the Goat* (Boston: Little, Brown, 1978) and *The Era of Trujillo, Dominican Dictator* by his political opponent Jesús de Galíndez (Tucson: University of Arizona Press, 1973). Gleave's description is in the pamphlet "Santo Domingo" (Washington, D.C.: Pan American Union, 1938).

Page 70: On Carmen Miranda and wartime Good Neighbor images in Hollywood, Allen L. Woll, *The Latin Image in American Film* (Los Angeles: U.C.L.A. Press, 1977).

Page 72: Somoza's gifts to FDR are described in Diederich's *Somoza*, p. 21.

Page 73: The anecdote about Ambassador Stewart is in Krehm, *Democracies and Tyrannies*, p. 120. Carías's circular, "As partners of the great nation . . ." is in ibid., p. 95.

Page 74: On Arias and Nazism in Panama, see LaFeber, *The Panama Canal*, pp. 90–98.

Page 80: The events of 1944 in Guatemala are described in Stephen Schlesinger and Stephen Kinzer, *Bitter Fruit: The Untold Story of the American Coup in Guatemala* (Garden City, N.Y.: Doubleday, 1982), pp. 25–35; North American Congress on Latin America (NACLA), *Guatemala* (New York and Berkeley: NACLA, 1974). The Ubico period is summarized in Richard N. Adams, *Crucifixion by Power* (Austin: University of Texas Press, 1982), pp. 174–183.

Pages 83–85: Major Harris is cited in Thomas P. Anderson, *Matanza: El Salvador's Communist Revolt of 1932* (Lincoln: University of Nebraska Press, 1971), pp. 83–84. The photographs and other Salvadoran government documents were given to the Guatemalan journalist Alfredo Schlesinger and formed the basis of the account by his son, Jorge Schlesinger, *Revolución Comunista* (Guatemala City, 1946). The description of Chico Sánchez's execution is in Anderson, *Matanza*, p. 126.

FOUR: BAD NEIGHBORS: 1947–67

Page 87: Stimson's remark to McCloy is in Stephen E. Ambrose, *Rise to Globalism: American Foreign Policy, 1938–1976* (New York: Penguin, 1976), p. 116.

Page 89: On the dangers of the Truman Doctrine, see Robert Dallek, *The American Style of Foreign Policy: Cultural Politics and Foreign Affairs* (New York: Knopf, 1983), chapter 6; and Frederick F. Siegel, *Troubled Journey: From Pearl Harbor to Ronald Reagan* (New York: Hill and Wang, 1984), chapters 2 and 3. Richard M. Freeman's *The Truman Doctrine and the Origins of McCarthyism* (New York: Knopf, 1972) is an excellent general work on the period.

Page 91: Beals's comment is noted in John A. Britton, "Carleton Beals and Central America after Sandino: The Struggle to Publish," *Journalism Quarterly*, Vol. 60, no. 2 (Summer 1983), pp. 240–45.

Page 92: On corruption in Cuba, see Hugh Thomas, *The Cuban Revolution* (New York: Harper and Row, 1971), chapters 24 and 25. The anecdote about Roger Alden is taken from Herbert L. Matthews, *The Cuban Story* (New York: Braziller, 1961), p. 56.

Pages 96–101: The standard accounts of the Guatemalan coup of 1954 are Schlesinger and Kinzer, *Bitter Fruit*, and Richard H. Immerman, *The CIA in Guatemala: The Foreign Policy of Intervention* (Austin: University of Texas Press, 1982).

Page 98: The reference to May 1954 as the high point of the Cold War is in David Caute, *The Great Fear: The Anti-Communist Purge under Truman and Eisenhower* (New York: Simon and Schuster, 1978), p. 11.

Page 103: See Dana Gardner Munro, *The Five Republics of Central America* (New York: Russell and Russell, 1967), and his *Intervention and Dollar Diplomacy in the Caribbean, 1900–1921* (Princeton: Princeton University Press, 1964).

Page 105: Typical of the flood of right-wing books on Cuba, which invariably blamed Matthews for his role in Castro's rise to power, are Nathaniel Weyl, *Red Star over Cuba* (New York: Hillman, 1961) and Daniel James, *Cuba: The First Soviet Satellite in the Americas* (New York: Avon, 1961).

Pages 106–7: The most complete account is Peter Wyden, *Bay of Pigs: The Untold Story* (New York: Simon and Schuster, 1979).

Page 109: The classic narrative of the Missile Crisis is Robert F. Kennedy, *Thirteen Days: A Memoir of the Cuban Missile Crisis* (New York: Norton, 1969). Dean Rusk's revelation is in J. Anthony Lukas, "Class Reunion: Kennedy's Men Relive the Cuban Missile Crisis," *New York Times Magazine*, August 30, 1987.

Page 109–10: The prisoner-release scheme is described in Milton S. Eisenhower, *The Wine Is Bitter* (Garden City, N.Y.: Doubleday, 1963), pp. 282–83.

Page 113: A good critique of the Alliance for Progress is Jerome Levinson and Juan de Onis, *The Alliance that Failed* (Chicago: Quadrangle, Twentieth Century Fund, 1970). LaFeber's *Inevitable Revolutions*, pp. 146–60, contains a good, concise treatment. Figures on the Peace Corps are taken from Gerard T. Rice, *Twenty Years of Peace Corps* (Washington, D.C.: Peace Corps, 1982). Harris Wofford's *Of Kennedys and Kings* (New York: Farrar, Strauss, 1980), is also useful.

Page 114: "Free elections are stopped . . ." is from *I. F. Stone's Weekly*, April 15, 1963. See Neil Middleton, ed., *The I. F. Stone's Weekly Reader* (New York: Random House, 1973).

Pages 116–18: The account of the 1964 Panama riots is taken from LaFeber, *The Panama Canal*, pp. 132–45.

Page 119: Piero Gleijeses, *The Dominican Crisis: The 1965 Constitutionalist Revolt and the American Intervention* (Baltimore: Johns Hopkins University Press, 1978) is the most thorough analysis. See also Abraham Lowenthal, *The Dominican Intervention* (Cambridge: Harvard University Press, 1971) and Howard J. Wiarda and Michael J. Kryzanek, *The Dominican Republic: A Caribbean Crucible* (Boulder, Colo.: Westview, 1982). LBJ's decision to increase troop strength in Vietnam as a result of public support for the Dominican invasion is noted in Larry Berman, *Planning a Tragedy: The Americanization of the War in Vietnam* (New York: Norton, 1982), p. 63.

Page 120: Master Sergeant Luke Thompson's story is told in Philip Taubman, "The Secret World of a Green Beret," *New York Times Magazine*, July 4, 1982. The comments by Sontag and Berger on the death of Che Guevara are taken from the collection of tributes *Viva Che!* (London: Jonathan Cape, 1968).

FIVE: THE DEMOCRACY GAME: 1967–82

Page 126: On the 1972 election, see Raymond Bonner, *Weakness and Deceit: U.S. Policy and El Salvador* (New York: Times Books, 1984). Duarte's own recollection of the episode, and his subsequent lobbying in Washington, is in his autobiography *Duarte, My Story* (New York: Putnam, 1986), pp. 70–90. The "soccer war" is recounted in Thomas P. Anderson, *The War of the Dispossessed: Honduras and El Salvador, 1969* (Lincoln: University of Nebraska Press, 1981), and in William H. Durham, *Scarcity and Survival in Central America: The Ecological Origins of the Soccer War* (Stanford, Calif.: Stanford University Press, 1979).

Page 127: Information on the 1972 fraud is taken from Enrique Baloyra, *El Salvador in Transition* (Chapel Hill: University of North Carolina Press, 1983). "My welcome to the United States . . ." is from Duarte, *My Story,* p. 89.

Page 133: The Somoza public-relations campaign is detailed in Lars Schoultz, *Human Rights and United States Policy Toward Latin America* (Princeton: Princeton University Press, 1981).

Page 136: There are valuable insights into the Mariel episode in Wayne S. Smith, *The Closest of Enemies: A Personal and Diplomatic History of the Castro Years* (New York: Norton, 1987), chapter 8.

Page 139: A moving account of the life of one of the churchwomen is Ana Carrigan, *Salvador Witness: The Life and Calling of Jean Donovan* (New York: Simon and Schuster, 1985). A series of reports by the New York-based group Americas Watch detail human-rights abuses in El Salvador since 1981.

Page 141: The Solaun speech is reported in Diederich, *Somoza,* p. 145. Somoza's own account, which is largely written in this vein, is: Anastasio Somoza, with Jack Cox, *Nicaragua Betrayed* (Boston and Los Angeles: Western Islands, 1980).

Pages 143–44: A detailed survey of public opinion on U.S. policy on Central America is William M. LeoGrande, *Central America and the Polls* (Washington Office on Latin America, May 1984). "The Cubans are there . . ." Av Westin, *Newswatch: How TV Decides the News* (New York: Simon and Schuster, 1982), pp. 199–200. There are a number of valuable analyses of press coverage of El Salvador, unfortunately none of them recent. See Jonathan Evan Maslow and Ana Arana, "Operation El Salvador," *Columbia Journalism Review,* May/June 1981; Michael Massing, "About-Face on El Salvador," *Columbia Journalism Review,* November/December 1983. On photography in wartime, Anne Nelson, "Images and Icons," *Columbia Journalism Review,* March/April 1985.

Page 148: The most accurate short version of events on Nicaragua's East Coast in 1981–82 is in Cynthia Brown, ed., *With Friends Like These: The Americas Watch Report on Human Rights and U.S. Policy in Latin America* (New York: Pantheon, 1985), pp. 156–79.

SIX: UN-AMERICAN ACTIVITIES: 1983–1988

Page 155: Two helpful books on the events in Grenada are Hugh O'Shaughnessy, *Grenada: Revolution, Invasion and Aftermath* (London: Hamish Hamilton, 1984) and Kai P. Schoenhals and Richard A. Melanson, *Revolution and Intervention in Grenada: The New Jewel Movement, the United States, and the Caribbean* (Boulder, Colo.: Westview, 1985).

Page 156: "The victories won by American arms . . ." is from Richard Hofstadter, *The Paranoid Style in American Politics* (New York: Knopf, 1965), p. 175.

Pages 156–58: Krauthammer's comment on revolution is from his book, *Cutting Edges: Making Sense of the Eighties* (New York: Random House, 1985).

Page 158: A complete analysis of the Nicaraguan election was published by a delegation from the Latin American Studies Association: *The Electoral Process in Nicaragua: Domestic and International Influences* (Pittsburgh: LASA, 1984). Roy

Gutman's *Banana Diplomacy* (New York: Simon and Schuster, 1988) reconstructs the sequence of events that led to the withdrawal of Arturo Cruz.

Page 160: Bunau-Varilla, "Look at the Nicaraguan postage stamps . . ." is in Mc-Cullough, *The Path Between the Seas*, p. 285.

Pages 165–66: There is substantial material on the contra-drug connection in Leslie Cockburn, *Out of Control* (New York: Atlantic Monthly Press, 1987).

Page 167: Peter Davis's *Where Is Nicaragua?* (New York: Simon and Schuster, 1987) is one of the few attempts to come to grips with that country's place in the American imagination. The most influential account of the Nicaraguan revolution in shaping discussion in Washington is Shirley Christian's extremely conservative reading, *Nicaragua: Revolution in the Family* (New York: Random House, 1985). Of the innumerable other books on the subject, Peter Kornbluh's *Nicaragua: The Price of Intervention* (Washington, D.C.: Institute for Policy Studies, 1987) is probably the most complete account of the covert war. Peter Rosset and John Vandermeer, *The Nicaragua Reader* (New York: Grove, 1983, revised edition, 1986) is a useful compilation of source documents. Christopher Dickey's *With the Contras: A Reporter in the Wilds of Nicaragua* (New York: Simon and Schuster, 1985) is a vivid description of the early days of the contra war.

Page 171: A number of Herblock's Nicaragua cartoons are in two recent collections: *Herblock Through the Looking Glass: The Reagan Years in Words and Pictures* (New York: Norton, 1984) and *Herblock at Large* (New York: Pantheon, 1987).

Page 178: Dean Acheson's comment on the banana peel is cited in LaFeber, *Inevitable Revolutions*, p. 15.

PICTURE CREDITS
AND SOURCES

INTRODUCTION

Page ii: Constantino Arias/Center for Cuban Studies. Page x: José Gómez de la Carrera, "Avenue of Royal Palms," driveway to the residence "Quinta de Palatinos," also known as "Las Delicias," at the Cerro, Havana, Cuba, 1889. Albumen, 9¼" x 7¾". The Ramiro Fernandez Collection, Museum of Arts and Sciences, Daytona Beach, Florida. Page xii: Jim Dobbins/*Boston Herald-American*. Page xiii: Paul Plaschke/*Louisville Times*. Page xiv: *The Oregon Journal*. Page xvi: Warren/*The New York Journal*. Page xvii: Tony Auth. © 1983, *Philadelphia Inquirer*. Reprinted with permission of Universal Press Syndicate. All rights reserved. Page xviii: Saatchi & Saatchi DFS Compton. Page xx: Used by permission of *The Washington Post National Weekly Edition*.

CHAPTER ONE

Pages 1 and 3: Author's collection. Page 7: New York Public Library Picture Collection. Page 8: Eadweard Muybridge, Las Nubes, Guatemala, 1875. Page 10 (top): Author's collection; (bottom): Lorillard, Inc. Page 12: Author's collection. Page 13 (top): Author's collection; (bottom): George Black. Page 14: Author's collection. Page 15: *The Detroit News*. Page 16: Author's collection. Page 18 (top): *The Minneapolis Tribune*; (bottom): Edith H. Williams and Joanna H. Noel. Page 19: *Scientific American*. Page 20 (top): *The Columbus Dispatch*; (bottom): Author's collection. Page 21: Library of Congress. Page 22: R. C. Bowman/*The Minneapolis Tribune*. Page 23: G. W. Rehse/*The St. Paul Pioneer Press*. Page 24: Karen Glynn & Eddie Becker Archive. Page 25: Clifford Berryman/*The Washington Star*. Page 26: McKee Barclay/*The Baltimore Sun*. Pages 27 and 28: Karen Glynn & Eddie Becker Archive.

CHAPTER TWO

Page 30: Karen Glynn & Eddie Becker Archive. Pages 33 and 34 (both): Chiquita Brands, Inc. Page 35: Karen Glynn & Eddie Becker Archive. Page 37 (top): New York Public Library; (bottom): Author's collection. Page 38: Author's collection. Pages 39 and 40: Copyright 1931 by Doubleday, a division of Bantam, Doubleday, Dell Publishing Group, Inc. Reprinted by permission of the publisher. Page 41: William "Billy" Ireland/*The Columbus Dispatch*. Page 43: U.S. Marine Corps/Karen Glynn & Eddie Becker Archive. Page 44: Karen Glynn & Eddie Becker Archive. Pages 46 and 47: U.S. Marine Corps/Karen Glynn and Eddie Becker Archive. Page 48 (top): Wide World Photos; (bottom): Karen Glynn & Eddie Becker Archive. Page 49: Copyright 1928 by the New York Times Company. Reprinted by permission. Page 50: Wide World Photos. Page 52: Jerry Doyle/*The Philadelphia Record*. Pages 55 and 56: Karen Glynn & Eddie Becker Archive.

CHAPTER THREE

Page 58: Wide World Photos. Page 63 (top): Author's Collection; (bottom): Karen Glynn & Eddie Becker Archive. Page 65: Tichnor Bros. Boston/Author's Collection. Page 67: Karen Glynn & Eddie Becker Archive. Pages 68 and 69: Pan-American Union. Page 70: New York Public Library Picture Collection. Page 71 (top): Bettmann Newsphotos; (bottom): Author's collection. Page 72: Luis Marden © 1944 National Geographic Society. Page 74: U.S. Army Photo. Page 76 (top): U.S. Navy photo; (middle): Luis Marden © 1942 National Geographic Society; (bottom): Luis Marden © 1944 National Geographic Society. Page 77 (top): The Coca-Cola Company; (bottom): Franklin D. Roosevelt Library. Page 79 (top): Wide World Photos; (bottom): Karen Glynn & Eddie Becker Archive. Pages 81 and 82: Luis Marden © 1944 National Geographic Society. Page 82 (bottom): Susan Meiselas/Magnum. Pages 83, 84, and 85: Karen Glynn & Eddie Becker Archive.

CHAPTER FOUR

Page 86: Karen Glynn & Eddie Becker Archive. Page 89: © 1987 by Herblock in *The Washington Post*. Page 91: Luis Marden © 1944 National Geographic Society. Pages 93, 94, and 95: Constantino Arias/Center for Cuban Studies. Page 97: Copyright 1952 Time Inc. All rights reserved. Reprinted by permission from *Time*. Page 99: Cornell Capa, *Life Magazine*, © Time Inc. Pages 100 and 102: Bettmann Newsphotos. Page 103: Copyright 1957 by the New York Times Company. Reprinted by permission. Page 105: © 1960 by *National Review* Inc., 150 East 35 Street, New York, NY 10016. Reprinted with permission. Page 107: Wide World Photos. Page 108: Department of Defense. Page 109: Bettmann Newsphotos. Page 111 (top): Department of Defense; (bottom): Anne Nelson collection. Page 112: Peace Corps Photos. Page 115: Reprinted by permission of Newspaper Enterprise Association, Inc. Page 117: Wide World Photos. Page 118: North American Congress on Latin America (NACLA). Page 119: *The Chicago Tribune*. Page 121: George Cohen. Page 122: Bettmann Newsphotos.

CHAPTER FIVE

Page 124: James Nachtwey/Black Star. Page 128: Wide World Photos. Page 129: Bettmann Newsphotos. Page 130: Author's collection. Pages 131 and 133: Bettmann Newsphotos. Page 134 (top): Burt Glinn/Magnum; (bottom): Susan Meiselas/Magnum. Page 137: North American Congress on Latin America (NACLA). Page 139: A.B.C. News/video still by Steve Rubin. Page 140: Susan Meiselas/Magnum. Page 142: © Under Fire Associates, a Greenberg Brothers Partnership. All rights reserved. Page 144: Etienne Montes/Gamma-Liaison. Page 145: Jean-Louis Clariond. Page 146 (top): Susan Meiselas/Magnum; (bottom): Etienne Montes/Gamma-Liaison. Page 147: Matthew Naythons/Gamma-Liaison. Page 149: Bruce Hoertel. Page 150: Karen Glynn & Eddie Becker Archive. Page 152: Anne Nelson.

CHAPTER SIX

Page 154: Bettmann Newsphotos. Page 157 (top): Department of Defense; (bottom): Center for Cuban Studies. Page 159: Bettmann Newsphotos. Page 160: Author's collection. Page 161: Karen Glynn & Eddie Becker Archive. Page 163: Sovfoto/Eastfoto. Page 164: Copyright © 1986 Time Inc. All Rights Reserved. Reprinted by permission from *Time*. Page 165: White House Photo. Page 168 (top): Tony Auth. © 1983, *Philadelphia Inquirer*. Reprinted with permission of Universal Press Syndicate. All rights reserved; (bottom): Paul Conrad/Los Angeles Times Syndicate. Page 170: M. G. Lord/*Newsday*. Page 171: © 1987 by Herblock in *The Washington Post*. Page 173: Bettmann Newsphotos. Page 174: White House Photo/*The New York Post*. Reprinted by permission. Page 175 (top): White House Photo/*The New York Post*. Reprinted by permission; (bottom): White House Photo. Page 176: Paul Conrad/Los Angeles Times Syndicate. Page 177: Richard Gardner/*The Commercial Appeal*. Page 178: Eugene Richards/Magnum.

INDEX

ABOUT THE AUTHOR

George Black was born in Scotland in 1949 and was educated at Oxford University. Formerly editor of *The NACLA Report on the Americas,* he is now foreign editor of the *Nation.* His writings on Latin America and the Caribbean have appeared in the *New York Times,* the *Los Angeles Times, Mother Jones,* the *New Statesman,* and many other publications. He has lived in New York City since 1981, and is married to the writer Anne Nelson.